25-00

ALSO BY WENDY LAVITT

American Folk Dolls
The Knopf Collectors' Guides to American Antiques, *Dolls*

ALSO BY JUDITH REITER WEISSMAN

The Knopf Collectors' Guides to American Antiques, *Folk Art*

LABORS of LOVE

PHOTOGRAPHS BY SCHECTER LEE

STUDIO VISTA   LONDON

LABORS of LOVE

AMERICA'S TEXTILES AND NEEDLEWORK, 1650–1930

JUDITH REITER WEISSMAN AND WENDY LAVITT

STUDIO VISTA

an imprint of
Cassell Publishers Limited
Artillery House, Artillery Row
London SW1 1RT

First published in Great Britain 1988

British Library Cataloguing in Publication Data
Weissman, Judith Reiter
Labors of love: America's textiles and needlework, 1650–1930
1. Needlework—United States—History
I. Title II. Lavitt, Wendy
746'0973   NK9112

ISBN 0-289-80011-0

Printed in Japan

FOR HAROLD AND MICHAEL

FOR MEL, KATHY, JOHN, AND MEREDITH

Acknowledgments

Many people were kind enough to lend their help in the preparation of this book. We want to thank the museums and individuals who supplied information and made their collections available. We are especially grateful to Schecter Lee, whose beautiful photographs enhance the book, and to Alice Quinn and Susan Ralston, whose editorial perceptions guided *Labors of Love: America's Textiles and Needlework* to completion. We also want to thank the following institutions, private collectors, scholars, and dealers.

Gloria Allen, DAR Museum
Albany Institute of History and Art
Joshua Baer, Morningstar Gallery
Dexter Cirillo
Gallery 10 of Arizona
Guthman Americana
Vernon S. Gunnion, Pennsylvania Farm Museum of Landis Valley
Marion Hall, Museum of American Textile History
Mary-Ellen Earl Perry, The Margaret Woodbury Strong Museum
Jan Christman, The Shaker Museum
Kelter-Malcé
Bill Copeley, New Hampshire Historical Society
Joy Piscopo, F. O. Bailey Antiquarians
Maud Margaret Lyon, Louisiana State Museum

Mary Alice McKay, New-York Historical Society
Sandra Vlodek
Valentine Museum
Minnesota Historical Society
Philadelphia Museum of Art
School of American Research, Santa Fe, New Mexico
Cynthia Nakamura, The Denver Art Museum
Natural History Museum Los Angeles County
American Museum of Natural History
Gillian Moss and Sarah Seggerman, Cooper-Hewitt Museum
Laura Fisher
Margo Paul Ernst
John Ernst
Christopher Selser

Benson Lanford

James Economos

George Terasaki

Bob Kapoun

Jean Mailey, Metropolitan Museum
   of Art

Elizabeth Teitel, Metropolitan
   Museum of Art

Tony Berlant

Mary Davis and S. Alexandride,
   Museum of the American Indian,
   Heye Foundation

William Channing

Eleanor Tulman Hancock

Rosalind S. Miller

Lillian and Jerry Grossman

Sylvia Pines

Evelyn Haertig

Jeannine Dobbs

Sweet Nellie: A Country Store

Margie Dyer

Sam Herrup

M. Finkel & Daughter

Arne Anton

Tandy Hersh

Sheila Rideout

Glee Krueger

Dena S. Katzenberg

A. E. Dreyfuss

Cynthia Rubin

Pamela Larson

Warren Roberts

Lesley Heathcote

Celia Oliver, Shelburne Museum

Polly Mitchell, Shelburne Museum

Bob Shaw, Shelburne Museum

Ken and Robin Pike

Marion Hall, Museum of American
   Textile History

Ford Ballard, Litchfield Historical
   Society

Elliott and Grace Snyder

Bettie Mintz / "all of us americans"
   folk art

Betty Ring

Barbara Johnson

Chris van Alstyne

Dr. Siri von Reis

Ligia Marcial

Nancy Druckman, Sotheby's

The Brooklyn Museum

CONTENTS

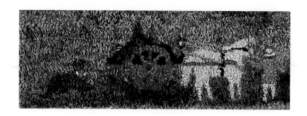

INTRODUCTION

The needle, unlike the pen, has always been thought a woman's instrument. Without it, women would have been unable to fulfill their wifely duties, and would have passed many an idle and boring hour. With it, they were able to express themselves in a socially acceptable form, and make beautiful objects for themselves, their families and homes.

By the sixteenth century in England and on the Continent, needlework was no longer limited to garments and hangings for kings and churchmen. Secular embroidery, some of it worked by amateurs rather than professional guild members, was becoming a popular form. When the first settlers came to the colonies in the early seventeenth century, some brought with them their valued bed hangings and embroidered silk quilts, as well as trinket boxes covered with tiny beads or the raised embroidery called stumpwork. For the most part, however, little remains of those early treasures, and most of what is known about them comes to us only through the written records of letters, diaries, and estate inventories.

The first decades of settlement left little time for anything but producing the basic necessities of food, clothing, and shelter, and in the beginning the small areas of cleared land were needed to grow food. By 1640, however, the planting of flax or hemp for linen was required by both Connecticut and Massachusetts. Raising sheep for wool also became a priority, so that the colonists would not have to depend on England for cloth.

What cloth they had was precious, and except in the very wealthiest families, was used until it literally wore away. By the eighteenth century, life in what were by then substantial towns—Salem, Providence, Philadelphia, and Boston—had become quite sophisticated. Cabinetmakers had developed their own distinctive forms of high style furniture. Luxurious silks and satins, and fashionable printed and painted cottons from France and India were easily bought at the shops. And

girls of well-to-do families were being sent to young ladies' academies to learn the skills they would need later on in life: good manners and posture, reading, dancing, and above all, needlework.

By 1706 the *Boston Newsletter* carried advertisements for private boarding schools for girls, and by the end of the eighteenth century hundreds of such schools were established throughout the newly independent republic. A young lady's needlework skills, like her manners and looks, were counted a part of what made her desirable as a wife, and all who could afford to give their daughters such an education did so.

By the first quarter of the nineteenth century, young women had ceased to do the very fine canvaswork embroidery of the previous century, work so fine that the canvas might have as many as fifty-some threads to the inch. They continued, though, making samplers both simple and elaborate, and began embroidering pictures of silk on silk, usually with the faces, hands, clouds, sky, and water painted in rather than stitched.

Many fashions in needlework came and went over several decades, such as mourning pictures with their familiar willow trees, mourners, and tombstones bearing the names and dates of the dead. Stenciling on cloth—both the painted velvet pictures of fruit and flowers and the patterned bedcovers and tablecloths—was popular in the early nineteenth century, as was white work, which flourished between about 1790 and 1830.

By this time, with domestic cotton printing factories firmly established and peddlers carrying cloth throughout the countryside, pieced quilts were being made more and more. Before this period, the majority of quilts had consisted of large pieces of cloth seamed together to form a solid-color quilt rather than of the much smaller pieces used in making patchwork. Earlier quilts were made of linsey-

woolsey, calamanco (glazed wool), or the expensive imported chintzes, which were often cut out and appliquéd on a plain white ground to make the precious fabric go further.

The establishment of the cotton-printing industry made possible what is usually thought of as the quintessential American quilt—pieced or appliquéd cotton, composed of small squares, diamonds, or triangles arranged to form an all-over design. The block method of quiltmaking, where the design depends on the repetition of the same motif in block after block, seems to have been an American innovation, and one that also contributed to bringing quiltmaking to its peak in the mid-nineteenth century.

By the latter part of the century, some writers in the ladies' magazines such as *Godey's* and *Peterson's*—both read by large numbers of women—began to deplore the waste of time it took to make such an unfashionable bedcover as a cotton patchwork quilt, recommending instead the use of silk, satin, and velvet patchwork as a worthwhile way of spending one's time. While the piecing of quilts continued uninterrupted in certain areas of the country—and does so today—the women who read these magazines gradually gave up cotton patchwork. They turned instead to the varied forms of elaborate Victorian needlework—among them, silk crazy quilts and Berlin wool work, done by transferring precolored designs from a kind of graph paper to a fairly coarse canvas (no more than twenty threads to the inch), and working them in the strong colors dictated by the prevailing taste.

A great variety of rug types, shirred, yarn-sewn, hooked, braided, and even knitted and crocheted, developed during the nineteenth century, adding many new forms to the woven striped and plaid rag rugs that were among the earliest rugs made here. Through the early years of the twentieth century, rugmaking, like quilting, continued to be of interest to certain women, but not until the 1920s

and 1930s, when there was a renewal of interest in American crafts, was there much innovation in either form.

By the 1920s, however, antique buffs had begun searching back roads and country villages for old rugs, quilts, and early needlework. Homer Eaton Keyes, the first editor of *The Magazine Antiques,* included numerous articles on these forms in the early issues of the magazine, and helped save many examples of at least one form, the bed rugg, some of which had managed to survive unrecognized as work from the first quarter of the eighteenth century.

Needlewomen and quilters began to take an interest in recording the history of their art around the same period, and the first of many works appeared: Candace T. Wheeler's *The Development of Embroidery in America,* in 1921, and Ethel Stanwood Bolton and Eva Johnston Coe's *American Samplers* in the same year. Ruth Finley focused on *Old Patchwork Quilts and the Women Who Made Them* in 1929, and Carrie A. Hall and Rose Kretsinger wrote *The Romance of the Patchwork Quilt in America* in 1935, dedicating it to "Quilt Lovers—Everywhere World Without End."

An interest in women's lives as well as their art was a related but separate development, producing work like Julia Cherry Spruill's *Women's Life and Work in the Southern Colonies* (1935). The women's movement of the 1970s and the Bicentennial celebration in 1976 both, in different ways, gave further impetus to careful scholarly investigations into the history and nature of needlework, labor that occupied a good part of women's lives from the first years of colonial settlement until today. The work that follows, like the forms it illustrates and discusses, is meant to be part of these larger traditions, and like the needlework itself, has also been a "labor of love."

New York City
February 1986

LABORS of LOVE

THE PEDDLER'S WAGON.—DRAWN BY C. G. BUSH.—[SEE PAGE 394.]

"The Peddler's Wagon," drawn by C. G. Bush, appeared in *Harper's Weekly* (June 20, 1868). Amid an endless supply of brooms and containers, the peddler offers a precious piece of cloth for scrutiny. 16″ × 10½″. (Courtesy of Wendy Lavitt. Photograph, Schecter Lee.)

ONE

CLOTH

The President of the United States, on the day of his inauguration, appeared dressed in a complete suit of homespun cloaths; but the cloth was of so fine a Fabric, and so Handsomely finished, that is was universally mistaken for a foreign manufactured superfine cloth.
—Gazette of the United States, May 6, 1789

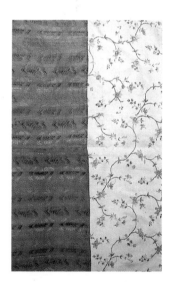

The need for cloth prompted the development of American textiles from homespun beginnings to sophisticated manufactures. Reflecting American ingenuity and myriad patterns of immigration, cloth production eventually prospered despite severe trade restrictions and stiff competition from European imports. How well a particular material fared depended on how difficult it was to manufacture and how it stood up to its European counterpart.

Textiles played an enormous role in the economic life of the colonies. Estate inventories valued bedding and bed curtains only slightly less than property or silver, and textiles composed the largest category of newspaper advertisements. Despite the rigors of settlement and the scarcity of skilled craftsmen and equipment, American textile production tried to follow the fashions set by the Europeans. Yet until the Industrial Revolution, elaborate prints and fine materials were beyond the capabilities of most fledgling American firms. Even after a variety of imported and domestic fabrics became available in urban centers, rural households were often forced to depend upon the fruits of their own labors for clothing and bedding. The end of the nineteenth century saw farm women still thumbing well-worn copies of outdated ladies' magazines for guidance in making simple garments.

A hand-blocked, printed floral linen fabric with a striped backing, from western Connecticut. It may have been used as a christening blanket, c. 1800–20. 25″ × 12″. (Courtesy of the Litchfield Historical Society.)

HOMESPUN LINEN

Early inventories attest to the importance of "home made cloth," revealing that spinning and weaving played integral roles in early American households. One observer in a nineteenth-century rural settlement noted: "For many years, almost every article worn by man or woman, young or old, in this town, was spun, woven, colored and made here. Every woman knew how to do her part."[1]

Diaries mention the custom of taking spinning wheels on social visits. It was not uncommon between 1770 and 1785 to see groups of women lugging their wheels in the streets en route to spinning contests. These affairs, forerunners of the popular nineteenth-century quilting bees, offered a welcome break in the daily routine. In Goshen, Connecticut, a young lady won one contest by spinning several runs of yarn (normally three and a half days work) in one day. To help the cause, "Her distaffs were all prepared, her yarn reeled and even her food put in her mouth."[2] The host of the contest, the town, or the local minister often received a share of the spun yarn. In 1769, Dr. Ezra Stiles hosted a match to which thirty-seven spinners brought their flax and their wheels, producing ninety-four skeins of fifteen knots each, after which, in return for his share of the skeins, Dr. Stiles provided supper.[3] During a period of economic hardship, the *Massachusetts Gazette* published the following ditty:

Let a friend at this season advise you.
Since money's so scarce and times growing worse,
Strange things may soon hap and surprise you.
First then throw aside your high topknot of pride,
Wear none but your country linen,
Of economy boast. Let Your pride be the most
To show cloaths of your own make and spinning.[4]

The pleas for increased production would probably have gone unheeded were it not for the strong linen-making heritage of the English and Scotch-Irish settlers. While Massachusetts reflected its English origins, New Hampshire, particularly Londonderry, established itself as a Scotch-Irish province whose linen-making reputation impressed European travelers. In 1750 James Birkit observed, "This province [New Hampshire] also produced . . . Exceeding good flax of which the Irish Settled at Londonderry Make very good cloth & fine Ounce thread, Some of the Cloth I see was choise good Shirting Linnen and I am informed this little town increases very much."[5]

Clothmaking in New Hampshire and other states was the first home manufacture sponsored by popular country fairs. With an eye to improving the quality of cloth produced in the country, fair organizers gave cash prizes to reward fine clothing made at home. In the October 29, 1821, edition of the *New Hampshire Patriot,* an editorial observed, "The premiums offered for fine cloths have already had a good effect: much fine and well-colored cloth has been exhibited where formally coarse and inferior cloth was produced."

Although much of this linen was produced by women working at home, some weaving was done on a professional basis by both men and women. A few ambitious women not only equipped their homes with linen goods but wove for other families as well. "Spinsters" and widows sometimes earned needed income by spinning for various households. The routine of daily spinning was seldom interrupted,

This early historical ("liberty") fabric was so popular that it was printed in blue as well as brown, c. 1800. (Courtesy of the Litchfield Historical Society.)

save for illness or catastrophe. In 1807 Mrs. Jane Hazelton of Newfane, Vermont, grew so tired of her lifetime work that on her hundredth birthday, "she spun a full day's work and then she called her son and told him to set her wheel away, as she had spun her last thread."[6]

During the Revolution domestic linen production expanded as spinning clubs such as the Daughters of Liberty and the Association of Plantation Maidens held competitions to meet the increased demand. While the end of the Revolution prompted the resumption of imports, some women continued to spurn English goods. The *Salem Gazette* (Jan. 31, 1782) printed a letter by a homesick British exile complaining about the attitudes of American women attending a dance for British officers: "The women are seldom or never persuaded to dance; even in their dresses the females seem to bid us defiance; the gay toys which are imported here they despise; they wear their own homespun manufactures and take care to have in their breast knots and often in their shoes, something that resembles their flag of thirteen stripes."

Feelings of patriotism notwithstanding, American women were eager to give up the wheel for store-bought goods. By the end of the eighteenth century, wealthy women made frequent shopping trips in which their purchases included "factory cloth." With the advent of factory-made cotton in the first quarter of the nineteenth century, the making of linen by hand waned. Some women in rural areas continued to spin flax so they could afford the ready-made goods available in general stores. In Ohio, Kitturah Penton Belknap wrote in her diary of 1839: "I have been spinning flax all my spare time thru the Winter. Made a piece of linen to sell, got me a new calico dress for Sunday and a pair of fine shoes. . . ."[7] Kitturah Belknap also used her spinning abilities to prepare for a trip westward. To withstand the rigors of the Oregon Trail, she set to work:

> [Nov. 15, 1847] Now I will begin to work and plan to make everything with an eye to starting out on a six months trip. . . . So the first thing is to make a piece of linen for a wagon cover and some sacks. . . .

> [Jan. 1848] I have to make a new feather tick for my bed.

> [Feb. 1, 1848] . . . the linen is ready to go to work on and six two bushel bags all ready to sew up that I will do evenings by the light of a dip candle for I have made enough to last all winter after we get to Oregon. . . .

> [Apr. 9, 1848] I have made 4 nice little table cloths so am going to live just like I was home.[8]

The linen she wove was likely to measure 39 to 40 inches in width, probably the distance she could easily throw a shuttle from one side of the loom to the other. After weaving, she would most likely wet the cloth and bleach it white in the sun. Although she does not mention them, Kitturah Belknap also probably made linen bed ticks that she filled with feathers. While the covers were washable, few ticks were all-white. Usually, blue-and-white checked, plaid, or brown-and-white checked tops hid the plain bottom panel.

When the owner of this small-scale checked linen tick searched her scrap bag, she obviously could not find a matching check; so she repaired her bed tick with a large-scale linen remnant. Pennsylvania, 19th century. (Courtesy of Tandy Hersh.)

Six linen ticks show the many ways of varying stripes and checks. Note the hand-woven tapes. Pennsylvania, 19th century. (Courtesy of Tandy Hersh.)

This linen bag probably represents a Civil War campaign to exempt firemen from military service. 14½″ × 19½″. (Courtesy of Lillian Grossman. Photograph, Schecter Lee.)

Linen sufficed for a variety of mundane articles. In the 1797 Hancock, New Hampshire, book of rules and regulations governing volunteer firemen, it was required of each man to have two linen firebags with his name applied. The purpose of the drawstring bags was to save as many valuables as possible from a fire by stuffing them into the bags (during the eighteenth century saving the house itself was often impossible).

By the middle of the nineteenth century handmade linen was already considered a curiosity, with many examples regarded as heirlooms to be exhibited at country fairs and expositions as part of America's heritage. However, the Civil War affected the availability and the cost of muslin and cotton in many communities, inspiring a short-lived resurgence of the art. In Ephrata, Pennsylvania, Elizabeth Spangler reminisced about this in reference to her mother's large collection of homespun plaid linens:

> My mother was born September 1st, 1855, Louisa Plean.—At eleven she was taught the art of spinning by her aunt. The war between the States was the cause of the raising of flax, its preparation, spinning and weaving, because muslins and calicos [prints] were scarce and expensive, from 50 c to $1.00 per yard. Mother did not weave. She and Aunt Betsy carried the yard to a man by the name of Kiddinger. He wove linen cloth at 14 to 50 cents per yard.[9]

WOOL

During the seventeenth and eighteenth centuries American-bred sheep furnished much-needed wool for rural families. Although the wool of American sheep was coarse compared to the fine wool from the Spanish Merino sheep favored by English clothmakers, it provided simple clothing and blankets. In 1767 Governor Moore of New Jersey marveled: "The custom of making these coarse cloths (woolen and linsey-woolen) in private families prevails throughout the whole province, and in almost every home a sufficient quantity is manufactured for the use of the family. . . ."[10] While imported woolen fabrics such as calamanco, camlet, cheyney, and harrateen were used by the wealthy for bed curtains to alleviate the cold of unheated bedrooms, many families relied on homespun "serge, stuff or woolen."

In a time when textiles were valued almost as much as silver and land, sheep were accorded special privileges, including unlimited grazing on the commons, and were protected by statutes forbidding their slaughter before the age of two. Dogs who killed sheep were hanged; their owners were directed to pay back twice the cost of the unfortunate sheep. In Virginia a yard of homespun woolen cloth could be exchanged for six pounds of tobacco at the county courthouse, while a dozen pair of knitted stockings merited twelve pounds of tobacco.[11]

England, intent upon protecting its monopoly and believing that the Americans "had no right to manufacture even a nail or horseshoe," regarded the colonists' wool raising with a jealous eye. In 1699 all sailing vessels bound for England from the colonies were forbidden to carry any "Wool, Woolfells, Shortlings, Moslings, Wool Flocks, Worsteds, Bays, Bay or Woolen Yarn, Cloath, Serge . . . etc."[12] Later the Crown restricted transportation of woolen goods from province to province. Despite these bans, domestic wool manufacture continued to flourish. By the time of the Revolution, when many patriotic citizens refused to wear imported wool or eat mutton, Americans were able to survive their self-imposed boycott of English goods. However, it was not until the nineteenth century, when sheep were bred in the United States with wool fine enough for worsted fabrics, that America could begin to compete with English products. The problems inherent in fine-wool production continued well into the century, as noted by the following exchange in 1841:

> The domestic Cloth made from fine Wool, in many cases, wears as long again, and in all cases, half as long again as the Cloth made from coarse Wool. Many of the neighboring women, who had the strongest prejudice against fine Wool, after trial, now always prefer it to coarse. I will give the testimony of a neighboring female, who is in the constant habit of making her husband's woolen garments. A neighboring female enquired of my wife for some fine Wool. Upon asking what difference she found in the wear of the fine Wool to the coarse, she replied, "It makes just this difference: 'When I make my husband clothes from the coarse Wool, two suits last him a year. When I make them of fine Wool, three suits last him two years.'" The Wool she spoke of as fine Wool was half-blood or grade wool. Those who desired to lighten the labor of their wives commit a great mistake in giving them coarse Wool to make into Clothes.[13]

The steps involved in turning raw wool into cloth were numerous and time-consuming. The wool first had to be scoured to remove its greasy coating before burrs and dirt were removed by "picking." Further cleaning and blending were accomplished by carding. Portions of wool were rubbed between two wire-studded

Two early wool blankets. Although a homespun weave, the work in the plaid blanket is very fine and even. The indigo embroidery adds a striking note. Vermont, c. 1800–25. 76″ × 78″. The striped blanket, from Pennsylvania, c. 1800–25, combines a blue weft with a black and orange warp. 68″ × 74″. (Courtesy of Kelter-Malcé. Photograph, Schecter Lee.)

boards or cards, combing it so that it was ready for spinning. Even when women could send out their wool to be carded, they still had to plan their work carefully and then find the time to process the wool. In Iowa in June–July 1842, Kitturah Belknap noted in her diary:

> [June 1] The sheep will be sheared this week. Then the wool will lay out for a few days to get the sheep smell off then my work will begin. Im the first one to get at the wool—25 fleeces, will sort it over, take off the poor short wool and put it by to card by hand for comforts, then sort out the finest for flannels and the courser for jeans for the mens wear. I find the wool very nice and white but I do hate to sit down alone to pick wool so I will invite about a dozen old ladies in and in a day they will do it all up.
> [July 1] My wool came home today from the carding machine in nice rolls ready to spin. First I will spin my stocking yarn. Can spin two skeins a day and in the evening will double and twist it. . . .[14]

It is estimated that the carding machine, first introduced in North Bennington, Vermont, in 1801, reduced labor by one third. By the middle of the century, factory mass production had made inroads on home wool manufacture. In the cities, women gladly renounced their spinning wheels; but many rural women remained behind the times for reasons of thrift or lack of opportunity. George Cummings recalled his boyhood on a farm in New England:

> By the middle of the forties [1840s] or a little before, father had begun to keep sheep, and mother would take the wool from the sheep's back, wash, card in rolls, spin, and weave, and make into clothes. She usually colored the yarn with indigo so the cloth would be bluish, and with the white warp the cloth had a checkered look. Sometimes father would take the cloth to a mill in Campton where it could be dressed, as it was called. Then it was rather nice looking. Mother made nearly all my clothes out of such cloth till I was almost twenty-one.[15]

Many farmers' wives bartered or sold surplus wool to country stores, whose proprietors relegated their homespun skeins to out-of-the-way corners: "Drygoods were arranged with some eye to effect. Red and blue and yellow fabrics made contrasting streaks, while various fancy articles dangled from thickset hooks in partitions of shelves. Under the counters were odds and ends of traffic. Thence came cotton batting and 'factory yarn,' and woolen skeins spun by farmers' wives."[16]

By the 1880s, when cheap woolen goods were readily available, women's magazines and books suggested decorating existing blankets instead of making them. In *Our Homes and Their Adornments*, published in 1882, Almon C. Varney explained how women could turn an old-fashioned homespun blanket into an object of Victorian splendor:

Old Blue Blankets—Another friend had a bare, cheap new cottage. Money was not abundant. Old grandmother-woven indigo blue blankets were. She began sewing in little figures,—stars, crescents, and odd stitches in colored silks,—and the woolen blanket became a gorgeous fabric. It was hung with wooden rings on a length of gilded gas pipe midway of the bare hall, and your first impressions upon entering were of Eastern richness.[17]

Homespun woolen cloth was now a novelty, an old-fashioned art that would not be revived until the renaissance of the craft movement in the 1970s.

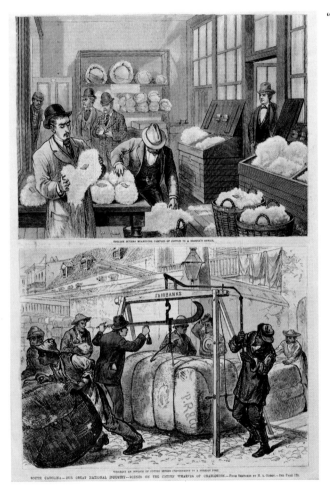

"SOUTH CAROLINA—OUR GREAT NATIONAL INDUSTRY—SCENES ON THE COTTON WHARVES OF CHARLESTON." From "Sketches by H. A. Ogden," appearing in *Frank Leslie's Illustrated Newspaper* (Nov. 16, 1878). The top scene shows English buyers examining cotton samples in a broker's office; the bottom panel is captioned "Weighing an invoice of cotton before consignment to a foreign port." 16″ × 10½″. (Courtesy of Wendy Lavitt. Photograph, Schecter Lee.)

COTTON

Although cotton was planted in America as early as 1619 by the Virginia colonists, it did not play a significant industrial role until after the invention of the cotton gin in 1793. American cloth production was revolutionized by this new machine that miraculously cleaned as much cotton in a day as it had taken one person a year to clean by hand. Before the cotton gin, the South had largely clothed its slaves with cotton woven and spun by black women. In a letter written in 1786, Thomas Jefferson noted:

The four southernmost States make a great deal of cotton. Their poor are almost entirely cloathed with it winter and summer. In winter they wear shirts of it and outer clothing of cotton and wool mixed. In summer their shirts are linen, but the outer clothing cotton. The dress of the women is almost entirely of cotton, manufactured by themselves, except the richer class, and even many of these wear a great deal of homespun cotton. It is as well manufactured as the calicoes of Europe.[18]

On George Washington's plantation at Mount Vernon, one white woman and five black servants wove enough cotton and other fabrics to fulfill the needs of twenty-five families.[19]

Whenever the colonists could inexpensively obtain imported cotton from the West Indies, they would extend its use by combining cotton wefts with linen warps. Cotton was considered so important that it often merited newspaper attention. The following item in the *New York Gazette* (Feb. 19, 1767) and an advertisement in the *Boston Gazette* (July 25, 1749) reveal how highly even small quantities of calico (printed cotton) were valued.

> SHOP LIFTER. Monday last a woman lifted a couple of Pieces of Callicoe off Mr. Milligan's shop window, but a Negro happily seeing it, immediately gave intelligence thereof, Whereupon a Pursuit was made, the Woman overtaken, and the Callicoe found upon her; She was carried before an Alderman who committed her to jail; and 'tis said she is to have her Trial today.

> Two bredths of white Calico "drawn and partly work'd with blewith thread," advertised as lost.[20]

The first successful cotton mill was established in Rhode Island in 1790, a forerunner of the mills that were soon to dot the New England landscape and employ thousands of young men and women. By 1832, an observer noted that by working in a mill, "a female can now earn more cloth in a day than she could make in the household way in a week."[21] However, because of a scarcity of equipment

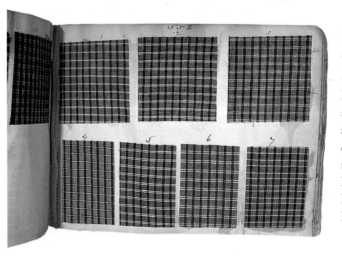

Swatches in an early sample-book (1848) from the Lancaster Mills in Clinton, Massachusetts. It is remarkable how the various plaids and checks look as if they could have been produced recently. (Courtesy of the Museum of American Textile History, North Andover, Mass.)

This cotton handkerchief with the printed portrait of Samuel Slater was distributed at the Cotton Centenary in Pawtucket, Rhode Island, in 1890, honoring the "Father of American Manufacturers." Slater had established his cotton spinning mill in 1790. 23″ × 22″. (Courtesy of Laura Fisher. Photograph, Schecter Lee.)

and skilled craftsmen, the early mills found it hard to compete with English goods. Advertisements in eighteenth-century newspapers attest to the existence of fledgling cotton-printing firms centered in Rhode Island, Boston, and Philadelphia. Usually, calico printing was regarded as a branch or extension of the printing industry. Since cotton was so valuable, many printers agreed to stamp patterns on faded or stained cloth brought in by thrifty housewives. Ads such as the one by James Franklin, a Boston printer, appearing in the *Boston Gazette* in 1720, notified the public of various printers' specialties: "The Printer hereof prints Linens, Callicoes, Silks &c. in good Figures, very lively, and durable colours, and without the offensive smells which commonly attends the Linnens printed here."[22]

An account of one of the first printing establishments in Providence, Rhode Island, describes the laborious process of direct printing: "In the year 1780 Alverson a painter & Jeremiah Eddy agreed to go into the Printing of cloth with oil colors. Jeremiah Eddy cut the tipes on the end of small pieces of hardwood and put on the paint on the tipes with a brush, stamping the cloth by hand in small flowers to please the eye. . . ."[23] Many of these small businesses could not compete with the long-established and more technically sophisticated European printers, and it was not uncommon to see advertisements offering the sale of printing tools, such as the one in the *Boston Newsletter* in 1773: "To be sold, very cheap for cash, by the person who prints dark callicoes, an excellent set of prints for the same. The person who has them to dispose of would Instruct the Purchaser in the use of them if required. . . ."[24]

The most famous early calico printer in America was the English immigrant John Hewson (c. 1745–1822), whose printworks was first announced in the July 2, 1774, edition of the *Pennsylvania Gazette*. Although interrupted by the Revolution, the business lasted until 1825, and was noted for its unusually fine block-printed floral patterns derived from English chintzes. Unlike the majority of Amer-

This bleached linen bag was dyed with indigo by the resist method. While the actual date is unknown, it was probably made in the late 18th or early 19th century. (Courtesy of the Pennyslvania Farm Museum of Landis Valley, Lancaster, Pennsylvania Historical Museum Commission.)

An 18th-century Pennsylvania German fragment of a resist-dyed cotton cloth from Berks County. Note the picotage dots throughout the fabric. (Courtesy of the Philadelphia Museum of Art.)

ican printworks, the Hewson establishment was relatively well documented. Even in Hewson's time the importance of his firm and its contribution to American manufacture were recognized. His achievements were acknowledged by his inclusion in the Grand Federal Procession in Philadelphia on July 4, 1788. Hewson's float in this patriotic parade was described in the *Pennsylvania Gazette*:

> Behind the looms was fixed the apparatus of Mr. Hewson, printing muslins of an elegant chintz pattern . . . on the right was seated Mrs. Hewson and her 4 daughters, pencilling a piece of very neat sprigged chintz of Mr. Hewson's printing, all dressed in cottons of their own manufacture . . . on a lofty staff, was displayed the callico printer's flag, in the center 13 stars in a blue field, and thirteen red stripes in a white field; round the edges of the flag was printed 37 different prints of various colours, as specimens of printing done at Philadelphia.[25]

In addition to newspaper accounts, advertisements, a journal, and Hewson's will, there exist ten known surviving examples of the firm's work (two bedspreads, six patchwork quilts, and two handkerchiefs). As research continues to unearth the story of eighteenth-century textiles, perhaps more of these beautiful Hewson "documents" will be discovered.

We know of an Irish immigrant, Archibald Rowan (1751–1834), who worked as a calico printer on the Brandywine River near Wilmington, Delaware, from 1797 to 1799. Although his business was short-lived, it appears to have produced as fine a body of work as John Hewson's printworks. Rowan's most important legacy was his surviving pattern book, comprising 140 designs, which is now in the collection of the Winterthur Library, along with his autobiography and two chintz fragments printed at his mill.

Of the many fabrics used in America during the eighteenth and early nineteenth century, the "blue-resists" or "India-blues" have inspired the most comment and conjecture. The question of their origin (American or English?) has baffled many textile historians—although the noted scholar Florence Pettit believes them to be probably American.[26] These decorative cotton fabrics, printed in two or more shades of blue on white (undyed) ground, are characterized by large, fanciful designs of birds (peacocks, pheasants, owls, etc.), fruit, exotic flowers, extensive foliage, and occasionally pillars and baskets. Picotage dots accentuated the designs and were part of the six-step printing process that used a paste/wax formula to form the resist patterns.[27] By alternating the placement of the paste mixture while submerging the cloth in vats of indigo in successive dippings, two or more shades of blue designs were produced. Metal pins attached to wooden printing blocks were responsible for "printing" (actually "reserving") the resist dots.

The variety and quality of American printed fabrics during the eighteenth and early nineteenth century could not compare to the British imports. In the first quarter of the nineteenth century English block prints incorporated "bizarre, fantastic and exotic" designs that appealed to more sophisticated Americans. Patriotic subjects made expressly for the American market were also popular, as were Ori-

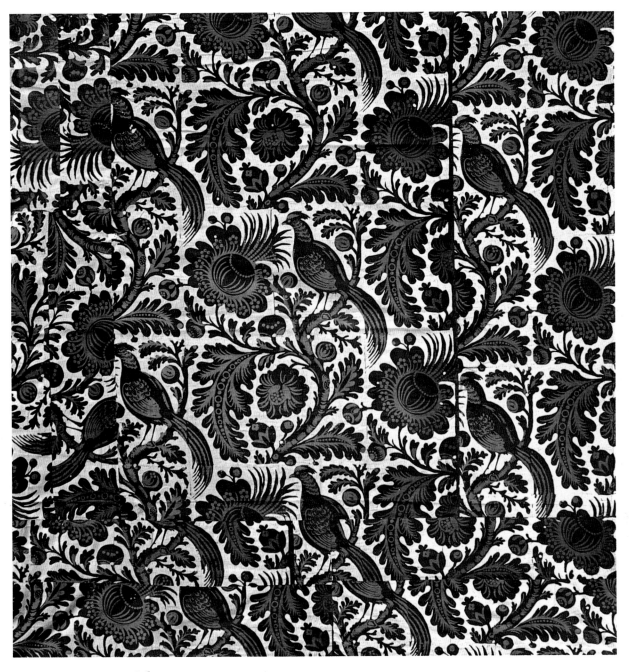

"American Pheasant"—a dramatic resist-dyed bedcover found in
one of the oldest homes (built in the 1600s) in East Hampton, Long
Island, and thought to have been made in the early 18th century.
Wooden hand blocks were used to dye each 20″ × 30″ square.
72″ × 97″. (Courtesy of the Shelburne Museum, Shelburne, Vt.)

ental motifs introduced by intrepid sea captains. Plates from Audubon's *Birds of America*, printed in the 1830s in several color combinations on fabric, were obviously a commercial success, as they continued to be offered for years.

The most important advance in the history of printed cottons was the introduction of roller printing. In 1815 Thomas Cooper described the new process in his book *A Practical Treatise of Dyeing and Callicoe Printing*: ". . . callicoes are printed by rollers, made of copper, accurately turned, and engraved with a pattern.—Callicoes may thus be printed a single colour, at the rate of a piece every five minutes very easily. By means of a series of these rollers, three . . . even four colours have been printed."[28]

The copperplate printing technique called for the plates to be inked, then wiped clean, thus leaving color only in the incised lines. The pressure of the rollers caused the ink to be drawn out onto the cloth. By 1835, two rollers could be run together; by 1840, colors could be printed consecutively, and the same cylinder could be inked in different colors. These improvements in textile manufacturing offered the consumer new designs and color combinations in dress and upholstery fabrics.

Factory cottons could easily be obtained in the East by the mid-nineteenth century, but pioneers in the West regarded storebought cloth as an expensive novelty: "On some occasions, the men could purchase a calico shirt . . . for which they paid $1.50 or $2 in skins or furs. And if a woman had one calico dress . . . she was considered a finely dressed lady."[29]

Even thread commanded premium prices and was always one of the most eagerly awaited staples in the peddler's pack. When it was not available, women made their own. In Smithfield, Utah, "Thread was very scarce, and when it could be obtained it sold for $1.25 a spool, but cross bar thread was made by unravelling factory threads, which was put on the spinning wheel, crossed and twisted. If dark thread was needed, these threads were blackened with soot from the stove."[30]

When hand-me-downs were beyond repair and cotton or muslin was unavailable, flour and grain sacks were turned into quilt linings and underwear. Printed advertisements often amusingly decorated "unmentionables"; one woman recalled: "Someone had said that the real pioneer in Kansas didn't wear any underwear, but this was not true of the Ellis County pioneer, and the clothes lines with undergarments advertising I. M. Yost's High Patent Flour were the best evidence."[31]

In the South, a uniquely regional type of weaving developed among the Louisiana Acadians descended from eighteenth-century French-Canadian immigrants. Using simple two-harness looms, Acadian women produced a variety of sturdy textiles in many shades of blue, brown, and white. They continued to use brown cotton—called nankin, coton jaune, cotonnade, or "slave cloth"—after most Southern commercial cotton growers had ceased producing it.[32] Many Acadian weavings are enlivened by *cordons* (strands of heavier yarn creating a ribbed effect) and *boutons* (raised, button-shaped nubs at the right-angle intersections of *cordons*). Although these textiles were generally intended for home use, "Acadian cottonades" were being advertised in New Orleans as early as 1821.[33] Late nineteenth-century magazines and women's organizations promoted them, but until recently Acadian textile traditions have been a well-kept secret.

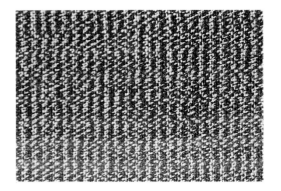

Mme Delhomme wove this Acadian, cottonnade material about 1865, probably planning to use it for men's trousers, jackets, or other outerware. (Courtesy of the Louisiana State Museum.)

Skeins of blanket-weight yarns of undyed brown and white cotton in a native Chitimacha Indian basket. (Courtesy of Cynthia Rubin.)

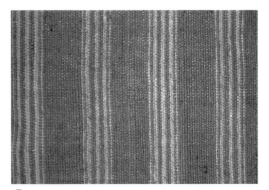

Detail of a 19th-century *coton jaune* blanket. Although it was intended for use as a serviceable bed covering, its handsome weave is of a superior quality. (Courtesy of the Louisiana State Museum.)

A turn-of-the-century ruffled Acadian pillowcase with warp and weft *cordons*. (Courtesy of the Louisiana State Museum.)

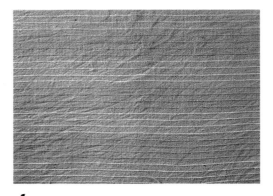

Acadian clothing fabric spun and woven by Mme Delhomme, c. 1865, in Vermilion Parish, Louisiana. The use of a heavier-weight yarn for the *cordons* creates an interesting textural effect. *Cordons* were normally used for bedspreads; it is rare to find them in clothing-weight textiles. (Courtesy of the Louisiana State Museum.)

SILK

Because of its high cost and relative scarcity, silk was used sparingly in eighteenth-century America. Unsuccessful attempts by the Virginia Company to raise silkworms in the seventeenth century, during the reign of James I, preceded equally

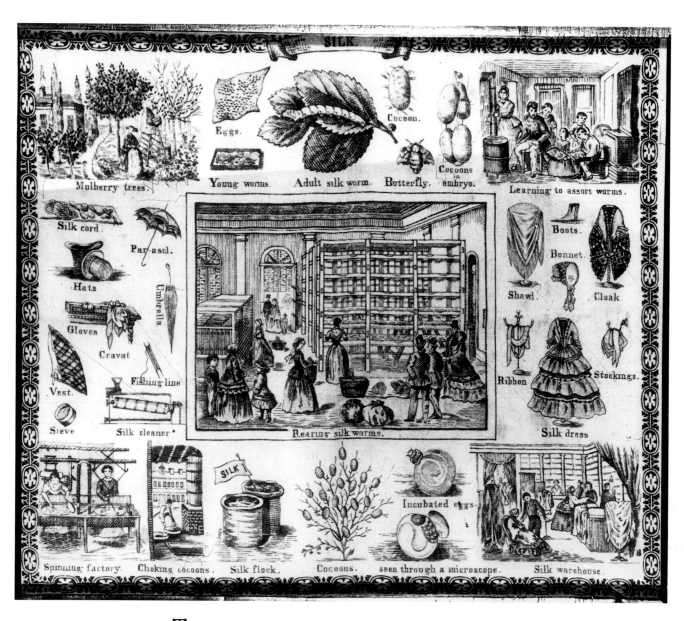

The arduous steps in rearing silkworms and manufacturing silk are graphically depicted in this printed pink-on-white cotton handkerchief, c. 1850–55. 10″ × 8″. (Courtesy of the New York-Historical Society, New York City.)

unproductive experiments in South Carolina and Georgia in the eighteenth century. Most silk was imported and did not become a feasible staple until the nineteenth century. At the time of the Revolution, ads appeared in newspapers aimed at those fortunate persons who already possessed their own silk. *The Pennsylvania Packet* (Aug. 15, 1774) contained a notice stating that "any person having silk of their own may have it manufactured into . . . silk stockings, sewin silk, ribbons &c."

Among the early silk producers, the Shakers were highly successful, especially in Kentucky and southern Ohio. By the 1830s the Kentucky community was producing enough silk for every sect member to own a silk handkerchief.[34] As with all Shaker products, their silk was of the finest quality. One observer of the handweaving process noted in 1847: "They [silk handkerchiefs] were a plain white cloth with a twill'd border. They are very handsome, and better than they can buy to wear to meeting."[35]

Other mid-nineteenth-century silk-making establishments included John Schwartz of York, Pennsylvania, who manufactured 200 yards of silk from his own cocoons in 1848. According to the *Hanover Herald* (October 1882) of Hanover, Pennsylvania, Mr. Schwartz eventually had a stockpile of 80,000 silkworms. He "passed his shuttle back and forth 9,000 times for every yard of silk he made, which was 27" wide."

In the Midwest, Ernst Valeton (1810–1894), a French immigrant, bought land in Kansas and persuaded several French families to join his cooperative community, which boasted seventy acres of mulberry trees. By 1870 the community was weaving 224 yards of silk ribbon a day.

On September 18, 1824, General Lafayette arrived in Troy, New York (one stop on his triumphal tour of America), where joyful crowds greeted him. Many people wore silk badges printed by Myron King of Troy in Lafayette's honor. (Courtesy of the Daughters of the American Revolution Museum.)

Abolitionist sentiments inspired the transfer-printed design on this silk drawstring bag. Many fashionable ladies and gentlemen of anti-slavery persuasion wore jewelry and carried purses proclaiming their beliefs. c. 1820–30. Height, 9". (Courtesy of the Daughters of the American Revolution Museum.)

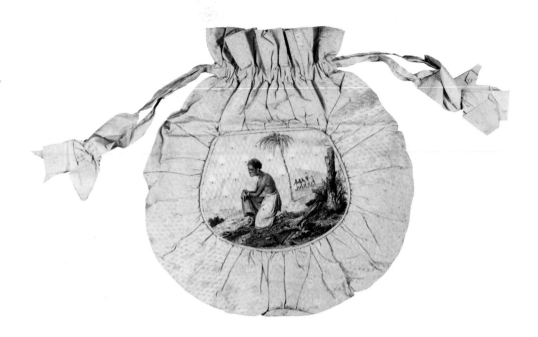

Three generations of one Alabama family named Weber wore this silk masonic apron bearing the name "Willis B. Jove," dated April 1, 1825. 21" sq. (Courtesy of Lillian and Jerry Grossman. Photograph, Schecter Lee.)

Four neckerchiefs indicative of the variety and quality of Shaker products. The green-lined linen kerchief with the pink stripe has finely cross-stitched initials, "I.W.," and "51" for 1851. The blue-and-white linen neckerchief was made by the Shakers of Sabbathday Lake, Maine; the silk neckerchief came from Kentucky; and the fringed taffeta neckerchief was made by the Church Family in Canterbury, New Hampshire. (Courtesy of the Shaker Museum, Old Chatham, New York. Photograph, Paul Rocheleau.)

As an industry, silk production appealed to individual entrepreneurs, including a Georgia woman who sold her silk in antebellum South Carolina at two to three times the cost of imported silk. She explained: "The people of South Carolina were all for living on their own resources, and having no dependence on other countries; they therefore, readily paid double prices for silks grown and manufactured at home, because it shut out the foreign trader, and kept all the money in the country."[36]

In 1836 the *New Hampshire Patriot and State Gazette* reported a new invention by Betsey Kimball: a spinning machine "to aid the common spinning-wheel for the formation of the ordinary silk thread from several fibres of cocoon." To stimulate silk production she often appeared in public wearing silk clothing of her own manufacture, eliciting praise from admiring neighbors. However, despite Betsey Kimball's efforts, silk manufacturing in New Hampshire proved economically unfeasible.[37]

The process of raising silkworms, reeling, dyeing, and knitting was a difficult business at best, and the steps involved were often remembered over a lifetime. In a letter written in 1845, Laura Brooks Vosbough willed a silk day cap she had made in 1780:

> I wish Elizabeth to keep what is marked with my name and to remember me and my industry by keeping the silk that I have made from the mulberrys which I raised from the seeds sown with my little fingers when quite small, with my father's help and encouragement. The feeding of the worms and the reeling of the balls, the knitting and the dyeing . . . I also did.[38]

In Utah, where the Mormons tried to develop home industries in silk production, whole families were involved in its manufacture. Annie Tanner remembered:

I don't know how mother ever spared us to go off and pick mulberry leaves for the silk worms. I suppose it was because President Young was promoting the silk culture in Utah. Aunt Nancy, father's third wife, secured some sheets of paper on which were silk worm eggs, and emptied her rooms to make a place for shelves and scaffolds on which the leaves were spread over the hungry worms.

Aunt Nancy reeled the silk from some of the cocoons and dyed the skeins which we used. . . .[39]

Although sporadic attempts were made throughout the country during the nineteenth century, the silk industry as a viable manufacturing presence never really took hold.

DYES

Before the availability of dyebooks in the nineteenth century, home dyeing depended upon the ingenuity and hawk-eyed observations of the dyer. For those who could not bring their cloth to the dyers and bleachers who advertised in local newspapers, the arts of "colouring" were almost as essential as the skills of spinning and weaving. Despite the drab costumes of the Puritans, most eighteenth-century Americans desired a variety of colors. One European observer marveled at the range he saw: ". . . you'd be surprised to see what beautiful colours some families will have in their garments, which commonly are streaked gowns, skirts, and petticoats of the same stuff. This we have borrowed from the Dutch, as well as the art of producing so many colours from the roots and barks of our woods, aided with indigo and alum. . . ."[40]

All year long, women collected roots, barks, berries, leaves, and nuts for dyeing. Successful homemade recipes commanded great interest, and on occasion were jealously guarded. Pink was a particularly hard color to obtain, and legend has it that one New England woman who had discovered its formula refused to divulge her secret. "Wyndym pink," as it came to be known, was named after the town where this possessive woman lived.[41] Nor was the spirit of competition unknown among pioneer women in the West. Of nineteenth-century Spanish Fork, Utah, Margaret J. Luudlow recalled: "I have heard my mother, Alice C. Jones, say that there was a great rivalry among the ladies when it came to the dyeing of the yarns. Each one tried to outdo the other in producing shades and tints from the mineral and vegetable matter which they gleaned from the earth."[42]

Most women, however, regarded dyeing less competitively, as just another step in the arduous task of clothmaking. Their most important goal was to find stable dyes that would survive many harsh washings. At first, only the blue obtained from indigo dye could be guaranteed colorfast, promoting many colonial housewives to consider the indigo vat an indispensable addition to the home.

Although it has been noted that "the indigo tub was almost as common an article of furniture as the churn," women hated the long, odorous task of indigo dyeing. Even the addition of herbs could not offset the stench of chamber-lye (urine) that was needed to set the dye. When they could afford to, they were glad to send cloth to the professional dyer. Colonial advertisements make it clear that women were eager to forgo the difficulties of indigo home dyeing, and reflect the popularity of the color. Whenever advertisers mention color, they speak of blue, deep blue, pale or "pail" blue, or "blew." Evidently blue was considered very desirable.[43]

The colonists had little difficulty obtaining indigo as it was imported from the West Indies and even grown at home in Georgia, Louisiana, Virginia, and especially South Carolina, where its success was due to a young girl, Eliza Lucas Pinckney. Her efforts in producing indigo yielded her first commercial crop in 1744, when she was twenty-two years old.[44] Indigo became an important export of South Carolina until the destruction of most indigo plantations during the Revolution. Until the introduction of aniline dyes in the late 1850s, women depended on indigo for their blue dyeing and found it readily available in cakes carried by the peddler or the general store. In the Southern Highlands some women even grew indigo in their gardens. However, even the usually reliable indigo occasionally presented problems for the home dyer, as illustrated by the woeful tale of Daniel Webster's schooldays, "when he sallied out in a suit of fresh blue homespun, was the sad experience of many another youth. A sudden shower was fatal to snowy linen, for the rain soon washed the color from the coat into the shirt."[45]

By experimenting, women found mordants that could render a variety of dyes permanent. These mordants were often discovered among their kitchen supplies: vinegar, salt, lye, and soda. Each area supplied its dyes from local vegetation. In parts of Utah, for example, green was made from sagebrush with alum or creosote, brown-green from peach leaves, red and purple from madder, brown from walnuts, yellow from rabbit brush, and black from squawbush twigs.[46] Even small children searched the countryside for natural dyes. Hannah Dalton recalled:

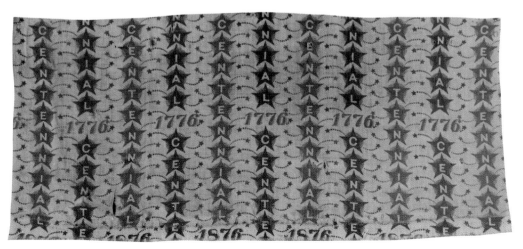

*C*entennial yard goods— some quilts have been found made of this printed cotton. (Courtesy of the Cooper-Hewitt Museum, Smithsonian Institution, New York City.)

I was . . . too small to spin, but I would gather the yellow blooms from the rabbit brush to color yellow; the peach leaves to color green; the log wood for black, and it was a great outing for us to go the mountains and get madras for red, and in every up-to-date home the blue dyepot, made of indigo, had a prominent place by the fire. All these things made pretty colors and we would get copperas from the foot hills to set the dye, so it would not fade.[47]

In another part of the country, almost identical hues might be produced from different materials. Recipes were cherished and handed down in families. These handwritten instructions could be incredibly complex. In a homemade book of dye recipes (found wrapped in a sheet of newspaper published in 1784), directions for the color "Clarret" stated:

Take Butternut bark of the body and boil it one hour / then take it and Copperis it / then fling away your old dy and Rence your Cloth Clean / then

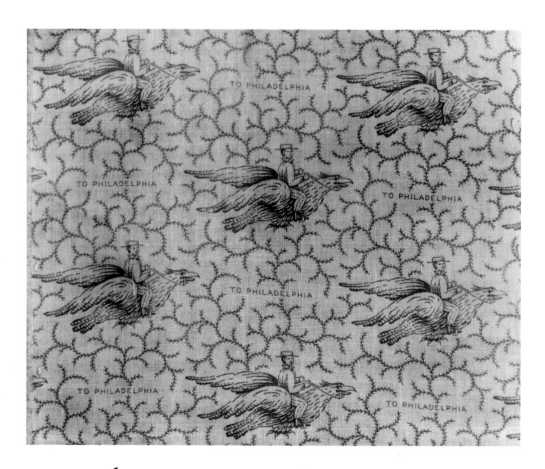

All roads led to Philadelphia during the Centennial—even if one had to fly on the back of an eagle, as this amusing fabric suggests. (Courtesy of the Cooper-Hewitt Museum, Smithsonian Institution, New York City.)

new vamp your dy with redwood and allum and boil it one hour / then take
it out and put in more redwood and allum and boil it one hour more / then
potash it also / put 2 pounds of redwood to 3 yards of Cloth &c.[48]

In the Southern Highlands women were experts at dyeing, using centuries-
old recipes. Sarah Dougherty in the 1930s reminisced:

> Our formula for madder was one that was used in England in the fifteenth
> century, according to an old book on dyes. This formula has been handed
> down in our family. It calls for ash lye, sour bran water, madder root, and
> alum. The process is different for different shades. My great-grandmother,
> Nancy Smith Flannery, was a professional indigo dyer and I have her for-
> mula for dyeing blue.[49]

By the close of the nineteenth century packaged aniline dyes had reached the
most remote settlements, and the era of home dyeing virtually ended.

By the 1880s, women could buy yardage imitating the popular crazy quilt patterns. This particular fabric, marked "PML"
(Pacific Mills, Lawrence), was made in Massachusetts.
It contained "new" and amusing motifs including a tennis
racquet and a frog with the motto "Fine Morning Sir." (Courtesy of the Litchfield Historical Society, Litchfield, Conn.)

A handsome Centennial fabric. 9″ × 8″.
(Courtesy of the Litchfield Historical Society,
Litchfield, Conn.)

According to family legend, Lucretia Street Hall (1773–1851) of Charlemont, Massachusetts, embroidered this vibrant bedcover with homespun and home-dyed yarns as a wedding gift for her niece in about 1837. 96″ × 97″. (Courtesy of Historic Deerfield, Inc.)

TWO

BLANKETS,
COUNTERPANES,
AND BED RUGGS

$\mathcal{C}$ontrary to popular myth, America's first bedcovers were not patch-work—tiny scraps of cloth pieced together—nor were they made of cotton. In fact, only a very small number of the bedcovers used by the colonists before the mid-eighteenth century were even quilted, and most of those were expensive imports, often of silk, from England or the Continent. Trousseau linens for well-to-do young ladies of fashion were usually ordered from abroad. Before Judith Sewall's marriage in 1720, her father, Judge Samuel Sewall, sent to England for "Curtains and Vallens for a Bed with Counterpane Head Cloth and Tester made of good yellow waterd worsted Camlet [a wool fabric possibly mixed with silk or hair] with Triming well made and Bases if it be the Fashion."[1]

Early textile historians believed that patchwork quilts came to the Massachusetts Bay Colony with the first settlers, but later researchers, going carefully through wills and probate records, have found evidence to disprove that view. Sally Garoutte examined seventeenth- and early-eighteenth-century records from Plymouth, Massachusetts; Providence, Rhode Island; Hartford, Connecticut; and New Hampshire, and discovered that among more than five hundred listings for bedcovers only ten were quilts. Quilts were expensive as well as rare in that era, their average value five times higher than that of the blankets listed. For the most part, seventeenth-century bedding seems to have consisted of "woolen blankets, woolen bed ruggs, and coverlets—which were sometimes woolen and sometimes linen."[2]

Determining exactly what a bed rugg or coverlet looked like in the first one hundred fifty years of this country's settlement is extremely difficult because no seventeenth-century examples have survived, and because written records are confusing in their use of multiple terms for bedcoverings. Coverlet (coverlid), derived from the French *couvre* and *lit,* in some contexts refers to the outermost layer of bed-clothing and in others to the woolen bedcovers woven by home and professional weavers. Elsewhere the word seems to refer to what today are called bed ruggs.

Various meanings have been suggested for counterpane (counterpin) and rug, some of them all-inclusive, like Alice Morse Earle's idea that even flannel sheets may have been included under the term "rug": "Flannel sheets also were made and may appear in inventories under the name of rugs, and thus partially explain the untidy absence, even among the possessions of wealthy citizens, of sheets."[3] The word "rug" also meant a type of cloth—a coarse wool—used for both garments and bedding.[4] "Counterpane," like coverlid, is generally agreed today to refer to the outermost and most elaborate bedcover, the one used for decoration rather than warmth.

Despite the confusion in terms, we know that the New England colonists slept under many layers of bedclothing, a combination of whatever rugs, blankets, and coverlets they could gather, to ward off the extreme cold in the ill-heated, drafty houses. Like their forebears across the ocean, they might even have used bed-staves (or staffes), sets of six tall wooden pins inserted in both sides of the bedstead to keep the heavy layers of bedclothing from slipping off.[5]

Beds themselves were of various widths and lengths; many four-posters were only four feet wide. The wider the bed the more expensive it was to build, with the cost rising at "2 pence per inch" as the bed became wider than four feet.[6] With no standard bed sizes, the size of covers also varied considerably, often requiring adjustment when someone acquired a new bed.

The most frequent alterations found on surviving pieces are the square cut-outs at the bottom for a four-poster bed. Occasionally, the design of a piece appears unbalanced, with a skewed center and a border wider on one side than the other. Such a piece may have been cut down either to fit a bed or to remove a damaged part.

BLANKETS

"Blanket" is derived from the medieval French *blanchet* (pronounced *blanquet* in the west of France). Originally meaning a bedcovering made of white linen, the word came to be used for textiles woven of wool, silk, or cotton.[7] When the one hundred men of the Massachusetts Bay Company left England to form their settlement here, they numbered among their goods "50 Ruggs and 50 peare of blanketts of Welsh cotton," the latter a well-known woolen fabric of the period, named after its place of origin.[8]

Most common in the colonies were blankets of wool, first imported and later raised, spun, and woven at home. English blankets were exported and sold in pairs, the two lengths of blanketing woven together with a stripe between, indicating where they were to be cut in two. Witney blankets, from Oxfordshire, were considered the best, for their thickness and softness. As noted in *The Workwoman's Guide*, published in England in 1838, "Every bed should have one under blanket, and two or three upper ones. These last are usually the Witney, whilst the under blanket is of an inferior sort; they should be thick and light, with a soft nap or wool upon them. . . . The Witney blanket is considered the best."[9]

Both here and abroad, these plain white blankets were often decorated in the corners with simple embroidered designs. As early as 1653, the French Cardinal Mazarin owned several sets of English blankets with a blue crown worked in the corners—a design popular here as late as the eighteenth century.[10] In the colonies and in England, another embroidered motif was the compass rose (sometimes called "Wind rose"), divided like a compass into as many as thirty-two points and resembling a stylized rose. Evidence suggests they were quite popular—five rose blankets are listed in the 1797 inventory of Aaron Burr's home, and George Washington is known to have ordered some for the executive mansion in Philadelphia

A plaid woolen blanket from Pennsylvania, c. 1830 (twill-woven in the bird's-eye pattern). Made on a multiple-shaft loom, it is typical of Pennsylvania homespun blankets. 82″ × 84″. (Courtesy of Margo Paul Ernst. Photograph, Schecter Lee.)

This handwoven plaid wool and cotton blanket was embroidered with brightly colored woolen yarns with eight-pointed stars in each square. A tatted fringe edges two sides, suggesting it remains unfinished. Mid-19th century. 89″ × 72″. (Courtesy of the Shelburne Museum. Photograph, Ken Burris.)

A cotton summer bedspread with crewel embroidery made by or for
Susan T. Bartlett, dated August 2, 1827 (or 1821). 76″ × 88″.
(Courtesy of the Shelburne Museum. Photograph, Ken Burris.)

A member of the Spear family in Shelburne, Vermont, wove and embroidered this early 19th-century twill blanket using vegetable-dyed wool yarn. 77″ × 106″. (Courtesy of the Shelburne Museum.)

A 19th-century unfinished bedspread. The vase and some of the flowers are worked in reverse appliqué, a technique involving cutting out the design from the main ground and attaching colored fabric underneath (which shows through) to establish the design. 72″ × 78″. (Courtesy of the Shelburne Museum.)

in 1792.[11] Embroidered with long, loose stitches in multicolored wools, the roses were easily torn, and few that are found today have remained intact.

Later, in the nineteenth century, homespun blankets were sometimes embroidered with elaborate all-over designs in either indigo or multicolored wools, on solid white or blue-and-white-checked backgrounds. Many blankets had floral designs, often with the same motif repeated three or four times across, like the blocks of a patchwork quilt. Other designs were based on a central medallion format, with a large flower basket or other design in the middle, surrounded by multiple borders.

COUNTERPANES AND COVERLETS

These bedcovers, topmost on the bed, were the most elaborate of all, being intended for show and not for warmth. In the seventeenth century, they were made of imported silks, wools, or cottons, from fabrics the names of which have long since disappeared from the language: calamanco, camlet, cheyney, darnix, and sarsenet. They came from the Continent or the British Isles, almost exclusively via London.

In seventeenth-century homes, the bedstead was the most important and valuable piece of furniture. To date, no seventeenth-century American highpost bed is known, although there is evidence that they existed. In Quaker Philadelphia, a warning was given to the "Women Friends" in 1698 to have "no superfluous furniture be in your houses, as great fringes about your valances, and double valances, and double curtains. . ."[12] indicating the presence of high-post beds. The fabrics covering a high-post or four-poster bed, collectively called bed furniture, were usually the most valuable household property listed in an inventory, and almost invariably were worth more than the bed itself. A large number of pieces were needed to enclose such a bed completely, to keep out the cold air, and to provide some privacy in the bedroom, which, as a rule, was shared with other members of the family. A complete set of bed furniture consisted of as many as six side curtains, head cloths, tester cloth (the canopy), three or four valances, and bedspread or counterpane.[13] Usually of crewel-embroidered linen, very few complete sets have survived, in part because some pieces of the set got harder wear than others, but also because sets were often divided among heirs.

Of the few surviving sets, most of whose makers are unknown, one has been documented as the work of Mary Bulman of York, Maine. Made about 1745, it was worked while her husband, a surgeon, served and died in Nova Scotia during the siege of Louisburg. Elaborately embroidered in multicolored crewel on homespun linen, it contains large-scale floral designs, running vines in large and small scale, and valances with long lines of poetry, surrounded by naively drawn trees, flowers, and fruit. Clearly a labor of love, the pieces must have taken months, even years of work, and with their vivid colors and charming designs, suggest their maker was a woman rich in both talent and joy, despite the difficulties of her life.

The bedspread or counterpane of a set was of fabric that matched the other pieces. It might be a solid color, of silk, camlet or calamanco (glazed worsteds), or linsey-woolsey (a linen warp with a woolen weft). The latter two were frequently made in dark-blue indigo, red, or deep watermelon pink, and all shades were heavily quilted.

Sets of bed furniture were not limited to those decorated with crewel embroidery. Imported cottons and chintzes (glazed cottons) with multicolored designs, made especially in India for the Western market, were also popular. Harriet Beecher Stowe remembered sleeping at her aunt's house in a bed that was

"curtained with a printed India linen . . . brought home by my seafaring uncle. . . . I recollect the almost awestruck delight with which I gazed on the strange mammoth plants, with great roots and endless convolutions of branches, in whose hollows appeared Chinese summer-houses . . . with sleepy-looking mandarins smoking . . ."[14]

Following the beginning of copperplate printing in England in 1756, copperplate prints with designs of birds, patriotic subjects, and pastoral scenes, in red, chocolate, blue, or purple on white, became popular for bed furniture and remained in vogue well into the nineteenth century. About 1760, George Washington had his newly made English bedstead hung with "chintz blew plate cotton furniture," that matched the chair seats and window cornices of the bedroom.[15] By the Federal period, crewelwork bed furniture had declined in popularity, seeming old-fashioned and heavy against the background of the lighter, more delicate furniture and interiors of the era.[16]

Believed to be the work of Catherine Thorn, this bed rugg was
part of the marriage chest of her sister Mary Thorn. Both girls came
from Ipswich, Massachusetts. Mary married in 1724, the date on the
rugg. Initialed "CT." (Courtesy of the Wenham Historical
Association and Museum, Inc.)

BED RUGGS

Of all the early bedcoverings, these embroidered coverlets, needle-sewn, with multiple strands of twisted (multi-ply) yarn, are the most rare and least like any other type of bedcover. Sometimes mistaken for hooked rugs—of much later date, intended for the floor and worked with a hook rather than a needle—they were regarded until the 1920s as having no value at all. Homer Eaton Keyes, founder of *The Magazine Antiques*, first came across a bed rugg in Chelsea, Vermont, serving as a carpet pad. When the carpet wore out, the rugg, dated 1774 and cut in two, emerged from its hiding place, having been well preserved from both light and wear.[17]

Sewn of multicolored wool yarns on plain woven wool or linen, most often with a simple running stitch, bed ruggs were made, from start to finish, at home. Growing the wool, cleaning, dyeing, and spinning it were only the first steps in a very long process. Possibly because of the great amount of work that went into making them, or maybe because of their importance at the time, bed ruggs, unlike most other types of bedcovers, are almost always signed or initialed and dated. The dates on these ruggs—worked into the design itself, often at the center top—make it easy to document when they were made. No needlewoman could have been prouder of her rugg than Mary Comstock, who wrote her name so large that, with the date, it takes up two lines and fills the top fourth of her rugg: "Mary Comstock's Rugg Jan'y 30, 1810."

Where these ruggs, made from the early eighteenth through the first part of the nineteenth century, originated is unknown. No records or examples are found in England, and very few references to embroidered bed ruggs are found in colonial inventories. The strongest evidence of their existence in the seventeenth century is a written reference to a "yearne courlead" by Susannah Compton and another by an Ipswich, Massachusetts, man, Adam Hunt, in 1671, to an "embroadured couerled."[18]

Bed ruggs have been found all over New England, with the greatest numbers coming from the Connecticut River Valley. The origins for their designs, like the ruggs themselves, are unknown; most, however, were done primarily in combinations of blues, browns, and undyed yarns, and follow one of two typical designs: "One was that of three or more vines meandering vertically on the rugg face, an adaption of the Tree-of-Life motif. . . . The other pattern, more often used, was a branching floral bush with a surround or border of vinelike rondeaux."[19] While a few examples follow neither pattern, the majority do, suggesting some yet-to-be-discovered design source.

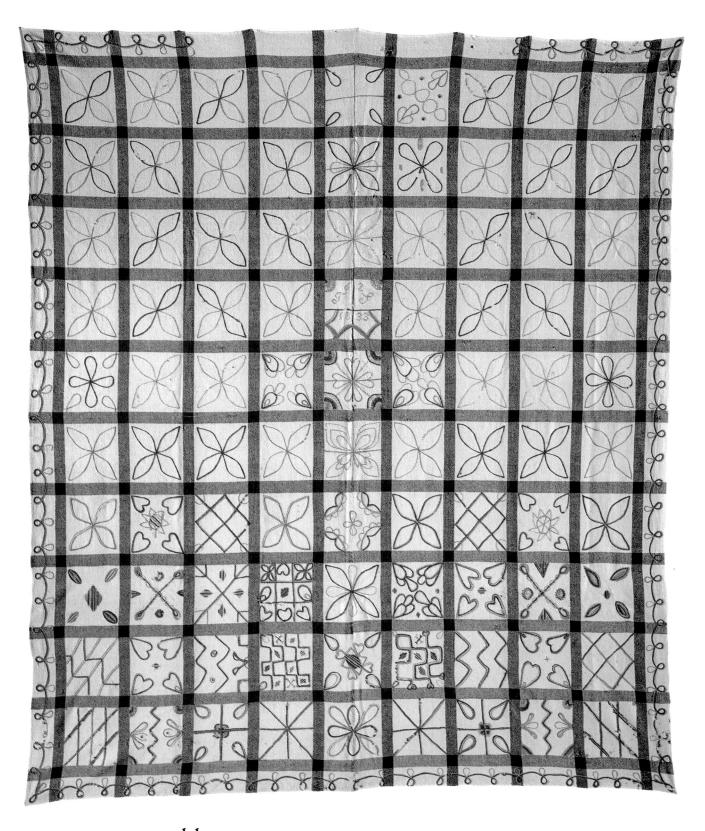

Homespun blankets were often embroidered with abstract designs. Made of two lengths of material, the pattern of this example is carefully matched at the center seam. Connecticut, dated 1833. 94″ × 83″. (Courtesy of Kelter-Malcé. Photograph, Schecter Lee.)

Central medallion patchwork quilt: a combination of several
patterns. This very large quilt is the unique creation of its Southern
maker. When found, it had a small note pinned to it that read
"Made by my father's aunt Leucetta Bosworth" and was signed merely
"Alice." Cotton. Probably Virginia. c. 1860. 94″ × 96″. (Courtesy
of Sweet Nellie. Photograph, Schecter Lee.)

THREE

QUILTS

The *earliest* quilted materials were made in the Orient, although no evidence exists to prove when or where the art of quilting originated. Dating from c. 3400 B.C., the carved ivory figure of an Egyptian pharaoh wearing a robe of incised diamond shapes suggests just how ancient a practice it is. Quilting is believed to have spread along the trade routes from the East to western Europe, and reached Britain by the thirteenth century, or possibly earlier.

Although quilting was used on bedcoverings by the Middle Ages, an even earlier use was for armor. Made of a sturdy material, like linen, and thickly padded and stitched, it was less effective than metal armor, which came later, but it offered at least minimal protection from the spears and arrows of war. When the metal variety came into use, quilted armor continued to be worn underneath, making the wearer more comfortable and cushioning the metal's weight.

Quilted bedcovers were in use by the thirteenth century, but the earliest surviving examples of bed quilts are three from Sicily, all made about 1400. Of stuffed and quilted linen, they are pictorial, illustrating scenes from the medieval legend of Tristan.

By the time the first colonists came to New England, New Amsterdam, and Virginia, quilted bedcovers were common in England and Holland, so it is likely that bed quilts were included in the household goods these settlers brought with them.

Evidence from seventeenth- and early-eighteenth-century New England inventories and wills suggests, however, that quilts were the least common type of bedcover as well as the most valued. Contrary to popular opinion, the earliest quilts were not made of scraps and were not the everyday bedcovers in most homes. And their rarity implies that they were owned by well-to-do families. In surveying inventories written in the Salem, Massachusetts, area between 1635 and 1674, one historian found that "coverlets were mentioned 142 times and ruggs (for the

An 18th-century calamanco bedcover, possibly from Maine, quilted in a swirling pattern of onion-shaped designs with floral motifs. 97" × 107". (Courtesy of Shelburne Museum. Photograph, Ken Burris.)

bed) 157 times while quilts were listed only 4 times."[1] A review of other early New England records indicates that the average value given for a blanket was 10 shillings, while that for a quilt was 52 shillings.[2]

Very few of the quilts found in the colonies until the mid-eighteenth century were pieced or appliquéd. Rather, they were what are called today whole-cloth quilts, although they consisted of several lengths of cloth seamed together, usually in a solid color, and decorated with elaborate quilting. Made either of silk or wool, many of the woolen ones and all of the silks were imported:

Quilts and Rugs—Imported from London and Sold by Moses Belcher Bass at his Shop in Ann Street. . . .—*Boston Newsletter*, May 13, 1762.[3]

The most typical of the whole-cloth woolen quilts, frequently indigo-dyed to a rich blue-black, were very large, to cover the many layers of bedding piled on the bedstead during the day and the low children's beds hidden away underneath. Other colors used were lighter blues, bright pinks, yellow, deep green, and browns, some of which still retain their intensity today. Traditionally called linsey-woolsey, these deeply colored wool quilts with lavish quilting stitches were made of all-wool glazed worsteds currently known as calamanco or glazed camlet.[4] Linsey-woolsey, a combination of linen (for the warp) and wool (for the weft), was made in the colonies as well as in England, and was much used for clothing, including petticoats and aprons.

An indigo blue–glazed calamanco quilted coverlet. Note how the glazed worsted retains its original sheen. Probably New England. c. 1800–25. 104″ × 106″. (Courtesy of "all of us americans" folk art.)

Chintz appliquéd by a variety of stitches on a very fine linen ground and a 2-inch border of printed chintz form this very early bedcover. The ribbon swag motif has proven to be an enduring design element, as popular in 20th-century quilting as in earlier work. 93″ × 89″. (Courtesy of the Shelburne Museum.)

By the early 1800s, quilts using smaller squares of different-colored wools were also being made, although they seem to have been less common than whole-cloth wool quilts. One example, made by a Scotch-Irish woman in Pennsylvania, signed and dated "Sept. 13, 1809—MRMc" in the quilting, is constructed of sixty alternating squares of watermelon pink and black. Set in a diamond pattern similar to those on eighteenth-century painted floors and floorcloths, each square is quilted with an elaborate geometric design. So many different designs appear on the quilt that Tandy Hersh, its present owner, believes it to be a sampler of quilting designs recorded for future use, much like an embroidery sampler.[5]

Woolen quilts, made for warmth as well as decoration, were not the only kind of whole-cloth quilts. Chintzes—elaborately printed cotton from England and In-

dia, both quilted and plain—were very popular in New England and in the Southern colonies. In the 1790s, Sarah Anna Emery of Newburyport, Massachusetts, went to visit a recent bride in her new home and noted the profusion of chintz, which she called "patch," in the best chamber: "[It] was elegant with gay patch hangings to the high square post bedstead, and curtains of the same draped the windows."[6]

Indian chintz bedspreads, or palampores—from the Persian and Hindi *palangposh,* a bedcover—unlined, and unquilted, were hand-painted; the color was put on with a kind of brush or pen rather than a wooden block.[7] Intended to appeal to the European market, many had overall floral designs. Most common, though, was the large, central flowering tree or Tree of Life motif, a tall, many-

A very early example of pieced chintz, notably rare for its use of long, narrow strips to form the design. Pennsylvania. c. 1830–40. 70" × 78". (Courtesy of "all of us americans" folk art.)

branched tree rising from a rockery or mound of earth, and sprouting a variety of flowers. Appearing on Indian textiles from the late seventeenth century on, the motif had originally come to Europe from the East, probably as wallpaper designs or paintings, and was modified by the European trading companies to be painted on Indian goods intended for the West.

Caroline King remembered sleeping in a bed furnished with chintz hangings and counterpane that, according to family legend, had been pirated on the high seas:

> The tradition about that gorgeous bed furniture was that it was taken with other handsome things from an English vessel, by one of my grandfather's privateers, and that it was on its way to England to adorn the bed of some very reverent and potent seignior there. . . . Nobody called it piracy and I never heard the word *plunder* [her italics] applied to our gorgeous bed trimmings. . . . I never heard of any one's slumbers under those tropical blossoms being for one moment disturbed by the free and easy, not to say freebootery way in which it came into our family.[8]

A rare 18th-century *broderie perse* "Tree of Life" handwoven linen counterpane. Bedcovers with appliqués of the prized Indian palampores were held in as much esteem as treasured porcelains. 106″ × 103″. (Courtesy of the Shelburne Museum.)

Whole-cloth chintz quilts, lush and deeply colored, were very expensive; perhaps for that reason, a method of appliquéing small pieces of chintz to a white ground, called *broderie perse* (Persian embroidery), became very popular in the late eighteenth and early nineteenth centuries. Since this method required much less chintz, it provided an economical way of being in style. Both small and large motifs of flowers, foliage, and exotic birds were cut out and sewed down with tiny stitches, in the following way: "Stretch your background upon a frame, and paste the chintz flowers into position upon it. When the pasting is finished and dry, take the work out of the frame and stitch loosely with as little visibility as possible, all around the leaves and flowers."[9] So popular were quilts with appliquéd chintz cutouts that, by about 1800, fabric printers both here and in England began designing and printing squares of cloth with popular motifs, specifically made for use as the center in central medallion quilts. Floral baskets and urns, as well as variations of the Tree of Life motif, were typical. In Philadelphia, John Hewson, one of America's few documented textile printers, is known to have made such centers, the best known example having an elegant urn filled with flowers and ornamented with a butterfly and several birds.

This unbacked and unquilted *broderie perse* bedcover resembles the earlier, printed Indian palampores. Here the design is not printed but assembled from a variety of chintz motifs stitched to the background fabric. Made by Maria Boyd Schulz, c. 1855, in Charleston, South Carolina. 112″ × 117″. (Courtesy of the Charleston Museum. Photograph, Carlton Palmer.)

Chintz quilts, both whole-cloth and appliquéd, have been found in New England and the Middle Atlantic States, but nowhere were they more popular than in the South, as recently discovered examples are making clear. One related group made between 1800 and 1840 consists of nine quilts similar in design and technique—all are *broderie perse* and all were done in a central medallion format, in which one large motif is surrounded by multiple borders. All of the quilts, it turns out, were made in Mecklenburg County, around Charlotte, North Carolina, by well-to-do women who were members of the same social group. Such elaborate, elegant works were most certainly made as bridal pieces, and possibly were quilted at one of the bees, or "quiltings," held in the South with great regularity.

"I was so engaged in frolicking," Mary Warren wrote in a letter of 1800, "for there is nothing here among us but quiltings and weddings. . . ."

"I was to 4 quiltings, but not any dancing at one of them," lamented Ginny Alexander to her sister in 1803, suggesting that she favored more lively affairs than the ones she had been attending.[10]

Almost from the first, the social aspect of quilting, the chance to chat and work with other women, was one of the charms of quiltmaking. Alice Earle mentions a ten-day quilting bee held in Narragansett as early as 1752, and a Long Island woman tells of quilting with friends in 1826: "Clear and calm and very hot,

This calico top contains a patch that must have been sent as the invitation to a quilting party. It reads: "CALICO PARTY. Yourself and lady are respectfully invited to attend a calico party to be given at KIRBYHOUSE HALL, CANAJOHAIRIE. ON FRIDAY EVE FEB. 18, 1870." New York State. c. 1870. 90″ × 102″. (Courtesy of Margie Dyer. Photograph, Schecter Lee.)

the thermometer being as high as 108—4 persons sunstruck today and several yesterday . . . Sarah Baldwin, Frances and Jane Bergen, hear [sic] to help us quilt."[11]

Quilting bees or frolics seem to have been popular in all sections of the country, although different customs prevailed in different places. In Pennsylvania, when the women had finished their work at a bee, the quilt was taken out of the frame and each corner was given to an unmarried woman. A cat was thrown into the center of the quilt, which was "vigorously shaken; the young woman nearest the cat when she jumped out would surely be married within the year."[12]

Of all the customs associated with quilting, the quilting bee is the one most often fictionalized or remembered. In 1895, though bees were by then long out of fashion, Mary Wilkins Freeman published a story called "A Quilting Bee in Our Village," capturing the spirit of a time past, and suggesting what the "frolickings" Mary Warren wrote about in her letter of 1800 must have been like:

> The women had just finished the quilt and rolled it up, and taken down the frame, when Lurinda Snell spied Mr. Lucius Downey coming, and screamed out and ran, and all the girls after her. They had brought silk bags with extra finery, such as laces and ribbons and combs, to put on in the evening, and they all raced upstairs to the spare chamber.
>
> When they came down with their ribbons gayly flying, and some of them with their hair freshly curled, all the men had arrived, and Mrs. White asked them to walk out to tea.[13]

As much as with bees, quilts have traditionally been associated with brides, the best known custom being that of a young woman completing a baker's dozen of quilts before she married. In most cases only the tops were made; they were quilted and finished when the engagement was announced, as filling and backing were expensive investments. Twelve of the quilts were likely to be everyday bed-covers, but the thirteenth must be a girl's bridal quilt, as elegant and elaborate as she could afford to make it. Hearts were the traditional motif for bridal quilts, along with pineapples for hospitality, cornucopias for abundance, and doves for peace. Bridal quilts carried with them their own superstitions: putting hearts on a quilt before a girl's engagement was announced was considered unlucky. In some areas it was considered bad luck for a prospective bride to help stitch her own bridal quilt, although she might sign and date it when it was finished, as some girls did in cross-stitch with strands of their own hair.

Whatever its function as a social occasion, quiltmaking's main reason for being has always been a private one—the personal satisfaction it gives. The necessity for making quilts to keep warm in the early colonies has been stressed, but as the relative rarity of early quilts compared to other bed coverings is established, it seems likely that quilts were always made more out of choice than necessity.[14] Women whose lives were busy with an infinite number of tasks, all repetitive and many tedious, must have welcomed the opportunity to experiment with color and

Photograph showing boys and girls working on patchwork squares in the third quarter of the 19th century. Found in Massachusetts. (Courtesy of Pat Yamin.)

pattern as a means of self-expression. It has been said that in the early years, some women worked on two quilts at once—one very intricate and finely made, the other less complex and with cruder stitching, so it could be done in the evenings by candlelight.[15] Such a scheme would have met both needs: warm bedcovers and aesthetic pleasure.

THE BEGINNINGS OF PATCHWORK

The origins of patchwork—sometimes called pieced work—like the origins of quilting itself, are buried in history. The earliest surviving American pieced quilts date from the latter part of the eighteenth century. The earliest English example still in existence, made at Levens Hall in Westmorland of Indian calicos, dates from 1708, but it is likely that patchwork was made in England even earlier, since by 1726, Jonathan Swift was referring to it in print in *Gulliver's Travels*. In the land of the Lilliputians, Gulliver is outfitted in a garment that "looked like the patchwork made by the ladies in England, only that mine were all of a colour."[16]

By 1772, patchwork was being done in the colonies too, as an entry in Anna Winslow's diary shows: "Some time since I exchanged a piece of patchwork, which had been wrought in my leisure intervals, with Miss Peggy Phillips . . . for a pair of curious lace mitts with blue flaps . . . I had intended that the patchwork should have grown large enough to have covered a bed. . . ." But as the rest of her entry tells, she never finished more than the small piece mentioned.[17]

Unlike Anna Winslow, who chose to abandon her project, many children were not allowed to go and play until they had finished each day's required amount of patchwork, whether they liked it or not. "Ann Lizy's Patchwork," a short story by Mary Wilkins Freeman, gives an idea of what many children must have felt about the work: "Ann Lizy had not as much ambition as her grandmother, now she was engaged upon her second quilt, and it looked to her like a checked and be-sprigged calico mountain."[18] Not surprisingly, Lizy loses a patch she is working on while walking to visit a friend.

Whatever their feelings as little girls (Lizy was not yet eight years old), most nineteenth-century women grew up to make hundreds of quilts for themselves and their families. Of these, the majority were patchwork or pieced quilts, made from stitching together hundreds of tiny pieces of cloth—most often squares, diamonds, or triangles, as curved shapes demanded much more skill. Although a few pieced quilts were made in the late 1700s and early 1800s, the great majority date from about 1830 on, when the growth of the domestic textile industry made attractive, inexpensive cotton prints readily available.

Patchwork quilts may be made from scrap pieces of cloth, odd bits saved over the years, from the clothing of loved ones, or from material bought expressly to be used in a quilt. While scrap quilts might seem to require the least planning, they may in fact be the ones quilters spend most time thinking about:

"LeMoyne Stars": a 19th-century crib quilt encompassing a variety of calicos and toiles with clamshell quilting in the border. 39″ sq. (Courtesy of the Shelburne Museum.)

It took a woman a long time to plan the pattern, but she could not start making it until the outdoor work was over for the year, so while she sat cutting beans for the piccalilli, she had time to plan the quilt in her mind, looking at the yellow beans, the green peppers, the red tomatoes, and the differing shades of each blending into the whole, adding just a speck of red pepper to make it come alive.[19]

Quilts made from the clothing of loved ones were and still are among those most cherished, and are frequently passed down in a family because of their sentimental value. At a Louisiana quilting bee held as recently as 1974, a group of relatives worked on a quilt with some fabric with which they were all familiar, and commented as they worked:

"Boy, I'll tell y'all what. This black and white checkered diamonds is somethin' else to try to do."
"Oh, that's Aunt Dee's. It was something to sew! Lord!"
"The black checked?"
"Oh, I had a dress out of that."
"Oh, I did too."
"Aunt Dee had a skirt and vest."
"I had a skirt and top. . . ."[20]

Pieced quilts for which the material was bought were often of two or three colors; blue and white, red and white, and red, green, and white in solid colors or small prints were some of the most popular combinations.

Whether bought or salvaged, cloth was scarce and very precious, particularly on the frontier, where scrap quilts were the rule, and losing even a piece was a tragedy:

Calico cost fifty cents a yard, and everything was cut very sparingly, but mother would give me the tiny scraps to put in my quilt blocks that Grandmother Smith was showing me how to make. I was making a nine-patch block and sometimes I had to piece the pieces in order to get a little block one inch square. One day we had been playing down by the shed where we kept old Lina, the cow. I forgot to take my basket in the house with me, and when I went to get it, it was gone. Mother said she was afraid Lina had eaten it. I think that was the greatest loss I ever had in my life, and to this day I remember how badly I felt. My little heart was nearly broken.[21]

Their ragbag or scrap quilts gave women a source of pride and accomplishment, and occasionally protected their sanity: "I had no yarn to knit, nothing to sew, not even patches. . . . One day Mrs. Parrish gave me a sack full of rags and I never received a present before nor since that I so highly appreciated as I did those rags."[22]

An appliquéd child's cotton pillow. The figure of Jesus is framed by the words "Behold I stand at the door and knock." The back of the cover is pink printed calico with an appliqué of a young girl laundering her doll clothes. Probably late 19th century. 23″ × 16″. (Courtesy of the Shelburne Museum. Photograph, Ken Burris.)

Ellen German chose a variety of homespun fabrics and mattress ticking for her quilt. The late date (1901) suggests she probably saved scraps of fabric over a period of years. 75″ × 88″. (Courtesy of Laura Fisher. Photograph, Schecter Lee.)

A rare, pieced patchwork quilt featuring spatter work, achieved by brushing paint through a sieve onto the fabric which has been covered by a template. All told, there are 4,700 pieces in the quilt. Probably 19th century. 87″ × 88″. (Courtesy of the Shelburne Museum.)

QUILT STYLES AND PATTERNS

The earliest patchwork quilts in this country, like the Indian palampores and traditional English quilts, were made in the central medallion style, which consists of a large central motif—usually appliquéd—surrounded by multiple borders. By the second quarter of the nineteenth century, however, American quilters began developing the block-style quilt, in which the overall pattern was derived from a series of smaller repeating blocks (in some cases two different blocks would alternate), each with the same design. The block method was a boon for quilters, as it meant they could carry the blocks with them from room to room, or even on visits to friends' and neighbors' homes.

Most early quilts, whether pieced or appliquéd, were made in the framed medallion style—even whole-cloth solid-color quilts, in which the only design was the quilting itself. Thus, the change in format from a design that moved from the center outward to an overall design was a significant one, and one that took place slowly.

While this basic design change can be attributed to the first decades of the nineteenth century, few other stylistic changes were as sweeping or as easy to date. Consequently, although certain fabrics, fabric designs, and colors can earmark a quilt as having been made within a specific time span, with a few exceptions, quilt patterns generally are little help in dating a work.

The 1830s and 1840s saw the rise of the cotton patchwork quilt, both pieced and appliquéd, or some combination of both. Because piecing required less material than appliquéing, everyday quilts were more often pieced. Most women, however, tried to ensure that one or two of their best quilts would be appliquéd.

In the eighteenth and early nineteenth centuries, only a few quilt patterns seem to have had names. Specific names become common with the rise of the block quilting style. At first, women took their patterns from quilts they had seen, from a pattern shared by a friend or neighbor, or possibly from a peddler carrying patterns with his other wares. According to one story, a peddler traveling through Pennsylvania in the 1840s cut out an elaborate leaf and scroll design for the women of the family with which he spent the night, when they complained of having no new patterns. Whether he regularly did so for the families he visited is unknown.[23]

By the last quarter of the nineteenth century, ladies' magazines and newspapers began publishing and advertising printed patterns, making them easily available.

The names given to quilt designs were taken from the Bible, nature, politics, historical events, and even popular literature. An abstract geometric design constructed of triangles and called "Lady of the Lake," after Sir Walter Scott's romantic poem, published in 1810, was popular by the 1820s, and remained so well into the twentieth century. The Lincoln-Douglas debates in Illinois produced several patterns, including "Lincoln's Platform" and "The Little Giant," in honor of Stephen

An unusual aspect of this calamanco quilt is the design of multicolored squares set in a diamond pattern. The bedcover is heavily quilted in floral and leaf patterns. 1820–50. 89″ × 86″. (Courtesy of Historic Deerfield, Inc.)

"Railroad Crossing": unlike Pennsylvania Amish quilts, this example from Ohio is constructed of many small pieces. Holmes County, Ohio. c. 1920. 85″ × 62″. (Courtesy of Betty Osband. Photograph, Schecter Lee.)

"Diamond in the Square": the double borders, each with corner blocks in contrasting colors, and the elaborate, fine quilting are hallmarks of Amish quilts. Lancaster County, Pennsylvania. c. 1900–10. 76″ sq. (Courtesy of Stella Rubin. Photograph, Schecter Lee.)

A classic pattern from Lancaster County, Pennsylvania, this "Amish Bars" quilt has four different designs in its quilting: baskets, diamonds, tulips, and braids. c. 1890. 71″ × 78″. (Courtesy of Kelter-Malcé. Photograph, Schecter Lee.)

Douglas, allowing women to express their political preferences at home, if not at the polls.

As patchwork quilts reached the height of their popularity from 1850 to 1875, more and more patterns came to be known by specific names, and often the same pattern had several names at different times or in different parts of the country. The pattern "Rocky Road to Dublin" for example, after 1849 was also called "Rocky Road to California." A multicolored design called "Joseph's Coat" in other areas of the country, in Pennsylvania was known as "Scrap-bag." The geometric pattern "Ducks and Ducklings" was also referred to as "Hen and Chicks" and "Corn and Beans," all of these names revealing regional differences. As Texas became more heavily settled, quilt names changed again: a design elsewhere called "Cactus Basket," constructed of diamonds and triangles, was known there as "Texas Rose" and "Texas Treasure," although the pattern stayed the same.

Quilt designs and names came from a variety of sources. "Fox and Geese," a popular pattern, was probably taken from the lines on the board of a popular game of the same name—one played by Sarah Emery as early as 1796: "Uncle Joe and I occupied the form in the chimney corner of an evening . . . roasting apples and telling stories or riddles, or playing fox and geese on a board, chalked for the game, with a red kernel of corn for the fox and yellow for the geese."[24]

Some names reflect the background of those who introduced them. "The Reel," for example, is said to have Dutch origins, being found first in the Hudson Valley town of Kinderhook. Much later, in the Midwest, a popular product was dubbed Rising Sun Stove Polish, "Rising Sun" being the name of a very popular early quilt pattern.[25]

Names that now seem puzzling would have been easily understood in their own day. The pattern known as "Hole in the Barn Door" seems a mystery, but is easily explained by someone familiar with country life: "Before there was electricity in barns, small diamond-shaped openings surrounded by heavy frames were cut high in the barn door to let in light."[26] Elsewhere the same pattern was called "Churn Dash."

Of all the hundreds of named quilt patterns, none are more original than those of the Pennsylvania Amish, a religious sect whose laws prohibit its members from making quilts in anything other than abstract designs. Only solid colors, no prints, are permitted, and the characteristic palette is dark blues, greens, and purple, accented with red, fuchsia, or another brilliant color, often shocking in its intensity. The scale of the designs is very large, and the designs themselves very simple. Most popular are the simple "Bars" pattern, "Diamond in the Square," and "Sunshine and Shadow," all with multiple borders not unlike those of the early American central medallion quilts.

The best examples of Amish quilts in wools or cottons, sometimes homespun, were made from the 1860s through the 1930s; thereafter the Amish also used synthetics, which lack the true feel and color of the natural fibers. Not all of the Amish people remained in Pennsylvania. Some moved west into Ohio, Illinois, and Indiana, where their quilt designs were influenced by the quilts from the world outside their own communities.

Appliquéd "Oak Leaf" quilt: one interpretation of a popular design.
The well-thought-out border alternates stylized trees with birds and
potted flowers. Dutchess County, New York. c. 1850. 106″ × 89″.
(Courtesy of Betty Osband. Photograph, Schecter Lee.)

Although "Broken Star" is a pattern used by many quilters outside
the Amish community, this particular example was made by a
Midwestern Amish woman. Walnut Creek, Ohio. c. 1920. 79" sq.
(Courtesy of Betty Osband. Photograph, Schecter Lee.)

"Fox and Geese," also called "Crosses and Losses," is a Mid-western, cotton Amish quilt from the Borntrager family of Medford, Wisconsin. c. 1930. 70″ × 78″. (Courtesy of M. Finkel and Daughter.)

These Midwestern Amish quilts are made in patterns composed of many more pieces than the Pennsylvania Amish examples, often in a combination of light-colored prints and black. They still have their own particular, identifiably Amish look, distinguishing them from non-Amish patchwork quilts, even those in the same patterns.

Pieced cotton quilts continued to be very popular, particularly in rural areas, throughout the nineteenth century, despite the disdain of ladies like Mrs. Pullan, who in 1859 rejected cotton patchwork in favor of patchwork made of silks, velvets, and satin: "Of the patchwork with calico, I have nothing to say. Valueless indeed must be the time of that person who can find no better use for it than to make ugly counterpanes and quilts of pieces of cotton."[27] Miss Florence Hartley, however, who wrote *The Ladies' Hand Book of Fancy and Ornamental Work* (also in 1859) preferred what she called the "real old Patchwork of bits of calico" to "bits of silk sewed together for parlor ornaments."

> We own to a liking for Patchwork, genuine old fashioned patchwork, such as our grandmothers made, and such as some dear old maiden aunt, with imperfect sight, is making for fairs and charities. We love to see a bed spread with the pretty squares and rounds and curious shapes, which mingled with white look so clean and gay; and we even love the irregular, coarse, ill-matched pieces, put together by a perhaps over-tasked mother, or a little child trying her first efforts at being useful.[28]

That Mrs. Pullan and Miss Hartley were able to argue about the merits of cotton patchwork and that Miss Hartley—as early as 1859—viewed patchwork as something quaint and old-fashioned makes clear that by the mid-nineteenth century certain fashionable ladies were already rejecting cotton quilts as passé.

If there were questions about the value of making some types of cotton patchwork, other types continued to grow in popularity. The "Log Cabin," for example, reached the height of its popularity after the Civil War, when it was made in every imaginable fabric: inexpensive cotton prints, silks and satins, wool challis, and even heavy wool suiting. In this case, the name of the design refers to the way the individual blocks are constructed—each long strip is stitched down to the next, and the block built up strip by strip, as logs would be laid one upon the other to build a log cabin.

In the United States and Canada, this design seems always to have been called "Log Cabin," although it had other names elsewhere:

> The name Log Cabin must have been given to this pattern once it reached the United States, as in the north of England it is called Log Wood, in the Isle of Man Roof pattern, and in Ireland a Folded Quilt. It was at one time thought that the Log Cabin pattern had come to Ireland from America, but research has shown that it was used in Scotland during the 18th century and subsequently crossed the sea to Ireland.[29]

Whatever its origins, the Log Cabin—in all its variations—is one of the most enduring patterns, and probably the one that lends itself to the most variation. By manipulating shades of light and dark, or using deep colors or prints in combination with black, quilters have achieved graphic effects that rival in intensity those of the twentieth century's abstract painters.

In the 1840s and 1850s, a new fad appeared: the album quilt. Constructed of blocks, usually appliquéd but sometimes pieced, the album quilt was made by a number of women, friends or relatives of the person to whom the quilt was given. Like the friendship album, popular during the same period, these quilts were a form of remembrance, each quilt block—like each album page—offering a verse or picture and signature that would call its maker to mind.

Album quilts were made for various occasions and events—when a friend or clergyman moved away, when a young man reached twenty-one, as wedding gifts, even as engagement gifts for young men. In each case, the women contributing squares to the quilt would design and work their squares at home, then bring them along to a formal album party where the squares were merely looked at and admired, or sometimes set together, stuffed, backed, and quilted.

One such party was given in 1845 to celebrate the twenty-first birthday of Benjamin Almoney and present him with a freedom quilt: "[The party] was arranged by his sisters. A square block was brought by each young lady attending which she had designed, made and presented to him. The quilt was not quilted at that time"[30]

A slightly later form of album quilt was the autograph quilt, with the individual squares usually made by one woman who then had her friends autograph them. Some women made quilts with famous people's signatures, including one enterprising lady from Rhode Island who collected autographs by writing to prominent people of the day. So pleased was she with her idea that she wrote to *Godey's Lady's Book* describing what she had done. The magazine in turn published an article about it:

> We have lately received a pleasant letter from a young lady of Rhode Island, who is forming a curious and valuable collection of autographs in an original and very womanly way; the design is to insert the names in a counterpane or bedquilt. Each autograph is written with common black ink, on a diamond-shaped piece of white silk (placed over a diagram of white paper and basted at the edges), each piece the center of a group of colored diamonds, formed in many instances from "storied" fragments of dresses which were worn in the olden days of our country. For instance, there are pieces of a pink satin dress which flaunted [*sic*] at one of President Washington's dinner parties. The whole number of pieces required is 2780; of these 556 are to contain autographs.[31]

By far the most outstanding examples of the album quilt are the elaborate, highly styled pieces referred to as Baltimore album quilts. Large block-style quilts with brilliantly colored appliqués on white grounds, they vary in quality of design and workmanship. Of those so far identified, it now seems certain that the very

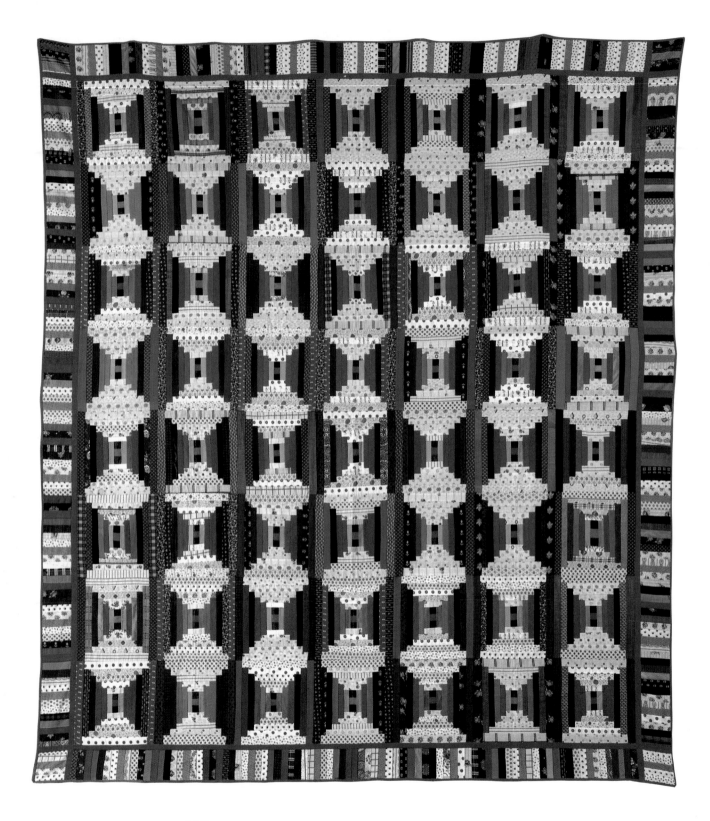

Wool challis Log Cabin quilt: a "Courthouse Steps" variation sometimes called "Spools," with a pieced cotton back and a hand-loomed silk tape binding. Berks County, Pennsylvania. c. 1860. 84″ × 94″. (Courtesy of Kelter-Malcé. Photograph, Schecter Lee.)

"Log Cabin: Light and Dark Variation." A talented quilter took a common pattern, altered it to her own taste, and chose colors that gave the design a great deal of movement. Pennsylvania. c. 1880. 84″ sq. (Courtesy of Kelter-Malcé. Photograph, Schecter Lee.)

A cotton Mennonite quilt in a pattern known as "Joseph's Coat" made for a boy named Joseph by his mother. Like the names of many quilt designs, this one comes from the Bible. Lititz, Pennsylvania (Lancaster County). 1890. 76″ × 80″. (Courtesy of M. Finkel and Daughter. Photograph, Schecter Lee.)

It is unusual to see such a riot of colors and fabrics in a house quilt.
Pennsylvania. c. 1920s. 92″ × 78″. (Courtesy of Sweet Nellie.
Photograph, Schecter Lee.)

best were created under the patronage of an experienced designer of *broderie perse* bedcovers, Mrs. Achsah Goodwin Wilkins. Positively identified by Dena S. Katzenberg as the driving force behind the most skillfully designed examples, Mrs. Wilkins did not actually sew the quilts, evidently because she suffered from a skin disease, but she took an active part in designing the individual blocks and laying out their overall pattern.[32]

The actual cutting and stitching, in Mrs. Katzenberg's view, was the work of a younger woman named Mary Evans, a protégée of Mrs. Wilkins. Although no quilt blocks signed "Mary Evans" have yet turned up, there are many inscribed with the names of their donors, all in the same handwriting, now believed to be that of Mary Evans, suggesting that she did the blocks for those donating them, working them and then signing the donors' names. As with other skilled needlewomen, Miss Evans's artistic signature survives in her work, in this case in her characteristic "triple bowknots, prominent white roses . . . [and] the use of rainbow fabrics to indicate contour. . . ."[33]

These appliquéd bedcovers, made in Baltimore in the 1840s and '50s, combine brilliantly colored imported and domestic fabrics with expertly cut and stitched appliqués in traditional as well as innovative designs. To the eighteenth- and early nineteenth-century design vocabulary of vases and urns of flowers, wicker baskets, and cornucopias of fruit, were added objects of local significance: well-known buildings and monuments, the Delaware State Seal, even a steam engine called a "one-armed Billy" that had its first run in Baltimore. A short-lived but important phenomenon, Baltimore album quilts were no longer popular by the end of the 1850s, suggesting further the probable influence on the finest examples of Mrs. Wilkins, who died in 1854.

At about the time that the women of Baltimore were using cottons to create some of the most elegant quilts ever made, women in other parts of the country, following the advice of authorities like Mrs. Pullan, were starting to use silks for their quiltmaking. *Godey's Lady's Book* (1830–98) and *Peterson's Magazine* (1842–98), two of the most influential women's magazines, frequently offered patterns accompanied by instructions for silk patchwork. All of *Godey's* designs were of English or Continental origin and were based on the English template system of quiltmaking, in which the fabric is basted around paper templates before the pieces are stitched together. The few American patterns offered were not identified by their traditional names and did not call for the running stitch, the usual method of sewing pieces together in this country.[34]

Very popular in silks was hexagon—also called honeycomb or mosaic—patchwork, each hexagonal patch being made of six small hexagons. In 1835, *Godey's* gave instructions on how to make such a patch: "The patches are made using a paste board model of the desired size. . . . Each patch must be a little bigger than the pattern so as to turn it over the filler [made up of old copy books or letters] while being basted to it. Each patch is joined to form a circle of five patches with one in the center."[35]

By the last quarter of the nineteenth century, silk patchwork, in all its varied patterns, was dying out. In 1877, S. Annie Frost noted its decline:

Dated 1847, this Baltimore album quilt top was signed by Mary
Orem and Owen D. French. Along with the usual fruit and floral
motifs, the makers included a full-rigged clipper ship, an eagle, and
two squares with the Fountain of Life. 68″ × 70″. (Courtesy of
Kelter-Malcé. Photograph, Schecter Lee.)

A Victorian crazy quilt made of silks and velvets—the remnants of
dresses and women's shirts—this quilt was more carefully planned
than it might look at first glance. The irregular patches were made
into nine large squares, stitched together to form the whole. The
small, square size indicates it was intended for use as a throw. 55″ sq.
(Courtesy of Wendy Lavitt. Photograph, Schecter Lee.)

Silk is also used in variously shaped blocks and patterns, for the covers of chairs and bedquilts, although we have known many pieces, started in tiny pieces to make an enormous bedquilt, end ignominiously in a very small pincushion. The taste is one that has nearly died out, although some beautiful specimens are still seen at fancy fairs.[36]

In its place, the silk crazy quilt—so called for its randomly shaped patches, which gave it the appearance of crazed porcelain—was to become the fashion. While the origins of the crazy quilt are uncertain, the fad seems to have been related to the great American interest in all things Japanese, stimulated by the arts and crafts shown at the Japanese Pavilion of the 1876 Philadelphia Centennial Exposition. Several contemporary magazines traced the crazy quilt to one particular source: "It is said that the idea for the crazy quilt is to a certain extent Oriental, some Japanese picture, in which was a sort of 'crazy' tesselated pavement composed of odd fragments, having suggested it."[37] Women collected any bits and pieces they could find and arranged them according to the contemporary taste. Straight lines, for example, were not acceptable: "It saves time [said Godey's] if a few of the smaller pieces are joined by a sewing machine, but we would suggest only a little of this being done, as it gives straighter lines. If, on completion, there are any angularities offending the eye, they can be hidden by the application of ovals or other curved forms of silk being put on the top and worked around."[38]

So ornate was much of this work that the primary function was no longer as a bedcover; mostly, these pieces were made for show, and ended up in the parlor, where, thrown over a chair, they served to display their maker's talents for all to see. In keeping with their function, few of these pieces were made large enough to cover a bed; most were the size of a lap robe or throw, a good bit shorter and narrower than a bed quilt.

In the early decades of the twentieth century, women in traditional communities like the Amish, and those in the small mountain towns of Appalachia continued, as they had always done, to make quilts. Few women in the mainstream of American life, however, kept up their interest.

Not until the Depression years of the 1930s did they again turn to quilting for what it could offer—socializing and solace. From that late day in the history of quilting came quilts that can hardly be mistaken for pieces of any other era. Using the period's pastels, women created quilts in a whole new palette—turquoise, pink, salmon, violet—in both solids and small-scale prints. Old patterns such as "Grandmother's Flower Garden" and "Double Wedding Ring" were revived, and new ones were made up, like the popular "Sunbonnet Sue" and "Overall Billy." Whether for economic or emotional reasons, quilting again took hold; women had weekly get-togethers to quilt, gossip, and trade patterns and fabrics. Newspapers and magazines carried quilt patterns, and quilters like Ruth Finley became so involved in the history of their craft that they wrote books about it. Later writers have pointed out inaccuracies in these early works, but they continue to be important as the first books in the field, and as evidence of women's interest in and commitment to quilting.

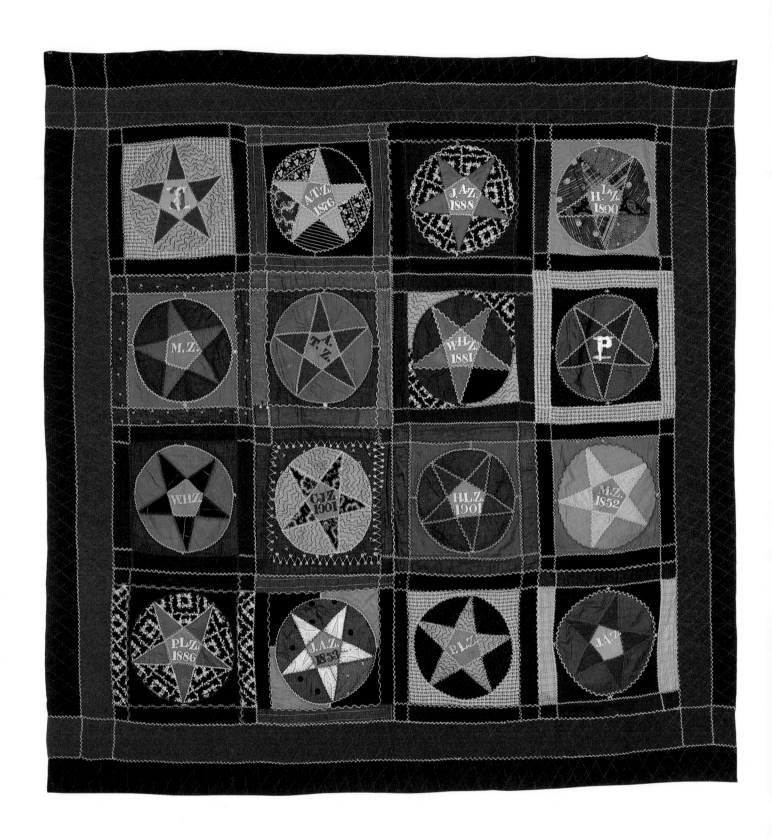

Star quilt. In this wool quilt all but two of the stars are initialed. The "Z" indicates the Ziegenfus family, through which the quilt has descended. Kunkletown, Pennsylvania. c. 1900. 69″ sq. (Courtesy of M. Finkel and Daughter.)

A rare combination of an all-white quilt with an off-center, multicolored star that is a Masonic symbol. Other Masonic motifs can be found in the quilting. Pennsylvania. c. 1875. 64″ × 82″. (Courtesy of "all of us americans" folk art.)

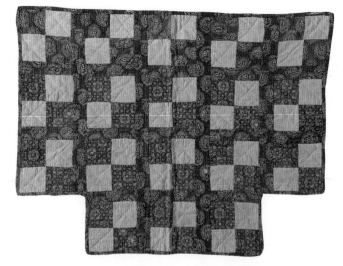

Doll quilts are very much admired by collectors as they exhibit in miniature all the characteristics of a full-size quilt. These two, the top one cut out for a four-poster doll bed, are typical of their era. Pennsylvania. c. 1830. Top, 17″ sq.; bottom, 14½″ × 19″. (Courtesy of Stella Rubin. Photograph, Schecter Lee.)

A large appliquéd pot of flowers was a popular motif for crib quilts in the second half of the 19th century. The red, yellow, and green calicos used in this Pennsylvania crib quilt are seen in many quilts of the period. c. 1865. 40″ × 42″. (Courtesy of "all of us americans" folk art.)

One of a pair of Baltimore album quilts, this one is distinguished
by the two deer at center. c. 1840–50. 98″ × 100″. (Courtesy of
Sam Herrup. Photograph, Schecter Lee.)

FOUR

WHITE WORK

O*f all the* varieties of quilting and embroidery, none is more elegant or more difficult to master than the white-on-white stitchery known as white work. Popular as early as the Middle Ages, it flourished during those periods when the use of color in embroidery and textiles was banned by the sumptuary laws, church edicts prohibiting excessive luxury in dress.[1] Ironically, white work, or "frost-worke," as it was sometimes called, became as elaborate and rich as the forbidden colored embroideries it replaced. A broad term, white work includes a number of different techniques, all of them having in common the use of white stitching on a white ground. The stitches may be of silk, cotton, or wool (or combinations of these for varied textures), worked on almost any fabric: cotton, linen, wool, or silk.

White work, in its embroidered, woven, and quilted forms, has been found continuously in England and on the Continent since the seventeenth century. Toward the close of the eighteenth century, quilted white work was common enough to be found in the furnishings of the cabin of a ship that crossed from Holland to Harwich: "The berths are ranged along the side walls in two rows like theatre boxes, one above the other; they have thoroughly good mattresses, [and] white quilted covers. . . ."[2]

In America, white work gained steadily in popularity until the 1790s, when it represented the height of fashion, so much so that entire bedrooms were done in white. Caroline King, of Salem, Massachusetts, visiting her aunt's house in Newburyport, Massachusetts, marveled at the whiteness of the bedroom: "The room was furnished in white painted furniture, the dimity drapery of windows and bed were white, the straw matting on the floor was white. . . . The great white bed stood like a snowdrift, crowned with a thick white 'comforter' or 'blessing' as we called the 'down puff' of those days."[3]

So popular was the idea of a white bedcover that by the middle of the nineteenth century women turned their white-backed patchwork quilts face down on

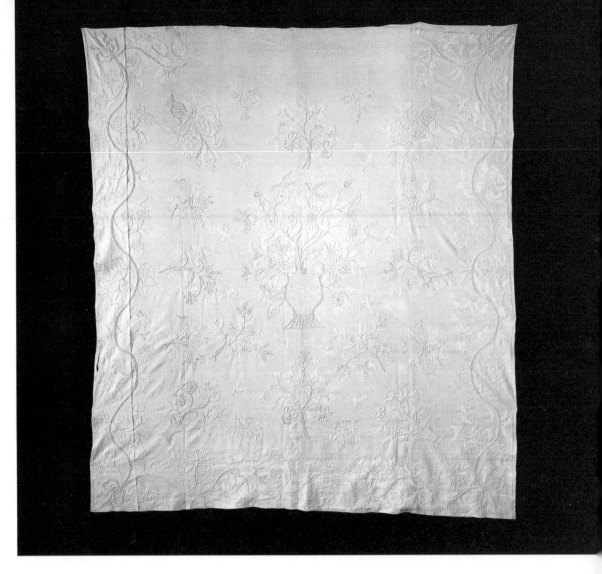

Victoria Montague, a descendant of Mary Ball (the mother of George Washington), embroidered a great variety of stitches on her twill cotton spread in the early 1800s. 93″ × 104″. (Courtesy of the Shelburne Museum. Photograph, Ken Burris.)

the bed, so that with the white-on-white quilting stitches uppermost, they looked like the desired all-white article. As one woman wrote, "I remember with regret the quilts I wore out, using them white side up in lieu of white Marseilles spreads. The latter we were too poor to own; the 'tufted' ones had worn out. . . . So I used the old quilts, making their fine stitches in intricate patterns serve for the design in a white spread, turning the white muslin lining up."[4] All-white bedcovers remained in vogue among fashionable ladies until the 1830s, and continued to be made in rural areas as late as the 1850s or '60s.

Along with the all-white quilted bedcovers came embroidered and candlewick spreads, "Marseilles quilts," dressing or toilet table covers (embroidered or quilted, or a combination of both), and all-white table covers and scarves. Most ambitious of all were the large—three widths across—bedcovers, worked in the tiniest quilting stitches, stuffed or corded, and often with several techniques combined on the same piece.

All-white quilts required great skill with the needle, and were attempted only by the most experienced needleworkers. They could take as long as several years to complete. Most would have been worked on only during the daytime, their fine white stitches on a white ground being too difficult to see at night in what artificial light was available.

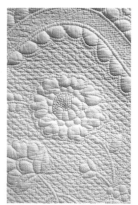

White work counterpane with stuffed work: Harriet Newell Robinson made this stuffed cotton bedspread with cornucopia and surrounding grapes for Martha Wheeler Sibley about 1810 in New Hampshire. 85″ × 75″. (Courtesy of Rosalind S. Miller. Photograph, Schecter Lee.)

Detail of a white work quilt made by Ann Pamela Cunningham, founder of the Mount Vernon Ladies' Association of the Union to Preserve Mount Vernon. The characteristic tiny quilting stitches create a stippled effect around the stuffed motifs. Laurens County, South Carolina. c. 1840. 105″ × 98″. (Courtesy of the Daughters of the American Revolution Museum.)

One quilting technique, all-over quilting with rows of small stitches worked very closely together, resulted in a stiff, heavy bedcover with an overall stippled effect. Rarely, however, was this tight quilting found alone; more often it was used as background stitching for a stuffed or corded design in a combination of patriotic motifs, urns, flowers, leaves, and vines. Whatever the quilting technique, though, the overall design of a central medallion surrounded by several borders remained a constant on all-white quilts.

Corded and stuffed work—two types of quilting common in England and Wales in the seventeenth and eighteenth centuries—were rare in this country until the white work craze of the Federal period. At that time, American women surpassed even their British sisters in creating white bedcovers, "with patterns of stuffed quilting hav(ing) no rivals in English or Welsh quilting"[5] in the view of Averil Colby, an English textile historian.

Of two, rather than three layers, stuffed and corded quilts are made by drawing the design on the back of the bottom, coarser layer of cloth; the design is then stitched through both layers, and stuffing or wadding inserted between. To stuff the quilt and create a raised design, threads in the backing are pulled apart so that small pieces can be pushed in with a bodkin (a blunt-edged needle), until the desired height of the design is reached.

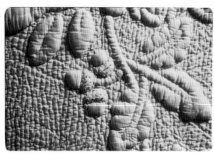

Detail of a quilted and stuffed cotton bedspread made by Orella Keeler of Ridgefield, Connecticut, as part of her wedding linens in 1823. According to family history, it was sewn entirely by candlelight and was used continuously for the next fifty years. 86″ × 84″. (Courtesy of the Daughters of the American Revolution Museum.)

Cording, used primarily for the linear elements of a design such as stems or tendrils,[6] is done by running candlewicking, a thick cotton cord or thread, through narrow channels formed beforehand by two parallel rows of fine running stitches. A quicker and easier method of cording was developed later: the pattern was drawn on the backing, the cording laid down on the pattern, and the top laid over both and stitched down with a row of quilting on each side of the cord. Clearly a shortcut, this less precise method was scorned by some needlewomen as the "lazy woman's way"[7] of cording.

MARSEILLES QUILTS

OPPOSITE, TOP:

An imposing eagle forms the center of this mid-19th-century Marseilles spread. Machine-made bedcovers of this type gradually replaced the time-consuming, handmade white-on-white spreads of the late 18th and early 19th centuries. 96″ × 102″. (Courtesy of the Shelburne Museum.)

OPPOSITE, BOTTOM:

A candlewick bedspread of handwoven cotton, skillfully tufted with snow-white wicking in an overall design of cornucopias, flowers, and foliage. It is believed to have been made by Nancy Stevens about 1850 in Alton, New Hampshire. 107″ × 102″. (Courtesy of the Shelburne Museum. Photograph, Ken Burris.)

Even before the first settlers reached these shores, a tradition of fine hand quilting flourished in the South of France, around Marseilles. These French quilts, elaborately stuffed and corded, were usually all-white and made of silk or linen, although colors, and cotton and wool, were sometimes used.[8] Marseilles quilts, as they came to be known (or Marcella, Marsala, or Marsyle), were imported into England, and from there shipped to the colonies throughout the eighteenth century in the form of bedcovers, yard goods, and petticoats. A letter of 1739 from Henry Purefoy to a London merchant confirms this and gives a clue to the weight of cloth so heavily quilted: "I received all the things in the box and returned to you the Marseilles quilt petticoat. . . . It is so heavy my mother cannot wear it."[9]

In 1763, an English patent was obtained for a loom-weaving process that produced woven cloth closely resembling the hand-stitched Marseilles quilting. From then on, until the early twentieth century, this less expensive, quiltlike fabric was much in demand both as yardage and bedcovers, despite the fact that it declined in quality as time passed. By 1850, colored Marseilles quilts were being offered for sale at Doremus & Nixon on Nassau Street in New York City: "Col'd Marselles Quilts—just imported . . . pink and white, blue and white, lilac and white. . . ."[10]

The older spreads are recognizable because they are heavier, thicker, usually very large, and most often have a central medallion format.

CANDLEWICKING

The demi-lune table cover pictured below features white embroidery and Dresden work on white homespun linen trimmed with ball fringe. Initialed "H.H.," it was made in Damariscotta, Maine, in the first quarter of the 19th century.

The dressing table cover (OPPOSITE) was probably used during the period when all-white bedcovers were fashionable. The stuffed floral basket in the center is surrounded by trailing vines of grapes and acorns. Signed "Ruth Cloyes," it was made in the second quarter of the 19th century. Embroidered and stuffed homespun linen. (Courtesy of Rosalind S. Miller. Photograph, Schecter Lee.)

Candlewicking, yet another type of white work, was so called for its soft, coarse yarn, very like that used for the wicks of candles, out of which the design was either woven or embroidered. On a loom-woven candlewick bedcover, the design is worked in as the piece progresses, as part of the actual fabric, with loops of yarn being raised up over wires or sticks to form the pile. Loom (sometimes called machine-made) candlewicks were usually made in one piece, and thus lack the seams characteristic of hand-embroidered examples, which were stitched together from two or three widths of cloth.

Embroidered candlewicks were worked with the same kind of yarn as the loom-woven ones, and in some cases with similar motifs (stars, pine trees, floral designs), although they are more realistic and less linear in the embroidered type. Several techniques were used to create the raised pile, including raising the loops over a small tool, twig, or even, in some locales, turkey-wing bones, to form the knots.[11] Sometimes the loops were clipped, and other times not, making for a different look. Various embroidery stitches were also used to create candlewick designs, most frequently the French knot, but also satin stitch, outline and stem stitches.

White-on-white embroidery took other forms besides that of candlewick bedspreads. White bedcovers were embroidered in thinner yarns and with flat stitches

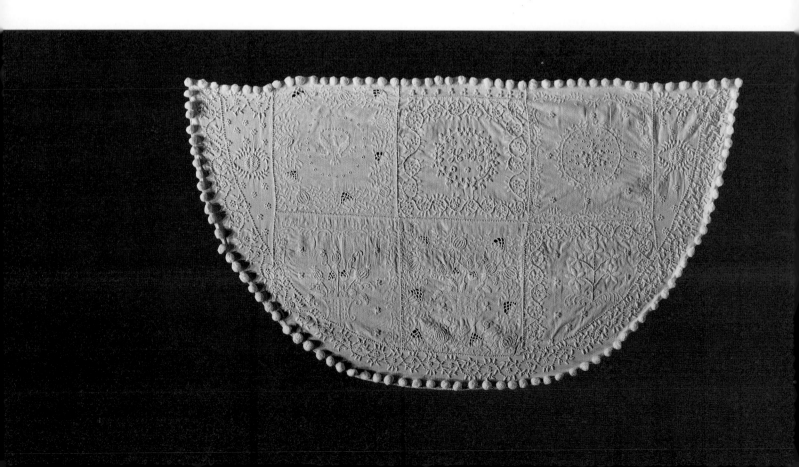

(as opposed to the raised, thick loops of the candlewick style); most were bridal pieces, judging from the names and wedding dates they bear. Much more delicate in feeling than the raised-loop works, they were made in the South, where white bedcovers were extremely popular for a longer period of time than in the North.[12] All types of white work bedcovers, in fact, were more common in the Southern colonies. According to Laurel Horton, "white whole-cloth quilts, whether imported or domestic, may have been the predominant form of fancy bedcovering. . . ."[13]

In addition to bedcovers, other articles, including clothing and household textiles, were part of the white work craze. Dressing table covers—stuffed, corded, or embroidered, often with a combination of all three techniques—were very popular. Personal items were lavished with the finest, most delicate work: a pair of white work pockets worn tied around the waist under a woman's skirts, and the small white cotton drawstring bags called reticules, or indispensables, that young ladies wore everywhere, swinging from their wrists, to hold small sewing implements or a handkerchief and scent bottle. White ruffles, fringes, tassels, drawn work, and sometimes inked verse further embellished these ladylike bags. Needlewomen were very skilled at creating a variety of designs and textures merely by using different weights of thread or altering the direction of the needle as it entered the cloth.

By the 1840s, the fad for white work had begun to wane, though dated examples from as late as the 1860s have been found. As the Victorian era progressed, perhaps the delicate, fragile whites began to seem passé and out of place. Only the machine-made Marseilles spreads, bland imitations of the old French originals, continued to be offered for sale in department stores—reminders of an earlier era when an all-white bedchamber was a young woman's dream.

A detail of a machine-woven candlewick spread, made about 1834 in Philadelphia. Both hand- and machine-made candlewick spreads were made in the first half of the nineteenth century, although the handmade ones took considerably more time. 98″ × 102″. (Courtesy of the Daughters of the American Revolution Museum.)

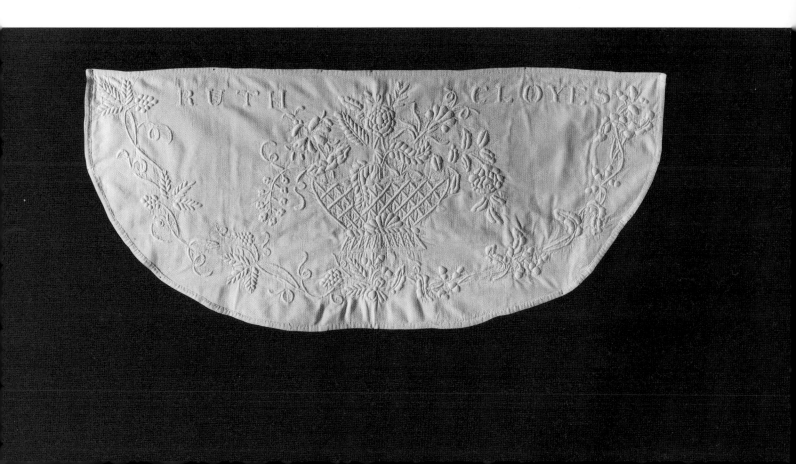

The account book of the illustrious weaver James Alexander contains an entry regarding Emily Downing in 1821, making this double-weave coverlet one of two examples that can be positively identified as his work. Born in 1770, in Belfast, Ireland, Alexander received his training in Scotland before emigrating to America. Although his first advertisement for "Flowered double and single Carpet Coverlids and counterpins of all descriptions . . ." appeared in 1817, he is known to have been working by 1800. New York State. 74″ × 95″. (Courtesy of Margo Paul Ernst. Photograph, Schecter Lee.)

FIVE

COVERLETS

While the ax and the rifle are credited in American folklore as the implements that tamed the land, the weaver's loom also played a vital role in the young country's survival. The spinning and weaving skills of the settlers provided warm coverlets to ward off the chill of drafty bedchambers. From the early days of colonization, when most coverlets were woven on small looms, weavers employed a variety of designs. Many of these patterns, or "drafts," as they came to be known, were handed down through generations. Professional weavers, who had been trained in the rigorous trade guilds of England, Scotland, Ireland, and Germany, brought their own drafts to America, often introducing the more intricate early patterns. The story of William Muir (b. 1818, Scotland), the son of a weaver, is fairly typical. When only six years old, "he was apprenticed as a draw boy and later he was placed at the loom and taught to weave silk fabrics, and later to weave paisley shawls and coverlets."[1] In 1836, when Muir came to America and eventually migrated to Indiana, his skills served him well as a weaver in an area where "Farmers kept sheep, clipped wool, washed and dyed it, then took it with a cotton warp to the weaver. They were the cheapest bedclothes they could get, besides being the most beautiful outside covers."[2]

Drafts have been found "written on brown paper, cardboard, backs of advertisements, and even on pineboards."[3] The various methods of composing drafts often reflected the nationality of the weaver. A pattern book written in German by Heinrich Muehlenhoff in Pennsylvania contained "44 coverlet patterns, a few drafts, over 100 folk medicine recipes and remedies, and some financial data; lengthy German prayers make up the rest of the book."[4]

As weaving demanded certain skills and time, families who could afford it often chose to pay for the services of the professional weaver. Many of these enterprising individuals operated out of home workshops, advertising their wares through local newspapers as did Stephen Miner of Stoningtonpoint, Connecticut,

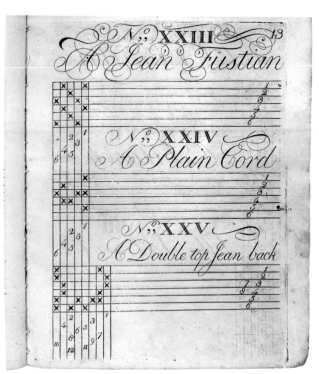

Pages from John Hargrove's draft book, 1792. The weaver would follow the diagram in threading and operating the loom. The drafts in Hargrove's treatise were printed from engravings rather than set in type. 8″ × 6″. (Courtesy of the Museum of American Textile History.)

who announced in the *Connecticut Gazette* (Mar. 3, 1775) that "he weaves Coverlids of all sorts . . . makes them and knots the Fringe, all in the neatest Manner, for one Dollar each."

Although romantic stories of itinerant weavers abound, the cumbersome looms actually precluded much traveling. More often than not the coverlet weaver was a local personage who combined farming in summer with weaving in winter. After the harvest, weavers or their representatives journeyed through the neighboring countryside obtaining orders and picking up handspun yarns from their customers to be woven later in the workshops. Coverlets thus represented a collaboration between the housewife and the professional weaver: she was responsible for the preparation of the wool, but the weaver actually made the coverlets. As late as the mid-nineteenth century, weavers still accepted yarn from rural families. In Pennsylvania, George Casley placed an advertisement in the *Chambersburg Whig* (Apr. 27, 1838) stating that "for the convenience of those at a distance, the subscriber will receive Wool and cloth at the following places. . . . Written directions should be attached to the bundle." Many weavers received goods instead of cash for their services. In Pennsylvania, "William Lowmiller, Lycoming County, wove coverlets and dyed yarns in exchange for firewood and potatoes. Jacob Royer . . . wove 170½ yards of linen and woolen in exchange for a stove and the borrowing of cash, while John Bossert paid for beef by blue dyeing."[5]

While coverlet weavers appear for the most part to have been respected members of the community, the following observation suggests that a few itinerants possessed the unkempt appearance of men on the road:

An overshot coverlet with an unusual blue linen warp and a wool pattern weft of red, dark green, and brown. The halves were so skillfully joined as to render the seam nearly invisible. Early 19th century. 95" × 78". (Courtesy of the Shelburne Museum. Photograph, Ken Burris.)

It is easy to see why in many areas this unusual four-colored overshot was called "Turkey Tracks." The undulating tracks create a dramatic, optical effect. It was also known as "Double Snowflake," the blocks of snowflakes enclosed by a "Wandering Vine" pattern. 69" × 91". Early 19th century. (Courtesy of Margo Paul Ernst. Photograph, Schecter Lee.)

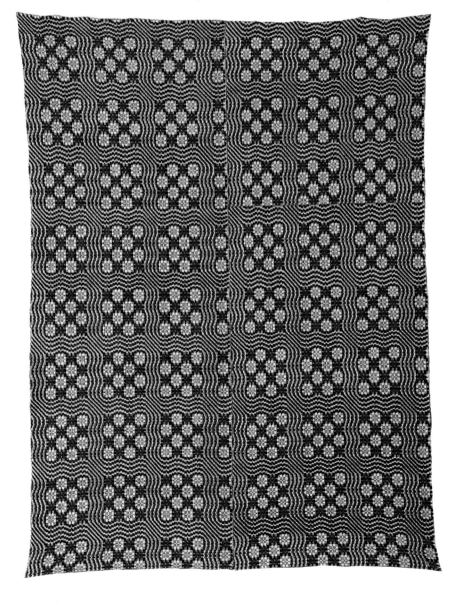

This Pennsylvania German hand loom, dated 1789, differed only slightly from European hand looms of the Middle Ages. When constructing his loom, the weaver probably had to rely on his memory of looms in the old country. (Courtesy of the Museum of American Textile History.)

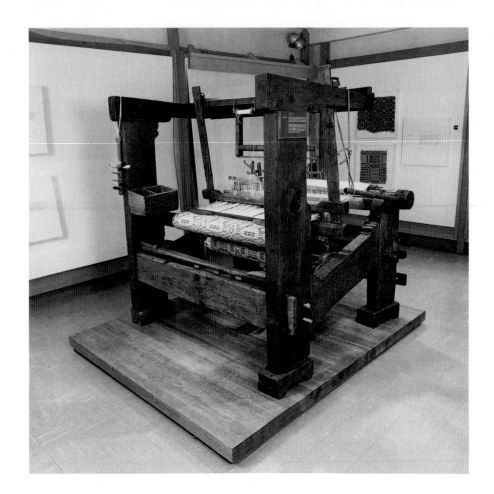

Thursday July 12 [1744] When I waked this morning I found two beds in the room besides that in which I lay. In one of which lay the great hulking fellows with long black beards, having their own hair and not so much as a night cap betwixt them both. I took them for weavers, not only from their greasey appearance, but because I observed a weaver's loom at each side of the room.[6]

Even though women at home wove overshot coverlets on simple looms for their families and for sale, the ranks of professional weavers utilizing industrial looms were mainly filled by men. In Indiana, Sarah LaTourette continued her father's coverlet business with her brother after her father's death in 1849. "Employing two men and one woman and using hand looms, the LaTourettes annually produced 200 coverlets valued at $500."[7]

She [Sarah LaTourette] used to weave on an average three coverlets a week [after the Civil War], and if a customer was impatient for his order to be filled she could make one a day. Forty pounds of homespun thread were required to string the loom. . . . Two thousands threads came down from the cross-piece of the loom, and when Sarah was working she could hardly be seen by a person coming in at the other end of the building.[8]

In Tennessee, Nancy Osborne Green (b. 1833), a professional weaver of overshot coverlets, often traveled as far as Virginia and North Carolina, staying for weeks with families for whom she wove.[9] In Warwick, Rhode Island, a black woman named Eleanor Eldridge (1785–1865) learned to be a weaver, specializing in coverlets and bed ticking.[10]

Coverlet weaving by women was encouraged and duly noted by local newspapers. *The New Hampshire Patriot and State Gazette* reported (Oct. 21, 1841) that an agricultural fair in Concord, New Hampshire, had featured coverlets "direct from the looms and hands" of the farmers' wives, which received praise from all those who attended. However, it must be noted that by the 1840s, except in outlying rural areas, almost all coverlet weaving was done by men in factories or workshops. A typical male weaver had one or two assistants and was hard-pressed to support his family and pay his apprentices on the proceeds recorded in surviving account books. He had to be accomplished both in plain weaving and more elaborate tablecloths and carpets. Many weavers were forced to uproot their families, moving westward to new frontiers as the demand for their services gradually diminished in urban areas.

Both home weavers and professionals assigned names to the various patterns that reflected contemporary interests or historical events. Many names simply described the weave or predominating motif. A single pattern could be known by one name in one area and another in a different locality. Popular names of quilts often served as titles for coverlets.

The overshot coverlet, woven in practically every community in America from colonial times through the late nineteenth century, may have derived from the seventeenth-century white-on-white table linens popular in England, Ireland, and Scotland.[11] Easily recognized by their floating wefts, which skip over a number of warp threads in regular progressions, overshot coverlets are characteristically composed of repeated geometric motifs broken only by a central seam. (Most early coverlets made on narrow looms contain center seams—the weaver had to throw the shuttle with one hand and catch it in the other.) While blue and white coverlets predominate, many other color combinations have been discovered. The all-white coverlet, sometimes woven in imitation of the fashionable Marseilles bedspread, being the least practical is considered the rarest. When overshot coverlets grew worn beyond repair, small pieces were often salvaged to be used as curtains, buggy throws, and even doormats.

A second type of coverlet, the handsome double weave, was more expensive to make, and at first could only be afforded by the well-to-do. Requiring a more elaborate loom than any household owned, the making of double-weave coverlets became the province of the professional weaver. Since twice as much yarn was needed for double-weave as for overshot coverlets, many families reserved their costly yarn for special gifts such as wedding presents.[12] The relatively high survival rate of double-weave coverlets may have been due to their value as heirlooms.

As the name implies, the double-weave coverlet consisted of two sets of warps and two sets of wefts that were joined together by interchanging threads at appointed intervals. One can identify a double-weave coverlet by pulling apart the two layers, as one would a pocket, and noting the mirror image of each side created by the interwoven threads. While historians believe the double weave's popularity

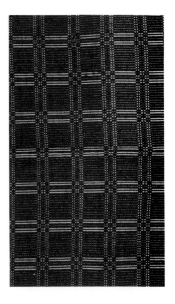

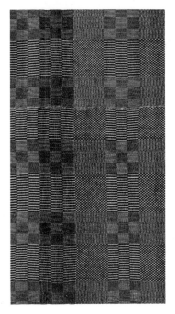

These two overshot coverlets' patterns are similar and appear often in various parts of the country. The red and blue coverlet (54″ × 70″) from the collection of Evelyn and Peter Kraus was found in Toronto, while the red and green example (62″ × 72″) from Alice Quinn's collection was probably made in Pennsylvania. Both 19th century. (Photograph, Schecter Lee.)

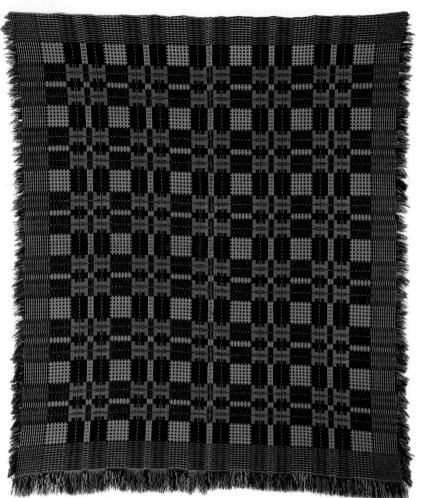

Warm, vibrant colors define this pre-Jacquard, double-weave coverlet. Its all-wool construction added to the warmth and probably to the original cost. The pattern consists of variations of "Table" and "Dog Tracks." 78" × 90". (Courtesy of Margo Paul Ernst. Photograph, Schecter Lee.)

The date (March 31, 1810) forms a repeat pattern in the corner blocks of this early double-weave coverlet. "Snowball and Stars" joined by a cross forming wheels compose the center field. The blue and white coloring is typical of New York State coverlets. 84" × 95". (Courtesy of Margo Paul Ernst. Photograph, Schecter Lee.)

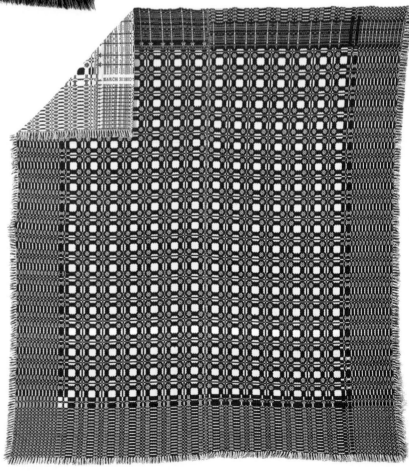

extended from 1725 to 1825, surviving examples date from 1800. Its construction was suitable for both hand looms and looms that were partially mechanized by the Jacquard attachment.

The Jacquard coverlet, named after the French inventor of the Jacquard loom, Joseph-Marie Jacquard, was first introduced to Americans in Philadelphia in the 1820s. The Jacquard mechanism was attached to the warp. As the weaver's shuttle carrying the crosswise yarns moved across the loom, the designated warp threads were lifted, and the pattern began to emerge. The revolutionary Jacquard attachment matched the warp and weft threads to holes on a series of punched cards that dictated the pattern. These cards, now hailed as the forerunners of computer cards, looked like the popular Victorian player-piano rolls. A skilled weaver could finish a coverlet in a day, instead of weeks, and it was possible to create endless varieties of designs composed of complicated curvilinear patterns. One could depict houses, trains, animals, and letters, the motifs limited only by one's supply of cards. A few weavers punched out their own pattern cards, but the majority bought cards from suppliers in Philadelphia and New York.

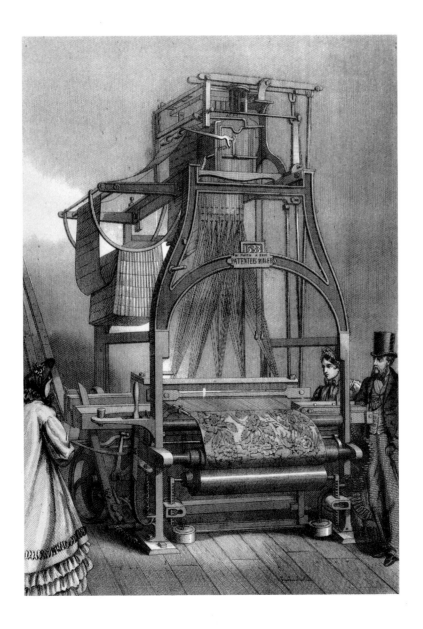

Steel engraving of the Smith brothers' patent loom that obtained a prize medal in 1862. Ladies and gentlemen marveled at the intricate weavings made possible by the Jacquard loom; the medal in question was awarded at the Philadelphia Exposition. (Courtesy of the Museum of American Textile History.)

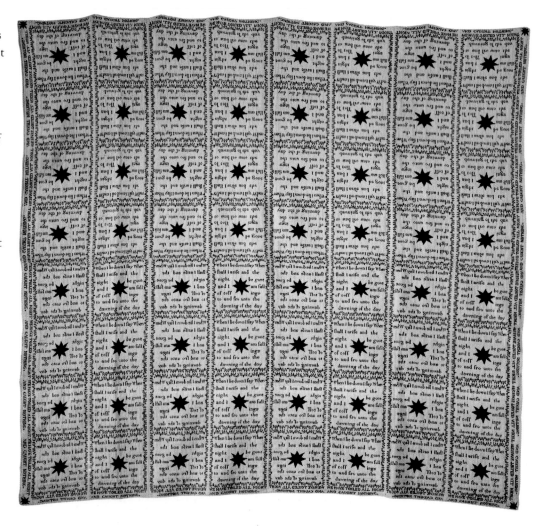

Greater variety was possible when weavers traded cards among themselves. Moreover, the appearance of a coverlet could also be changed by simply reversing the border cards with cards for the central area. Clients occasionally dictated the choice of border, field, and corner blocks, and often paid extra to have a coverlet personalized with their name, initials, and/or the date. However, the great similarity of borders found in coverlets ascribed to individual weavers indicates that most clients had a limited selection. The "signature blocks," also known as "advertising corners," were reserved not only for the weaver's signature and that of the customer, but also for the town, the date, and possibly an inscription. A wealth of genealogical information as well as political, moral, and religious sentiments of the times are revealed by the inscriptions found on Jacquard coverlets. Spelling errors, letter omissions due to lack of space, and number/letter reversals occurred in many coverlets. Weavers sometimes devised ingenious abbreviations for long words. Jacob Setzer (1819–1892) of Jackson Township, Pennsylvania, placed the first seven letters of "Township" on one line while putting the remaining "p" on the line below.[13] Some weavers identified themselves by their initials, while others used picturesque trademarks including sailboats, lions, eagles, flowers, and even a courthouse with a cupola on top.[14]

Woven on a draw loom, this c. 1820 double-woven coverlet contains sixty-four blocks of scripture from Job: 7:4, reading: "When I lie down I say when shall I arise and the night be gone and I am full of tossings to and fro until the dawning of the day." At the border of the coverlet appears a sentence from Luke: 5:5, "We have toiled all night and caught nothing." The coverlet was made in Salisbury, Vermont, for Roxy Farnham Graves, who was married in 1789. It is said she prepared the wool herself and had it woven by a man from Scotland. 80″ × 90″. (Naturally, the reverse shows white writing on a dark blue ground.) (Courtesy of the Shelburne Museum. Photograph, Ken Burris.)

When a weaver sat at his hand-powered loom to begin a Jacquard coverlet, he would measure the length of his warp threads at least double the length of the proposed coverlet. First, he would weave the bottom edge with its border and corner panel containing his "advertising square." He continued weaving the entire length of the coverlet, and, then, without cutting his work, reversed his pattern in the opposite direction until he finished the bottom edge of what would become the other side of the coverlet. After carefully removing the long strip of weaving from the loom (perhaps leaving a self-fringe of the warp threads), he would cut it in half and sew the unbordered edges together, thereby making a bed-size coverlet.[15] Jacquard coverlets were woven either in the single-cloth construction, resulting in two separate layers that could be pulled apart, or in the *Biederwand* weave. *Biederwand*, a German term, meant a compound weave combining a warp-faced plain weave and a weft-faced plain weave that reversed themselves throughout the coverlet, creating a ribbed effect. Tied *Biederwand* coverlets could not be pulled apart.

Occasionally, one finds a cradle-size Jacquard coverlet that can be differentiated from a cut-down piece by its small patterns and corresponding borders. Since a small coverlet only requires the width of a single loom, it will always be

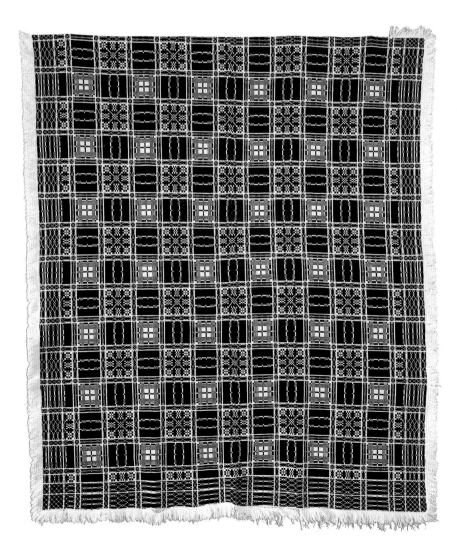

A double-woven coverlet of indigo blue wool and white cotton, made on a multi-harness loom. c. 1800–40. 79″ × 92″. (Courtesy of the Shelburne Museum. Photograph, Ken Burris.)

89

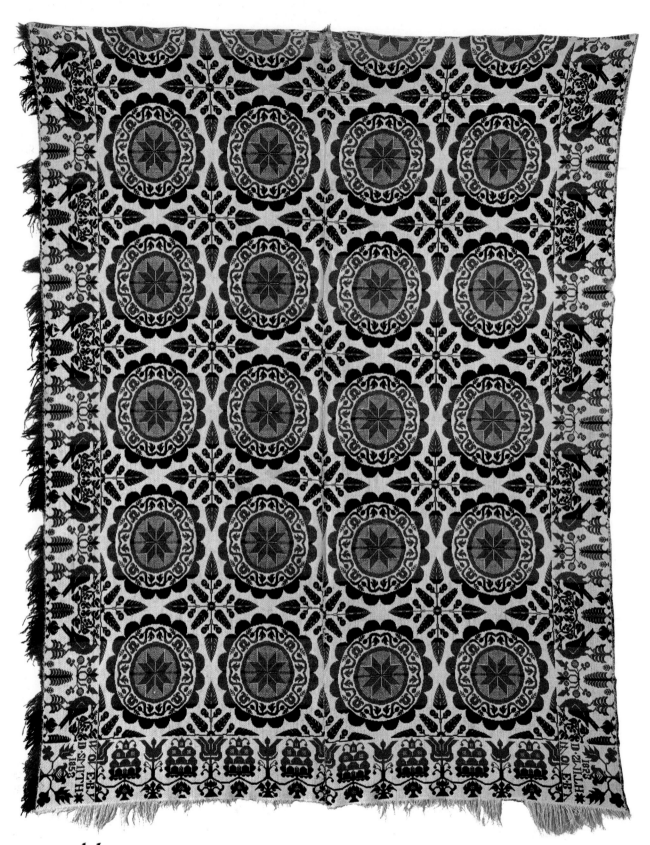

Medallions form the field of this Jacquard coverlet woven in 1853 by D. Smith. A panorama of birds, pine trees, and stylized flowers decorates its borders. The weaver might be Daniel S. Smith of Upper Hanover Township, Pennsylvania (listed in *A Checklist of American Coverlet Weavers*). 61″ × 92″. (Courtesy of Alice Quinn. Photograph, Schecter Lee.)

Asahel Phelps wove this Jacquard coverlet in Delhi, New York, in 1844; it is one of sixty-four pieces dating from 1835 to 1854 believed to have been woven by Phelps. The corner blocks of an eagle with an arch of stars appear in all of his coverlets. The border designs of weeping willow trees, birds, and flower-filled urns are frequently seen in Delhi coverlets. 80″ × 76″. (Courtesy of Janet LeRoy. Photograph, Schecter Lee.)

Acommemorative coverlet woven in memory of William Henry Harrison, who died after only one month in office. It is bordered by the heads of each President from George Washington to the ill-fated Harrison, and is executed in the *Biederwand* construction, using green and red wool and white cotton. The foliate pattern shows grapes, vines, and squares radiating triangles.
Ohio. c. 1841. 85″ × 90″. (Courtesy of Margo Paul Ernst. Photograph, Schecter Lee.)

An unusual moss green wool and natural color cotton coverlet in the summer and winter weave. Made in the early 19th century, its geometric design is reminiscent of a type of Irish chain. 78″ × 93″. (Courtesy of the Shelburne Museum. Photograph, Ken Burris.)

A child's coverlet in a one-piece summer and winter weave in the "Snowflake" pattern with a "Pine Tree" border. Cotton and wool. Found in Pennsylvania. c. 1830. 68″ × 48″. (Courtesy of Marston Luce.)

unseamed. A few examples of these "miniature" weavings have included children's names.[16]

Another popular type of coverlet, the summer and winter coverlet, resembles the double-weave coverlet in that it contains a dark and a light side in mirror images. But in structure, the summer and winter coverlet is closer to an overshot, as it is composed of pattern wefts "floating over" the background. Unlike the overshot, however, the summer and winter coverlet does not contain "floats" over more than two or three warps. Its tightly woven texture prevents the snags and tears found in the looser overshot coverlets. Since summer and winter coverlets were not double woven, the layers cannot be pulled apart by one's fingers. The fine honeycomb-like appearance (particularly noticeable on the lighter side) is another identifying feature. The origin of the title "summer and winter" has long been lost, but historians suspect that the name referred to the light and dark sides, for the coverlets were too warm for summer use. Summer and winter coverlets are the only

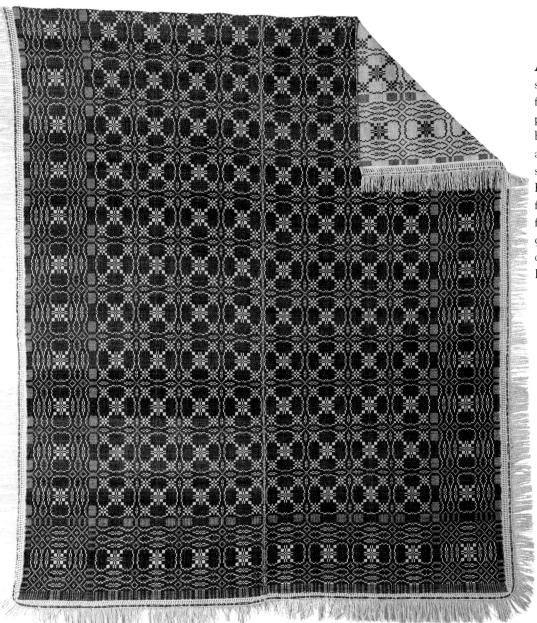

An early 19th-century summer and winter coverlet found in New York State. The pattern "Morning Star" is based on five "stars" joined by a "cross" forming "wheels"— sometimes called "Lover's Knot." The weaver added the fringe using the same yarns from the coverlet. 91" × 103". (Courtesy of Margo Paul Ernst. Photograph, Schecter Lee.)

coverlets whose weave appears to be solely American in origin, probably deriving from Mennonite weaving traditions.

A variety of fringes are found on coverlets, including self-fringes of weft threads and tape loom fringes, sewn on after the piece had been completed. As it was thrifty to use the remnants of the warps and/or wefts for fringe, many coverlets were self-fringed. In Pennsylvania and Maryland, weavers often preferred fringing two sides and the bottom of the coverlet. Unfortunately, few pieces have survived with their fringes in really good condition.

As more research accurately documents the makers and origins of America's coverlets, regional weaving traditions are increasingly revealed and usually found to be based on the weavers' backgrounds. In New York and New Jersey, for example, most of the weavers had migrated from the British Isles. They wove blue and white coverlets (with an occasional red and white exception) that were un-fringed or self-fringed at the foot. "The most common field motifs were flowers,

with the double lily, double rose, and double tulip predominating. Border designs often encompassed patriotic or Masonic imagery."¹⁷ Elaborate double-weave Jacquard coverlets were often made as wedding presents, with the marriage date woven into the corners. In neighboring Pennsylvania and Maryland, very different-looking coverlets stemmed from the German heritage of their weavers. A multicolor palette characterized Pennsylvania coverlets, with combinations of mustard and green, red and green, and red and white appearing frequently. Weavers often used a tricolored combination of red, white, and blue. Their coverlets can be easily identified by the tied *Biederwand* construction and by distinctive motifs appearing in other textiles deriving from Pennsylvania German decorative arts such as tulips, stylized birds and animals, and vases of flowers.

As the weavers moved west, they instilled their weaving traditions in their new communities. Many who migrated to Indiana came from the British Isles; their origins can be seen in the profusion of double-woven Jacquard coverlets. German, English, and Scottish weavers arrived in Ohio in equal numbers, producing both *Biederwand* and double-woven Jacquard coverlets. Many Ohio coverlets have been discovered with an unusual range of colors: reds and blues blended to create purple, turquoise and orange added to the palette, and an overall use of blocks of distinct color combinations. As more states complete research projects on their textile traditions, new weavers and coverlets will be discovered; slowly the puzzle pieces will reveal additional regional differences and similarities.

The Civil War ended the era of coverlets, as the country needed factory-made goods. Tastes changed: more elegant, sophisticated carpets and bed coverings came into vogue, even though the Philadelphia Centennial Exposition tried to revive coverlet weaving with patriotic and commemorative patterns. These aniline-dyed, mass-produced pieces never measured up to their handwoven counterparts. By 1900 coverlets were only being made in Appalachia, and in *Art and Economy in Home Decoration* (the last word on style in 1908) Mabel Tuke Priestman—suggesting that clever women cut up their old coverlets for decorative accents—condescendingly allowed that "the old blue and white coverlets, so dear to our grandmothers, are made into portieres and curtains which are more suitable for blue and white colonial rooms than almost anything else."¹⁸

Two details from an unusual red-and-white Jacquard coverlet attributed to a weaver in central New York. Since weavers customarily charged their clients more for dyeing their wool with madder or cochineal dye, red-and-white New York coverlets are rare. Natural cotton and red wool. Dated 1836 and marked with the initials "J.M.F." (identity unknown). 87½" × 76". (Courtesy of the Daughters of the American Revolution Museum.)

The alternation of color blocks and paired motifs, and the inclusion of several figural elements add to the interest of this Jacquard coverlet. Many weavings with similar rainbow-hued coloring have been found in Ohio. 80″ × 88″. (Courtesy of Laura Fisher. Photograph, Schecter Lee.)

An embroidered tea-table cloth, worked in a "theorem" design,
inscribed: "Isabella Henderson's work done in the year of our Lord
1826." Probably New England. 31″ sq. (Courtesy of Jeannine Dobbs.)

SIX

LINENS IN THE HOME

$\mathcal{A}$*n inventory* of linens used in the home of New York's Governor William Tryon in 1773 is notable for its variety. The detailed itemizing was the result of a terrible fire that destroyed the sixteen-room mansion, necessitating depositions of the contents for government compensation. The ample linen closet held:

14 Pr. of fine Irish cloth Sheets.

12 Pr. of coarse Ditto & Ditto.

22 Fine Irish Pillow cases.

12 Coarse Ditto Ditto.

8 Large India Huckaback Table Cloths.

12 Tea Napkins of Ditto.

2 Fine large Damask Table Cloths.

12 Tea Napkins of Ditto.

3 Birds-eye Diaper Table Cloths.

12 Napkins of Ditto.

4 Large Diaper Table Cloths each cover'd 2 Tables.

7 Diaper Table Cloths.

4 Damask side board Cloths.

6 Fine fringed breakfast cloths.

10 Glass Cloths.

4 Round Towels.

6 Dozen common Towels.

1 Dozen Knife Cloths.

6 Doyleys.

4 China Cloths.

4 Kitching Table Cloths.

38 Towels of diff't sorts.[1]

This rare glance at the contents of an entire linen closet—as if the clock had stopped in 1773—affords a preview of the "cloths" that graced the beds and tables of the colonists.

These mid-19th-century tablecloths were found in their original home in Beaver County, Pennsylvania. Their excellent condition implies they were reserved for special occasions. LEFT, 126″ × 136″; RIGHT, 126″ × 112″. (Courtesy of John Havenstein.)

TABLE LINENS

Whether seated at a rough-hewn trestle table in the backwoods or around an elegant Chippendale table in Boston, Americans enjoyed the best serving pieces, china, and table linens they could afford. In the early American home, the tablecloth was universally regarded as essential. Napkins and handkerchiefs (acting as substitutes for napkins) were, however, often omitted. A Frenchman noted in 1782: "A table in the American Style would seem extraordinary in France. The table is covered with a cloth, which also serves for napkins; it is ordinarily large enough to overflow on all sides, and each one wipes in front of himself (unhappily, they do not change it often)."[2]

When napkins were used, they were large rectangles or oblongs, designed to cover as much clothing as possible. The lack of forks until well into the eighteenth century and the use of common bowls made napkins a particularly welcome addition. To the more discriminating colonists and Englishmen, such as Samuel Pepys, the way napkins were folded mattered. Before an important dinner in his home for titled guests, Pepys noted in his diary (1668–69) that he was "mightly pleased with the fellow that came to lay the cloth and fold the napkins, which I like so well, as that I am resolved to give him 40s. to teach my wife to do it."[3]

The colonists placed boards on trestles for dining tables and called the cloths that covered them "borde cloths." Wealthy families might own a "a suite of Damaske, and a suite of fine Holland table Cloathes and napkins and side cloaths, and severall sorts of Diaper suites."[4] Warned by such notables as Governor John Winthrop to "come well furnished with linnen," seventeenth-century settlers brought and then imported linens whenever possible. While intricately patterned damasks were preferred, simpler linens served for everyday use. The Scotch-Irish immigrants continued their white-on-white weaving traditions in America, producing both homemade and factory cloths, and by the beginning of the nineteenth century, professional weavers were offering "a variety of damask and diaper table cloths and napkins . . . cotton doyles, or small napkins."[5]

Housewives and young girls intent on their dowries made simple damask tablecloths and toweling on four-harness home looms, passing down family patterns through several generations. For special occasions great precautions were taken to ensure the appearance of treasured damask cloths. Caroline Howard King of Salem, Massachusetts, noticed that before dinner parties given for her father's gentlemen friends in the early nineteenth century:

> The large tablecloth of finest damask, representing a landscape with trees and flowers and impossible lambs frisking among them, was ironed until its polished surface was almost as bright as that of the table. And it was never allowed to be folded. No crease must dim its brilliant smoothness, so it was hung over chairs in the spare-room until the day of the dinner party arrived. . . .[6]

While a variety of fabrics in many grades and textures were used for table linens, most appeared to be white, some with "blew stript," and a few "cheqd." The preference for white damask lasted throughout the nineteenth century and into the early years of the twentieth, with the approval of social arbiters of taste in numerous ladies' magazines. The February 1914 issue of *The Modern Priscilla* contained an article on "Dining Room Linens" by Ethelyn J. Morris, who advised: "In passing through the linen departments of the large shops, it will be noticed that all the finer, daintier, elaborate table linens are pure white. Occasionally there will appear some colored woven damasks. . . . These are for informal little luncheons . . . but for formal affairs and general use, there is nothing quite as satisfactory and durable as all-white table linens."

In rural areas, Americans often preferred the more practical turkey red checkered cloths embellished with animal, floral, and hunting motifs. Many of these damask cloths were made in England or Europe, but "the material by the yard . . . was being produced here by the time of the Civil War and probably some years before."[7] Like the popular summer and winter coverlets, these tablecloths were reversible, each side being a mirror image of the other.

BED LINENS

While wealthy colonists enjoyed sheets of fine linen, many households used coarser materials such as canvas, Holland, and hempen (a cream-colored, rough linen). Sheets were usually seamed in the center and hemmed at the ends. Most early linen was made by girls and young ladies for their dowries. As housewives they would mend and supplement their bedding when needed. During pregnancy, women focused on crib sheets and cradle linen, often embroidering them in anticipation of visitors. Fashions in bedding changed with the times: while a single bottom sheet served a pioneer bed, more elaborate bedclothes were prescribed by Victorian ladies' magazines. Describing the "dressing" of beds in 1882, *The Delineator* instructed: "The dressing is done after the most approved fashion, all the clothing being tucked in, so that the exquisite workmanship of the bed may be duly admired. The pillows are of the required shape, being almost square; while the spread is of Bolton [cotton] sheeting, left particularly plain."[8]

By the 1880s, two sheets for one bed were the norm, but earlier in the century travelers had frequently complained of poor sleeping accommodations and inadequate linens. When Charles West Thompson journeyed from Philadelphia to Lehigh County in 1823, he mentioned in his diary: "Here the dumb Dutchman did not know how to make a bed. There was just one sheet on the bed—no upper sheet."[9]

Even when a top sheet was omitted, bedding in Pennsylvania German counties and other rural areas consisted of colorful plaid, checked, and blue resist-dyed bolster covers, pillowcases, and the single sheet. Sheets made of tow instead of fine linen required several washings before losing their sandpaper finish. A few sheets were embroidered, with one amusing example stating in German, "This bed sheet belongs to me Elisabeth Herman—1838—whoever steals it is a thief—Elisabeth Scholl." Elisabeth not only sewed her married name but also worked in her maiden name.

For advice on bedding, a woman could consult various magazines. In 1869, *The American Woman's Home* warned:

It is poor economy to make narrow and short sheets, as children and domestics will always slip them off, and soil the bed-tick and bolster. They should be three yards long, and two and a half wide, so that they can be tucked in all around. All bed-linen should be marked and numbered, so that a bed can always be made properly, and all missing articles known.[10]

Traditionally, American women marked bed and table linens by embroidering initials and numbers on them to indicate the sequence of particular items. Thus, a sheet marked "4" would have been the fourth sheet made in a set. Not only could a woman keep track of how many sheets she made, she could also prevent uneven wear by rotating them by number. Some women turned a utilitarian practice into a form of art, creating elaborate embroidery using microscopic stitches. They often included religious mottos and romantic sentiments. A square of fine linen was marked by one woman in indelible ink:

1831
Mrs. Amanda Parker
Put your trust in God
No. 7

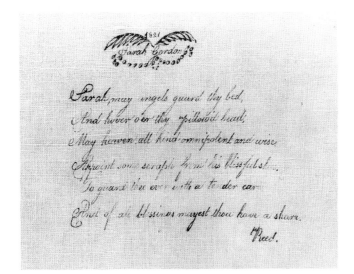

Whoever marked Sarah Gordon's linen pillowcase not only included Sarah's name and date, but added in a Spencerian hand a tender verse attributed to "Reed." (Courtesy of the New Hampshire Historical Society.)

While some nineteenth-century household specialists felt that India ink "disfigured" fine linens, other experts hailed its use. In 1861, *The Ladies' Hand Book of Fancy and Ornamental Work* intoned:

> One of the accomplishments which every lady should learn and try to excel in, is the ability to *mark* well in Indelible Ink. . . . We have used an Indelible Ink prepared by Mr. Blair, corner of 8th and Walnut Streets, Philadelphia . . . and never had it wash out or fade, and it is *free* in the pen, never blotting the article. . . . Some persons prefer a goose or crow quill to mark with, but a first-rate *steel* pen answers very well. . . .[11]

Certainly, Sarah Gordon of Bedford, New Hampshire, displayed a firm hand on her pillowcase, which was inscribed with her name, the date (1821), and a poem by "Reed":

> Sarah, may angels guard thy bed,
> And hover o'er thy pillow'd head,
> May heaven, all kind, omnipotent and wise
> Appoint some seraph from his blissful skies
> To guard thee over with tender care
> And of all blessings mayest thou have a share.
>
> *Reed*

Shaker textiles often contain initials and two sets of numbers, referring to the room in the dwelling houses (each room had a number) and the year the textile was made. Sometimes two sets of initials indicated an individual and the family with whom he or she shared the house.[12]

A variety of pillowcases, usually made of finely bleached linen, graced American bedrooms. Early pillow casings or "pillow-beares" had two to four linen twill ties at one end and were finished with narrow hems. Stuffed work, candlewick, and lavishly embroidered pillow shams that often accompanied matching spreads were reserved for holidays and visitors. By 1850 larger hems were in vogue, and buttons with buttonholes began to replace twill ties. Scalloping, fancy edgings, and embroidery became hallmarks of stylish late Victorian cases. Huge, square pillowcases and matching sheets featured elaborate monograms surrounded by a veritable orgy of white work.

A unique type of pillowcase was created by Pennsylvania German women between 1830 and 1860 to match appliquéd and pieced quilts. These decorative cases, called "show" cases, were often made in pairs and used to dress beds for special occasions, although some were used for everyday. According to Pennsylvania German custom, they were probably washed only twice a year.[13] This ensured the survival of a number of these cases, since unquilted patchwork and delicate appliqué tops rarely held up to repeated laundering. However, not everyone appreciated the practice. Margaret Van Horn Dwight good-humoredly recounted an overnight stay at Riker's Tavern in Hanover Township in 1810: "I never laughed so heartily in my life—Our bed to sleep on was straw—the pillows contained nearly a single handful of feathers and were covered with the most curious and dirty patchwork I ever saw—we had one bed quilt and one sheet—I did not undress at all. . . ."[14]

In well-made cases, unsightly seams were avoided by either carrying over the pattern on the front to the back, thereby creating a border, or doing the reverse. The detailed work of the front was not repeated on the back, but the material chosen for the back complemented the front. "Occasional" Pennsylvania German pillowcases might be edged with ruffles, fringes, or other trims, and some cases were embellished with embroidered names, dates, and inscriptions.[15]

Pennsylvania German pillowcases typical of the 19th-century cases that "dressed" beds for special occasions. Each about 14″ × 23″. (Courtesy of Kelter-Malcé.)

DECORATED PENNSYLVANIA GERMAN TOWELS

Another unique contribution of the Pennsylvania Germans, the embroidered show towel, displays a style of decoration distinctive in its origins. On early towels German verses appear, and if the maker stitched her name, she often gave herself the German feminine suffix "in."[16]

To Pennsylvania German families, decorated hand towels symbolized prosperity, cleanliness, and continuance of European tradition. A few eighteenth-century examples have been discovered; most show towels were made between 1820 and 1850, however, with the earlier towels longer and narrower than mid-nineteenth-century versions.

Cross-stitch embroidery along with other stitches embellished most show towels. At times intricate drawn work and bands of crochet and darned netting framed embroidered and plain sections. Using red cotton or red-and-blue cotton thread, young girls embroidered motifs resembling designs found on many Pennsylvania German samplers—flowers (mostly tulips), crowns, stars, birds, animals, people, hearts, and houses. By positioning symmetrical motifs in mirror images of each other, a unique, stylized effect was achieved.[17] Many girls worked on both samplers and decorated towels, using the same motifs and mottos for each. Like many decorated textiles, show towels were almost exclusively the work of adolescents, who had the time to spend on embroidery before taking on the added responsibilities of marriage and children.[18] Although Mennonite and Amish tradition prohibited frivolous decoration, exceptions were made for the show towel. The acquisition of needed sewing skills, the development of self-control, and the cultural disapproval of "idle hands" probably accounted for parental endorsement of the decorated towel.

The finished towel was proudly hung on a door. In the eighteenth century this was usually the door between the living room and kitchen, but at some point in the nineteenth century, people began displaying show towels on upstairs bedroom doors.[19]

THE LINEN CLOSET

The housewife's preoccupation with her linen closet was reinforced by contemporary magazines. In 1871, *Godey's* featured an article entitled "Labels for Packets of Linen" in which it prescribed *embroidering,* or marking in indelible ink, labels to identify various articles, including such particular items as "tablecloths for twelve."[20]

Sophia Elisabeth G. Witmer proudly inscribed her name on the show towel she made in 1860. The varied floral motifs and carefully executed birds together with the elegant tasseled fringe testify to her skill with the needle. 63½″ × 17½″. (Courtesy of the Philadelphia Museum of Art.)

The many hours spent by the American housewife in counting and caring for her linens might have inspired the invention of paper pillowcases with matching counterpanes by a papermaking firm in New Jersey in 1885. The *White Mountain Echo* of Bethlehem, New Hampshire, reported (Aug. 22, 1885): "Ornamental designs are stamped in the outer surfaces of the covers and cases, giving them a neat, attractive appearance. When . . . wrinkled from use, they can easily be smoothed out with a hot flatiron. The new paper bed clothes are 75 cents per set, and will probably become very popular."

Apparently, paper "bed clothes" did not catch on, and even in the high-tech circles of today's world the desire for beautiful linens has not abated.

The Victorian concept of a separate room in the house devoted to children led to the development of nursery linens. Outline embroidery patterns in magazines, kits, and booklets featured nursery-tale characters, animals, clowns, and other child-oriented motifs. Embroidery designs based on Kate Greenaway illustra-

OPPOSITE, TOP LEFT:

Elisabet Schefern's drawn work and pink embroidered motifs are typical of Pennsylvania German show towels. 51″ × 15″. c. 1840. (Courtesy of Rosalind S. Miller.)

OPPOSITE, TOP RIGHT:

Except for the central tulip and star motifs, all designs are mirror images in the drawn work panel of this Pennsylvania German show towel. 58″ × 18″. (Courtesy of Rosalind S. Miller.)

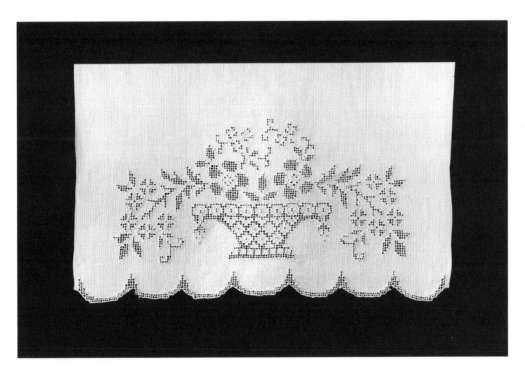

LEFT:

The drawn work design on this late-19th-century hand towel derives from the popular still-life motifs found on theorems and paintings. 17″ × 35″. (Courtesy of Alice Quinn. Photograph, Schecter Lee.)

tions in *Harper's Bazaar* (Jan. 11, 1879, July 23, 1881, Jan. 28, 1882), *Art Amateur* (September 1880), and *Godey's* (November 1880) proved so popular with the American public that the Kate Greenaway "look" stayed in fashion well into the twentieth century. Many women embroidered pillow shams, splashers for sinks, towels, tidies (antimacassars), and numerous other household linens with parades of children dressed in the quaint costumes favored by Kate Greenaway.

Fashionable Victorian women "revived" their family heirlooms by the addition of outline embroidery. Mail-order booklets contained patterns, monograms, and stamping instructions that were guaranteed. However, the following directions from the October 1908 booklet of *Modern Embroidery* might daunt today's reader:

OPPOSITE, BOTTOM:

Decorated Pennsylvania German hand towel by Konra Disler, dated 1862. Made of bleached linen with crochet lace and embroidered cross-stitching. 18½″ × 30½″. (Courtesy of the Philadelphia Museum of Art.)

Although originally handspun in 1824, this linen dresser scarf remained plain until a great-great-granddaughter embroidered these Kate Greenaway children on it. 32″ × 19″. (Courtesy of Rosalind S. Miller.)

Pillow shams decorated by embroidered (usually pink or red) mottos and scenes were popular with Victorian housewives. The stamped patterns, readily available by mail order or in department stores in the late 19th century, limited the individuality of this type of work. LEFT, 30″ × 25″; RIGHT, 31″ × 27″. (Courtesy of Rosalind S. Miller.)

For transforming perforated paper patterns to cloth. . . . Pour a little kerosene oil or benzine in a dish or cover, roll felt or cotton waste for pad. Saturate pad in oil, and rub over the paste, the colouring will absorb into the pad ready for use. Place the pattern smooth side up on the article to be stamped, rub the saturated pad over the pattern and get a clear line.

The figures chosen for outline embroidery reflected contemporary interests. The Japanese Pavilion at the Centennial Exposition kindled a vogue for Oriental design. Women's magazines gave directions for linens decorated by cherry blossom sprays, exotic birds on gnarled tree branches, fans, teapots, vases, and a host of other Oriental motifs. In 1883, *Peterson's Magazine* devoted an entire page to "Birds from Japanese Designs" and pronounced that "the superiority of the Japanese in designs of this kind, as also in designs for flowers, foliage, etc., is universally conceded."[21]

The Victorian taste for the elaborate and the bizarre, combined with the widespread desire to decorate in the latest style, resulted in an infinite variety of household linens. Fashionable linens were often bordered by sumptuous edgings of crochet, complicated drawn work, and other forms of white work, but many of these goods were not the handiwork of American women, but imported. In 1869, *The American Woman's Home* compared the prodigious output of eighteenth-century needlewomen with their Victorian counterparts':

> A bride in those days was married with sheets and tablecloths of her own weaving, with counterpanes and toiletcovers wrought in divers embroidery by her own and his sisters' hands. The amount of fancy-work done in our days by girls who have nothing else to do, will not equal what was done by these who performed, beside, among them, the whole work of the family.[22]

Magazines of the period began to question the value of spending so much time decorating household linens, suggesting that woodworking, marquetry, and other carpentry projects might better suit the modern woman. In 1883, *The Delineator* declared: "The hand-towel upon which days and days of cross-stitch and open-work are expended, and which serves its purpose no longer and no better than its prettily damasked but otherwise unornamented fellows, announces . . . that a large amount of time had been squandered upon a mere towel. . . ."[23]

The early 1900s saw the introduction of the Art Nouveau style and a move toward simplicity. By then, most women were buying their linens rather than making or hand-decorating them.

This linen hand towel might have served as a kitchen towel. It was probably made around the time of the Centennial, when depictions of George Washington were especially popular. 38″ × 18″. (Courtesy of Rosalind S. Miller.)

A country scene, a stroll in the afternoon, or a meeting of friends—all come to mind upon seeing this delightful embroidered hand towel. Unlike towels with stamped patterns, in this example the imagination of the home artist is apparent. Early 20th century. 16″ × 29″. (Courtesy of Alice Quinn. Photograph, Schecter Lee.)

"The Rose and Lily." Few silk pictures retain their color over time, so that this example is an especially important one. Although the school where it was worked has not yet been identified, it is known to have been in the Portland, Maine, area. Initialed "M.F.T." and dated 1817. (Courtesy of Mrs. Robert B. Stephens.)

SEVEN

EARLY NEEDLEWORK,
1650–1830

To understand from the vantage point of the twentieth century how central needlework was in women's lives in the seventeenth and eighteenth centuries requires a huge leap of the imagination. No woman, whatever her age, social class, or region, grew up without learning how to use a needle, a skill she was taught at five or six or even earlier, if she could manage it. So integral a part of a girl's education was needlework that Caroline King's father, who grew up in Salem in the eighteenth century, always recalled a sign he passed by as a boy that said: "Plain sewing and politeness taught within by Mrs. Bakeman."[1]

As a small child, each girl learned plain sewing and marking, and as she grew up, moved on to fancy or ornamental work. Never, though, could she give up the practice of earlier skills in favor of those learned later, for her entire household's linens and clothing too (though a professional seamstress might have made the latter) were her prime responsibility: "A girl should learn needlework to perfection, but principally the useful parts, and though the *ornamental* be highly commendable, yet it must not be encouraged to the prejudice or neglect of the *useful*."[2]

Plain sewing, the stitching and hemming of pillowcases, bed sheets, towels, undergarments, and clothing for infants, children, and adults, was the first requirement. Knitting—also considered plain work—of stockings, hats, mittens, gloves, and scarves was another part of the same time-consuming job. If less spectacular in what it produced than embroidered pictures or colorful samplers, plain sewing must have given, for those who found it other than horribly tedious, the pride of accomplishment in skills mastered. It may also have offered, as the author of *The Young Lady's Friend* (1837) put it, "a soothing and sedative effect . . .; it composes the nerves, and furnishes a corrective for many of the little irritations of domestic life."[3]

Marking, the stitching of initials and sometimes numbers as well, on bed linens, coverlets, blankets, clothing, and personal accessories such as handkerchiefs and petticoats, was another basic skill, and one no properly educated woman could be without. Marking linens with the owner's initials kept them from going astray if the washing was sent out or even if it was spread over nearby bushes at home.

Darning, another basic skill, seems always to have been less important here than in England and Europe, a fact much lamented by Ethel Bolton and Eva Coe, who wrote the first book on American samplers in 1921: "It is distressing to reflect that even at this early period our national sin of extravagance betrayed itself in our failure to train the young in the art of repairing and conserving."[4] In other countries, young women learned to imitate the various weaves so skillfully that no evidence of mended tears could be found. It seems likely, however, that colonial women at least, for whom cloth was particularly scarce, must have darned their textiles, even if they were less proficient at it than their overseas counterparts.

Whatever its satisfactions, plain sewing must still have been far behind fancywork in the amount of pleasure it gave. Sarah Anna Emery, who went to a Miss Emerson's school the summer she was eight, recalled years later her excitement in being shown how to do "ornamental marking and embroidery. This fancy work opened a new world of delight. I became perfectly entranced over a sampler that was much admired, and a muslin handkerchief, that I wrought for Mother, became the wonder of the neighborhood."[5]

The colored threads that Adele Messelir used to work her sampler were meant to demonstrate her skill at darning. The majority of American darning samplers were worked at Quaker schools. 1838. (Courtesy of Wendy Lavitt.)

Crewel embroidered pot holder initialed "RM" and dated 1792. Wool on cotton, backed with blue-and-white plain linen and bound with blue silk tape. Pennsylvania. 7″ × 6″. (Courtesy of the Pennsylvania Farm Museum of Landis Valley.)

Like clothing and the decoration of houses, fancywork has seen numerous fads and fashions, some more enduring than others. Much of the fancy needlework done early in America's history was what today we call crewelwork, meaning embroidery done in a variety of stitches with crewel yarns. Originally the word "crewel" referred only to the thread itself, a loosely twisted, two-ply worsted, rather than to the needlework technique, as it now does. As early as 1687, crewel yarn was imported into Boston from London, as evidenced by an order from Samuel Sewall for white cloth and "green worsted to work it."[6]

The designs for crewelwork, whether on bed furniture, pocketbooks, petticoats, or chair seats, came from many sources, including imported and domestic patterns devised by professional designers. During the eighteenth century, teachers of needlework also drew patterns for anyone wanting to buy them, and advertised their services in local papers:

> If any Ladies should think it too much trouble to draw their own patterns, if they will take the trouble to call on her, she [Mrs. Mary Mansfield] will endeavor to suit them. She draws patterns of any kind, either for muslin upon sattin, screens, pocket-books, spreads, etc.[7]

Print sources also inspired crewelwork designs—herbals, bestiaries, handcolored flower prints, and design books printed expressly for that purpose—all were used, sometimes being copied directly and other times providing ideas that the needlewoman interpreted as she chose.

In addition to bed furniture—which included valances, a headcloth, side curtains, and a counterpane—many other smaller objects were also worked in crewel. Among the most appealing are the single or paired pockets women wore tied around the waist under or over their skirts, which in the eighteenth century had no pockets. In these large pouches, housewives carried their small treasures and the tools of their trade: needles, pins, keys, scissors. Though many embroi-

In the 18th and 19th centuries, women wore tie-on pockets underneath their skirts, which had no pockets. Cotton with linen backs. c. 1780–1800. LEFT, 15½″ × 12½″; TWO ON RIGHT, 15″ × 11″. (Courtesy of Stella Rubin. Photograph, Schecter Lee.)

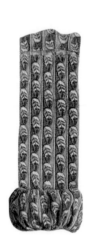

These three pockets (LEFT) are unusually well-documented. The calico example with the "lozenge" design was made in Norwich, Connecticut. The lower section contains an interesting assortment of articles:

1. an infant's well-mended linen and cotton cap with tape ties
2. embroidered muslin tabs for a lady's cap
3. a Reward of Merit card to Elijah Abeil
4. newspaper clippings from 1839
5. an engraved illustrated card with the poem *The Dying Christian*.

These date the pocket to 1839. 13″ × 14″.

The center pocket was made and painted by Mrs. Mary Floyd Talmadge in 1802 and given to Mrs. Farnam before her marriage to Mr. Horatio Farnam. It is a particularly elegant needlecase of ivory silk. 14″ × 4″.

The third pocket is made from scraps of many printed calicos, some dating from the 18th century. It has a linen lining. 16″ × 6″.

(All three pockets courtesy of the Litchfield Historical Society.)

A group of cotton needle roll-ups, also called huswifs. These cases were made of fabric scraps. Some had a pincushion as well. They rolled up tight enough to fit inside the larger pockets 18th- and 19th-century women wore under their skirts. New England. Height, 8″–16″. (Courtesy of Jeannine Dobbs. Photograph, Schecter Lee.)

dered or canvaswork pockets were very elaborate, and must have taken much time and care to make, few have been considered important enough for women to record them in their wills, although an occasional bequest is found. In 1795, for example, a New England woman left her daughter a dimity pocket along with its contents: "pocket-glass, comforter [a hand-warmer], and strong-waters bottle."[8]

So important to a woman's daily tasks were the contents of these pockets—made in plain linen, chintz, cotton, patchwork, and canvaswork as well as crewel—that it has been suggested the pocket should replace the spinning wheel as the traditional symbol of the housewife: "Whether it contained cellar keys or a paper of pins, a packet of seeds or a baby's bib . . . it characterized the social complexity as well as the demanding diversity of women's work."[9]

Related to these pockets is the much smaller, usually cotton, case called a "huswif" or housewife, an oblong pouch for needles, pins, and other smalls that rolled up and could be carried in the larger pocket. Usually made of scraps of calico or chintz, some were initialed in cross-stitch, as were pockets.

While pockets continued in use throughout the nineteenth century and even into the twentieth in some areas, by the mid-eighteenth century fashionable ladies were carrying small drawstring bags of silk or cotton, called reticules: "The insignia of the married state was a gayly embroidered or brocaded bag, in which were the household keys, snuff box, needlebook and piece of sweet flag to keep off qualms. At the side hung pincushions and little scissors swung from silver chains."[10]

Another type of pocketbook, this one carried by both men and women, was also in vogue in the second half of the eighteenth century: a canvas or crewelwork envelope bag, made in both single and double versions, and usually measuring about 4 by 8 inches. The single type has a flap closing, and the double one folds in the middle into two compartments of about equal size.

Men's bags were usually slightly larger than women's and, judging from advertisements for lost pocketbooks, held different items. An advertisement in the *Pennsylvania Gazette* of 1763 listed one man's pocketbook as containing: "some Pieces of Silver, some small Bills of Paper Money, sundry Invoices of Goods, a Ticket of the Leacock Lottery, endorsed Camalt, and a Receipt for Fifty Shillings, in Part of Land, with sundry Endorsements on it . . ."[11] Women's pocketbooks, if the following advertisement typifies what many held, evidently had much the same jumble of objects women's bags hold today: "a Pair of Stone Earrings, two Pair of Stone-Buttons which wanted mending, silver Thimble mark'd Hannah Bill, a large plain Stayhook in the shape of a Heart . . . and sundry Papers . . ."[12]

These hand-held pocketbooks were made either in crewelwork, usually in a floral design, or canvaswork, in a variety of stitches. Tent stitch, the hard-to-work Queen's stitch, cross-stitch, and most often, the Irish stitch, were used. Lined in brightly colored wool or worsted, many had a stiff interlining as well. Most were bound with hand-woven twill tape, sometimes ending in long ties that kept the pocketbook closed. By the end of the eighteenth century such bags had gone out of fashion, but those in existence must have been treasured, as a fair number of these small wonders survive.

Eighteenth-century canvaswork included not only pocketbooks but many

A pair of linen pockets with the inscription "Major Methold" and the initials "ECW" and "EPC" embroidered in typical Pennsylvania German fashion. Note the exquisitely small stitches and fanciful renditions of the peacocks, birds, and lions(?). Height, 10". (Courtesy of the Shelburne Museum. Photograph, Ken Burris.)

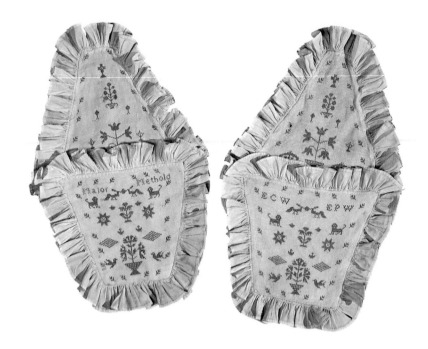

other objects, from tiny pincushions to large tent-stitch pictures of gentlemen and ladies in pastoral settings. These pastoral pieces, more than sixty of which have been discovered, vary in size, the largest being chimney pieces as much as 3 to 4 feet in width. Generally referred to as the "Fishing Lady" group, the pictures, samplers, and chair seats are similar in style and motif. The elegantly dressed lady, seen sitting by a stream holding a fishing pole, found in twelve of the pictures, is the source for the name of the entire group.

Worked in the Boston area in the eighteenth century by young women in their late teens and early twenties, the pictures are believed to have as their source domestic patterns drawn after English models by Mrs. Susannah Condy, a Boston teacher of embroidery. On several occasions, Mrs. Condy advertised that her patterns were available not only to her pupils but also to the general public. "She [Mrs. Condy] draws Patterns of all sorts, especially Pocket books, House-wives, Screens, Pictures, Chimney Pieces . . . etc. for Tent Stitch in a plainer Manner and cheaper than those which come from London."[13]

Of silk, wool, gold and silver threads, and bits of ribbon, with bead eyes and applied silver lace buttons, these tent-stitch pictures portray idyllic scenes in a primitive style. Couples sit peacefully enjoying nature while birds, stags, horses, sheep, and dogs fly or leap through fields and flowers. Although similar to the English needlework based on common sources, the New England versions are distinguished by "distinctly American details—stiff little ranks of steeplebush topping the hillocks and red-wing blackbirds in sportive flight."[14]

Less impressive in size but equally demanding of skill were the many other objects worked in tent stitch in a range of motifs—scenic, floral, geometric. Can-

A cotton drawstring bag or reticule, with pen and ink verses and floral decoration. Similar examples from the same area suggest that such bags were fashionable in this part of New England. Made by Sarah Bartlet in Campton, New Hampshire. Height, 9″. (Courtesy of the New Hampshire Historical Society.)

vaswork was very durable, and this was often the choice for chair seats, such as a set of eight intricately carved mahogany chairs with vividly colored tent-stitch seats made for an elegant dining room. Fire screens, designed to shield ladies' faces from the fire's heat, were made both as pole stands and in hand-held versions.

Books and Bibles were covered with canvaswork; pincushions, pinballs, sewing cases, tablecloths, and even wall pockets were worked in wools—and occasionally silks—on canvas. By the end of the eighteenth century, however, new fashions in needlework were gradually beginning to dominate, and the beautiful but time-consuming crewel- and canvaswork, among the finest examples of American needlework, appeared less and less often.

Already popular in France, tambour work, done with a hook rather than a needle, was taken up in America and in England during the second half of the eighteenth century. In 1768, Mrs. Bontamps, a milliner who had come from France, advertised tambour work in the *Pennsylvania Gazette* as one of her skills: "She also embroiders in gold, silver, silk and thread, upon the late invented Tambour."[15]

The technique itself is said to have originated in India or China, although the idea of working it on a hoop began in France. Quickly taking hold in the United States, it was taught in many of the academies, including Mrs. Saunders and Miss Beach's at Dorchester, Massachusetts. In 1803 they advertised that they taught, among other subjects, "Plain Sewing, Embroidery, *Tambour*, French Language . . . etc."[16]

The small tambour hook was inserted into a piece of fabric, and a loop of thread was pulled up from underneath, each motion creating a chain stitch on the

William Kingsley's canvaswork pocketbook, dated 1773 and stitched in the intense shades popular for these pieces at the time. Height, 6″. (Courtesy of Historic Deerfield, Inc.)

A velvet drawstring bag. Therorem painting, accomplished with the aid of stencils, was popular between 1810 and 1840. Pictures (on silk, velvet, and paper), bags, scarves, tablecloths, and bedcovers were all stenciled. Most showed flowers or fruit, and some added birds and trees as well. The other side of this bag has a different floral design. Oil on velvet with silk binding. Probably New England. c. 1825. 8½″ × 7″. (Courtesy of Jeannine Dobbs. Photograph, Schecter Lee.)

This crewel embroidered wallet is initialed "J.B." and probably belonged to either John Buell (1671–1746) or Jonathan Buell (1717–1796). It is lined with pink calamanco and edged in silk braid. 4″ × 6″. (Courtesy of the Litchfield Historical Society.)

surface of the fabric. A delicate art, tambour work was done with multicolored silks, wools, or cotton on "the lightweight muslins or silks of dresses, scarves, window draperies, and bed hangings. Tambour was easy to learn, quickly done, and as such, an instant hit."[17] In 1834, however, an M. Heilmann, of Mulhouse, France, invented and exhibited a machine at the Paris Exposition "by which a female could embroider with eighty or 140 needles, more accurately and expeditiously than she formerly could with one."[18] With the introduction of such machines, tambour work quickly lost its popularity.

Even more delicate than tambour work was the needle lace done in the eighteenth century and called Dresden or drawn work, or sometimes weave-lace. Such work required skill not only with the needle but the scissors. In drawn work, several threads are removed and the remaining ones drawn together to form a design. Sometimes embroidery is added to the drawn threads, and the cut threads are stitched to prevent their fraying. In some cases, no threads are actually removed; rather, they are merely pulled together with small stitches to form a design. Embroidery teachers from different cities including Boston frequently advertised that they taught Dresden and cutwork, but to date the only surviving lacework samplers are from the Philadelphia area.[19]

Early drawn-work pieces found today are all white, but "recent research by Susan Swan . . . suggests that these now pristine-white cutwork samplers were originally colorful, with brilliant silk quilled ribbon borders and rosettes. . . . Additionally, the sampler would have been mounted on a colored backing."[20]

Like much eighteenth- and early-nineteenth-century needlework, these pieces looked very different in their own time; just how different becomes clearer as early letters, diaries, and records are studied and contemporary styles and methods are revealed.

SAMPLERS AND NEEDLEWORK PICTURES

The earliest dated sampler found in the American colonies was made by Loara Standish, the daughter of Captain Myles Standish of Plymouth Colony, some time before 1656. Long and narrow, it measures 23 by 7 inches, and is similar both in shape and format to English samplers of the period. Samplers were made in England and on the Continent as early as the 1500s, their purpose being to serve as a record of designs, a personal pattern book, to which a woman could refer to refresh her memory or experiment with a new motif on a piece she was about to work. Early samplers were long and narrow—one seventeenth-century English example measuring 36 inches long by 7 inches wide. They were kept rolled up in a safe place, to be taken out when needed. Unlike later samplers, they bore no name or date, and were probably worked on over a period of time, being added to as new designs came to the attention of their maker.

An 18th-century pastoral scene in needlework, attributed to Mary Whitehead of Connecticut. Some of the blue yarn was once green, but has faded with time. Probably Norwich area. c. 1750. 17½" × 21½". (Courtesy of the Lyman Allyn Museum.)

The few seventeenth-century samplers known to have been made here and the greater number from the early eighteenth century are similar to contemporary English examples. By the second quarter of the eighteenth century, however, a distinctive American style had started to develop. For one thing, the shape of samplers changed; they became shorter and wider, and borders were added. In addition, regional differences in design and style began to appear around that time. A group of samplers depicting Adam and Eve were made in Boston, "the first recognizable group of samplers made in New England."[21]

The simplest samplers, consisting primarily of alphabets and numerals, were most likely worked at home or at a dame school, a small neighborhood school that both boys and girls attended, usually between the ages of four and nine.[22] Such pieces were marking samplers, to teach little girls the knowledge they would need to initial and possibly number their household linens later on; some even had the word "MARKT" embroidered on them along with their letters. More elaborate pieces, with houses, scenes, flowers, and other decorative motifs as well as long verses, were primarily made in seminaries or academies, private schools for well-to-do older girls ages twelve to eighteen.

Schools for young ladies are known to have existed as early as 1706, as evidenced by an advertisement in the *Boston News-Letter* of that year. Mistress Mary Turfrey advertised that she would board "Young Gentlewomen, if any Gentleman desires his Daughters should be under her education."[23]

Academies in the eighteenth century were geared to giving young women those skills it was thought necessary for them to have in order both to marry and

"The Hanging of Absalom,"
an embroidered scene worked
by Faith Robinson on a linen
ground. The treatment of both
figures and landscape is typical
of this type of embroidered
picture. Lebanon, Connecticut.
c. 1770. 18½" sq.
(Courtesy of the Lyman Allyn
Museum.)

to run their homes thereafter. While some schools, like Miss Sarah Pierce's Academy in Litchfield, Connecticut, offered solid work in academic subjects such as reading, writing, grammar, and French, many others focused only on more fashionable subjects: needlework, painting, dancing, etc. A letter to Nancy Shippen Livingston from her mother while Nancy was a pupil at Mistress Rogers' School for Young Ladies in Trenton, New Jersey, suggests the subjects considered important in 1777:

> Tell me how you improve in your work. Needlework is a most important branch of a female education and tell me how you have improved in holding your head and shoulders, and making a curtsy, in going out or coming into a room, in giving and receiving, holding your knife and fork, walking and seting [sic]. These things contribute so much to a good appearance that they are of great consequence.[24]

Samplers made under the eye of the instructor in eighteenth- and nineteenth-century academies were no longer meant to be rolled up and used only as a sort of reference; rather, they were show pieces—intended to be framed and hung prominently in a young lady's home as visible evidence of her accomplishments with the needle. At Mrs. Rowson's Academy (1797–1822) in Medford, Massachusetts, there was even an Annual Public Day or Exhibition at which "very beautiful specimens of Embroidery, Paintings and Drawings in watercolours, maps, etc. etc."

"Adam and Eve" sampler: silk on linen made by Sarah Bradstreet in 1754. Probably American. 10½" × 9½". (Courtesy of Historic Deerfield, Inc.)

were displayed to the public, which presumably meant her pupils' parents and relatives.[25]

Recent research has confirmed the presence of a number of schools, particularly in New England, that produced a large body of needlework—primarily samplers and needlework pictures—each with distinctive characteristics. Of those institutions, that of Mary (Polly) Balch, in Providence, Rhode Island (c. 1785– after 1831), is the source of what is at present the largest body of schoolgirl needlework identifiable as the work of one school.[26] Among the motifs frequently found on Balch School samplers are two trumpeting angels facing each other, Providence public buildings, and "the use of an imposing floral border, a vine growing from 2 double-handled vases, the latter usually worked in Florentine [Irish] stitch. The border flowers themselves are either highly stylized and worked in queen . . . stitch, or are worked in a more naturalistic way with roses, pansies, carnations, or even lilacs and forget-me-nots."[27]

The majority of eighteenth-century samplers, like those from Mary Balch's school, were complex pieces, in most cases designed by the school's needlework instructor. Patterns were available from England, but most teachers probably drew their own designs, which accounts for the similarity of design and motif in samplers from a particular school.

The more elaborate samplers almost always included verses, generally pious or religious ones, praising virtue, goodness, and industry. According to Susan Swan, the most popular source for verses was probably Isaac Watts's *Divine Songs for Children*, although verses from Shakespeare and the Bible were also frequently

used. Occasionally, a young girl, creating an original verse, immortalized her dislike of needlework in her sampler, as in "and she hated every stitch she did in it."[28]

Combining a large number of different stitches and motifs, most samplers made before 1830 were worked in multicolored silks on natural or bleached linen, the linen frequently being grown and spun at home. A small group of samplers dating from the first part of the nineteenth century were worked on a dark green linsey-woolsey ground, and, like the few surviving pieces with colored grounds, are rare. Tammy, or tannery cloth, a fine wool, and tiffany gauze, a thinly glazed cotton, were also used as foundation materials, the former being much more common in the British Isles and elsewhere, however, than in America. Salt bags made of hemp are also known to have been used for samplers.[29]

In addition to the more common alphabet, verse, and pictorial samplers there were several types made in much smaller numbers, and in some cases made only at certain schools. Map samplers, although found more often in England, were occasionally made in America. Young ladies stitched almost anything, ranging from one state to the entire Eastern and Western hemispheres. A typical American example is the state map of Massachusetts, worked in 1810 by Elizabeth Stevens, who stitched in the names of the towns, some horizontally and some vertically, and a sampler of North and South America made in 1798 by Frances Wade.

Three-dimensional silk globe samplers, showing either the earth or the heavens, seem to have been made only at the Friends Westtown Boarding School in Chester County, Pennsylvania, which was founded in 1799. Meticulously worked in silk on silk, the names of continents or planets were lettered in ink. Rachel

Amelia Quelch worked this silk-on-linen sampler, "finished in
the twelfth year of her age 1805." It has no alphabet but a variety of
motifs. English or American. 15½″ × 12¼″. (Courtesy of Lucette
and Lee Runsdorf. Photograph, Schecter Lee.)

A New England sampler executed on a linen ground by "Lucinda Linfield Randolph—aged 13." The tiny silk stitches show in sharp detail the small boat, picket fence, and the shuttered windows of the house. c. 1826. 17″ × 19″. (Courtesy of the Shelburne Museum.)

Copse, a student there in 1816, wrote to her parents about the globes she proposed to make:

> I expect to have a good deal of trouble in making them, yet I hope they will recompense me for all my trouble, for they will certainly be a curiosity to you and of considerable use in instructing my brothers and sisters, and to strengthen my own memory, respecting the supposed shape of our earth, and the manner in which it moves (or is moved) on its axis. . . .[30]

Another type of specialized sampler is the genealogical or family register. Horizontal rows of the names of a girl's ancestors were stitched, sometimes in tabular form, and frequently enclosed with an archway or floral border. A variation found in the Concord–Lexington, Massachusetts, area bears an embroidered tree with family names stitched on the apples hanging from its branches. Many genealogical samplers include the marriage dates of husbands and wives, and sometimes death dates too.

Samplers continued to be popular well into the nineteenth century, but by 1800 other needlework techniques had also come into vogue, among them, pictorial embroideries delicately worked in silk on silk. Instruction in this technique was given in the academies, as well as by teachers of needlework who advertised in local papers, as did Martha Logan: "Embroidery with Silk, Cruels, or Silver and Gold Thread."[31] Such embroideries were popular in England at the end of the eighteenth century and soon became so in America as well. The end of the Revolutionary War, which brought direct trading with China, meant less expensive silk

"Hector Taking Leave of Andromache," a needlework picture made with silk and metallic gold thread and watercolor by Katherine Wallace at Elizabeth Montgomery's "Ladies' English Sewing and Drawing School." c. 1818, Wilmington, Delaware. 24¼" × 27½". (Courtesy of the Daughters of the American Revolution Museum.)

thread and fabric for the embroiderers, and thus was also a factor in the increased number of silk-on-silk pictures.

Worked mainly in silks, sometimes with the addition of fine wool, these elegant pieces also used spangles (the eighteenth-century term for sequins), chenille yarns, and metallic threads. The faces, hands, and arms—when bare—were delicately painted, sometimes by the schoolgirl herself, or, more often, by the teacher or a professional artist such as T. C. Bell, Jr., a miniaturist who advertised in 1814 that he colored "(t)he Faces, etc. of Needle Work."[32] Large areas of sky, water, or clouds were frequently painted rather than embroidered, leaving the smaller areas for the more time-consuming needlework.

Subjects included biblical, classical, and literary scenes, many of them capturing dramatic or emotional moments, like the Parting of Hector and Andromache, evidently a very familiar theme judging from the number of surviving examples. "Prints showing allegorical representations of Hope, Charity, Faith, America, and the seasons were popular. . . . Other small prints copied for embroidery illustrated characters in popular novels. One of these was Maria, the heroine of Laurence Sterne's *Sentimental Journey*."[33]

Patriotic and historical subjects were also used, such as "Liberty, In the form

This silk needlework picture embroidered on white silk in grays and blacks was most likely the work of a very young girl depicting her own home. Maine. c. 1840. 7″ × 8″. (Courtesy of Kelter-Malcé. Photograph, Schecter Lee.)

of the Goddess of Youth, giving Support to the Bald Eagle," and the landing of Christopher Columbus. Both of these subjects, like those of almost all these needlework pictures, were based on a print source, either copied directly—as evidenced by those pictures with the same dimensions as their sources—or altered slightly. Sometimes the needlework is the mirror image of the print, indicating that the scene was somehow reversed in the process of being copied onto the fabric.

Such pictures were usually done in academies by girls who had already worked a sampler and were considered ready to move on to more difficult projects. The majority of silk pictures were framed, often with a rectangular or oval black-and-gold eglomisé mat. These frames are useful clues in determining where a particular picture was worked, as framers' labels remain attached to many. One framer, Bernard Cermenati, working in Salem, Massachusetts, whose label remains on several pictures, used this identification as a form of advertising: "Ladies' Needle-work framed in the most modern style, and the shortest notice [even in 1800, customers were in a hurry], as cheap as can be done in Boston."[34]

Silk needlework, like samplers, had its specialized forms, one of the most interesting being the silk embroidery referred to as printwork, so called because it looked very much like an etching or engraving. Worked "with a very fine needle in black silk, or in silk of different shades, from a jet black through all the gradations of a lead hue, to the palest slate-colour" on a white silk ground,[35] printwork was sometimes done with human hair as well as silk.

The design to be stitched, generally a memorial or landscape, was first penciled onto the silk, and then embroidered with the tiniest of stitches, in an effort to reproduce as closely as possible the look of the line and stipple engravings it imitated. Printwork pieces became popular in this country about 1800, although English examples are known from the 1780s. Their popularity, in part, is attributable to the needlemakers' art—they had learned to make extremely fine needles less than a hundredth of an inch in diameter—making possible the most minute stitches.[36]

Printwork was taken up in various parts of the country, including Providence, Rhode Island, where Miss Mary Balch advertised it as part of her curriculum in 1813. The printwork memorials from Miss Balch's school show great skill in the handling of the silk embroidery: "The blending of shades for marbleized monuments was unsurpassed; but most remarkable was the embroidered lettering . . . the most identifiable feature of the memorials from her school. The epitaphs were always embroidered with hair-fine black silk and flawlessly executed."[37]

Examples from Miss Balch's school survive, as do a number from New York's Upper Hudson Valley, but to date no school or schools where the latter group might have been made has been identified. Of these printwork pieces, a number have many of the symbols traditionally found in mourning pictures—the willow,

Silk and metal threads were embroidered on a velvet ground to create this mourning scene in memory of Mr. Abel Lord by Hepzibah Lord, c. 1804, in Connecticut. 17″ × 23″. (Courtesy of the Lyman Allyn Museum.)

symbolizing mourning and Resurrection; ferns for humility; and the broken oak tree, indicating a life cut short by death.[38]

Another form of silk embroidery—elaborate, stylized scenes of mourning with a central tombstone or altar, bearing the name and dates of the deceased, the willow tree, and weeping men, women, and children crowded around the tomb—also began appearing about 1800. While such scenes were to be ridiculed later in the nineteenth century, notably by Huckleberry Finn, who found they gave him the "fantods," they were all the fashion until about 1830. Various reasons are cited for their extreme popularity—great numbers survive—but the vogue for the sentimental and romantic was probably the most important. So fashionable were mourning pictures that young ladies evidently worked them as much for what they considered their beauty as to memorialize someone. Eliza Southgate, for example, suggested to her sister Octavia, who had asked for a needlework subject, that she do a mourning piece, "handsomer," she wrote, "than Landscapes."[39] Young women learned to stitch these embroideries in academies and from needlework teachers, the scenes, like those of other needlework pictures, usually taken from print sources.

Gradually, embroidered mourning scenes, like other needlework pictures, were replaced by pictures painted in oil or watercolor, on backgrounds of silk or velvet. The transition from needlework to paint was a slow one, the intermediate stages combining stitches and paint in the same work. This change, from the needle to the brush, is well documented in the advertisements of academies from about 1800 on, as Betty Ring has pointed out:

> Until about 1810, needlework in its various branches was of paramount importance, although painting on satin and velvet as well as paper work were offered in the school's advertisements [Mrs. Saunders and Miss Beach's] as early as 1805. After 1810 interest in painting courses notably increased, and by 1822 the academy's advertisement emphasized "PAINTING BY THEOREMS on velvet silk and paper. . . ."[40]

As painting on velvet or silk replaced needlework, manuals on how to sketch, paint, and use theorems began to appear with great regularity, among them Maria Turner's *Young Ladies' Assistant in Drawing and Painting* (1833) and Matthew D. Finn's *Theoremetical System of Painting, or Modern Plan, Fully Explained, in Six Lessons* (1830).

Explaining in Lesson IV how to paint with watercolors, Mr. Finn instructed:

> Rule II. The brush should be held perpendicularly to the paper, and worked with a circular motion of the wrist. . . .

> Rule XI. When your piece is finished, clean it off with the soft part of bread, (rather fresh) by rubbing it lightly over.[41]

Stencils, or theorems, as they were called in the nineteenth century, made it relatively easy for anyone to paint a picture. Theorems were made of stiff drawing paper coated at home with linseed oil and turpentine, and then dried, or were professionally cut by teachers or artists. Most often they had flower and fruit forms, although other designs are occasionally found.

By manipulating several large stencils or a great variety of smaller ones, the artist could create a simple or complicated composition. Although seemingly a mere mechanical skill, the great differences in quality of surviving theorem paintings show that much more than manual dexterity was required. Those artists with an eye for color, form, and composition created wonderful pieces, some lush and elegant, others misty and almost dreamlike. In contrast, theorem painters without such skills did works no better than those of poor freehand painters.

With the transition from needlework to paint complete, academies altered their curricula to meet the demands of contemporary students. By 1840, however, academic subjects were fast replacing skills like painting and needlework in young ladies' schools and the direction of women's education was changing rapidly. In some parts of the country, traditional needlework continued for several decades longer; but for the most part, needlework had moved very far from its beginnings, and the exquisite canvas work, crewel, and lace of the eighteenth century was gone forever.

An oil-on-velvet mourning picture, possibly from Mary Balch's school in Providence, Rhode Island, signed "Otis L. Allen." The foliage not only appears as a central motif but also frames the scene. c. 1825. 17″ × 19″. (Courtesy of Lillian and Jerry Grossman. Photograph, Schecter Lee.)

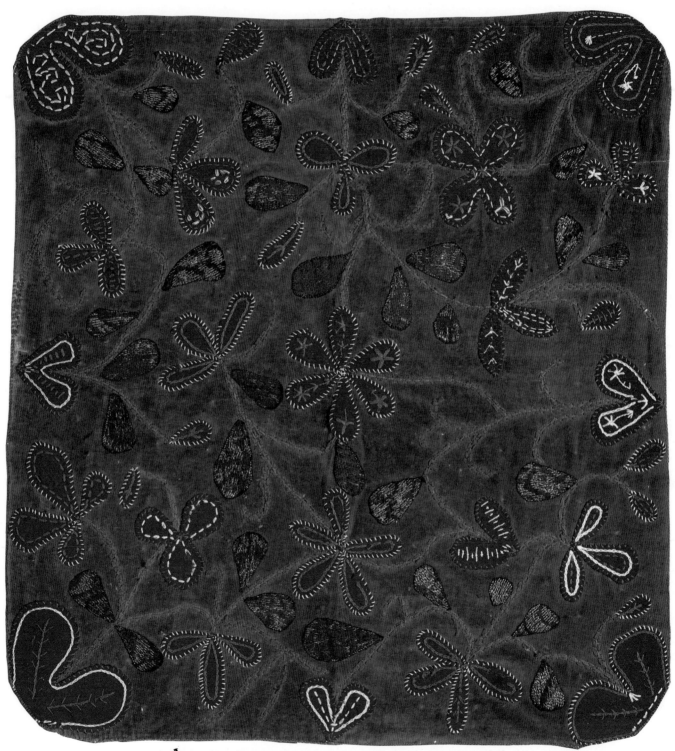

An embroidered and appliquéd velvet tablecover meant for a hall or dining room table. The floral motif is combined with a heart in each corner, from which the flowers spring. Probably New England. c. 1880. 48″ × 42″. (Courtesy of Jeannine Dobbs. Photograph, Schecter Lee.)

EIGHT

BERLIN WORK
AND VICTORIANA:
PRODUCTS OF "TASTEFUL BRAINS
AND INDUSTRIOUS FINGERS"[1]

T*he embroidery* and other fancywork of the Victorian era is clearly very different from that of the late eighteenth- and early nineteenth-century work that preceded it. By a gradual process, occurring in large part through the second quarter of the nineteenth century, as certain forms of needlework—the mourning picture, for example—died out, new ones, such as Berlin-work pictures, were replacing them. In general, by the 1840s the Victorian style of design—bolder, brightly colored, often beribboned, tasseled, or beaded—predominated.

Young ladies' academies and seminaries continued to flourish, but now the emphasis was on scholastic subjects, and little attention was given to what were formerly considered the female arts. Women still learned their basic needlework skills at home; but beyond that, their knowledge came not from small classrooms where the instructor personally supervised their work, but from the ever-increasing number of books on needlework that began appearing.

They were published in both Britain and America, and most of them had patterns and sets of instructions that were very similar, with the editors borrowing freely from other editions. For the next fifty years, a profusion of books appeared, with titles hardly distinguishable from one another, among them *The Ladies' Handbook of Fancy Needlework and Embroidery* (edited by an American Lady) in six volumes; *The Ladies' Handbook of Fancy and Ornamental Work; Dainty Work for Pleasure and Profit; The Lady's Manual of Fancy Work.* Along with these weightier volumes were the monthly periodicals, among them *Godey's Lady's*

Virginia Kramer sewed her wool needlework picture in 1842 or 1843 while she was a student at the Canton Female Seminary in Canton, Ohio. 18″ × 21″. (Courtesy of the Daughters of the American Revolution Museum.)

This floral still-life is the type of needlework that occupied the leisure time of Victorian women. The flowers were worked in wool; the background and the vase were beaded. 18″ × 18½″. (Courtesy of the Margaret Woodbury Strong Museum, Rochester, New York.)

Lambrequins, meant to adorn shelves or mantels, were especially popular during the 1860s and 1870s, the probable dates for these decorative examples. A melange of beadwork, needlepoint and silk embroidery. 9½″ × 22″. (Courtesy of the Margaret Woodbury Strong Museum.)

Book, which had a circulation of 150,000 in 1858, and *Peterson's Magazine,* both of which were published until 1898.

Magazines like *Godey's,* which flourished under the editorship of Sarah Josepha Hale, saw their mission as more than merely providing patterns for needlework. Their goal was considerably larger, as stated in the February 1864 issue: "This, then, is our aim: to diffuse and make popular the simple but efficient lessons of home happiness and goodness. Much is in the power of the mothers and wives of our land to make happy families, and thus insure a happy nation."[2]

Inherent in the view that *Godey's* and others set forth was the idea that the home was a kind of sanctuary, a place where all must be peaceful and beautiful, and that the homemaker's job was to make it that way. Decorating their homes with the myriad objects pictured in magazines like *Godey's* became the primary

Mrs. Woodruff of Litchfield, Connecticut, originally intended her needlepoint spaniel for a footstool in the 1890s, but instead it was framed at a later date. Note the beadwork on the pillow, and the glass eyes. 24″ × 18″. (Courtesy of the Litchfield Historical Society.)

135

occupation of large numbers of women, who read frequent articles praising the "home decorator . . . for beneath her touch uncomely objects gain grace and beauty."[3]

Achieving the desired "grace and beauty" was not, however, so easy, as much Victorian furniture, in the view of such contemporary authorities as Janet Ruutz-Rees, the author of *Home Decoration,* was ugly, "constructed of the commonest material, and almost always of unsightly shape and harsh outline. The sooner [they are] covered up the better."[4]

Covering up ugly furniture, window frames, or mantels was a job that kept women constantly supplied with handiwork. *Godey's* and *Peterson's* were full of suggestions for ways to beautify the home. No matter that the parlor was already more than filled with textiles in varied forms; contemporary taste dictated that more was better. Should women run out of ideas for what they might make, they had only to read over one of the fancywork manuals, such as Mrs. Pullan's. Lists of objects, like the following, described as "suitable for presents," were easily found:

Antimacassars
Doyleys. Braided on linen or muslin, netted, crocheted or
   knitted, jewelled doyleys.
Lambrequins, or mantel drapery—Berlin work
Mats. Ottomans.
Travelling Footstools[5]

Chairs, sofas, even rockers, required some sort of decoration. *Needle and Brush* provided an illustration and instructions for how to cover an upholstered rocker with a long velvet scarf. Of two shades of velvet, it was to be

A turn-of-the-century beaded needlepoint handbag. The metal frame is marked "Emilie Wochatsch"; the ends of the bag are made of soft leather. 8″ × 10″. (Courtesy of the Litchfield Historical Society.)

decorated with long stitches done with gold floss in imitation of sun rays . . . arranged upon [the rocker] to fall over the back and below the seat, all the edges being bordered with thick cord. The ends are trimmed with bullion fringe, and bullion tassels are fastened to the corners. Wide ribbons fastened to the scarf at the lower part of the back are tied above the frame at the meeting of the back and seat. . . .[6]

Along with elaborately decorated furniture, beribboned and embroidered whisk-broom holders, and beaded elbow cushions, the Victorians favored the wall pocket. "Probably no one article of modern invention and ingenuity has afforded greater satisfaction than wall-pockets," wrote one writer in 1875.[7] Made in a variety of shapes and sizes, and wall-mounted, the wall pocket's function was to keep conveniently at hand papers, magazines, toilet articles, or whatever items the maker intended it to hold. "Some of them were shaped like portfolios, their front covers held in positions by chains, cords, or ribbons; still others were pouch-shaped. All were decorated lavishly."[8]

Besides objects for the home, personal items and accessories for both men and women were also popular types of fancywork. Recommended were gentlemen's braces (suspenders) and house slippers; ladies' boudoir or work bags; foot muffs, penwipers, and various kinds of scarves, including Rigolettes (warm headdresses) and Nubians (3 yards long and half a yard wide—and knitted).

Fancywork, which encompassed a variety of techniques—patchwork, embroidery, tatting, crocheting—also included Berlin work, a type of wool-on-canvas embroidery that originated in Berlin in the early 1800s. By the middle of the nineteenth century it was worked in German wool yarns, also known as Merino, German, or zephyr wool, which replaced almost totally the crewels and worsteds used previously.

Mrs. Sally Pierpont embroidered this cotton square attached to a muslin backing using raveled silk in 1849. It is initialed "S.P.—83," signifying Mrs. Pierpont was eighty-three when she finished her painstaking work with its multicolor design of crewel stitches. She died in 1851, two years after the embroidery was sewn. 9″ × 8″. (Courtesy of the Litchfield Historical Society.)

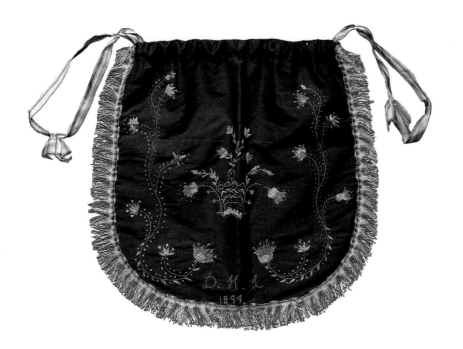

Initialed "D.H.L." and dated 1844, this embroidered silk bag might have been a gift from a friend, probably the maker. A drawstring bag like this would have been used either as a workbag at home or as a reticule. New Hampshire. Height, 9″. (Courtesy of Kelter-Malcé. Photograph, Schecter Lee.)

Julia Kane made this Berlin work sampler in the late 19th century. The initials at the right suggest a Nova Scotia origin. Wool on linen. 15″ × 11″. (Courtesy of Lucette and Lee Runsdorf. Photograph, Schecter Lee.)

Maggie Morrison included in her Berlin work sampler the name of her school, "NENTHORN PUBLIC SCHOOL," and dated it "April 21st, 1887." The date testifies that samplers were worked almost until the turn of the century. 15″ × 11½″. (Courtesy of Lucette and Lee Runsdorf. Photograph, Schecter Lee.)

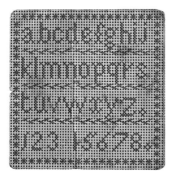
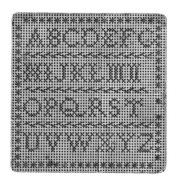

The miniature alphabet samplers were enclosed in the embroidered case beneath them, decorated with a fruit-filled compote. Height, 3″ to 5″. (Courtesy of Rosalind S. Miller. Photograph, Schecter Lee.)

Jean Peterson's wool-on-linen sampler includes a profusion of stylized motifs: a pair of stags, a house, fruit basket, hearts, and initials. Dated 1842. English or American. 14″ sq. (Courtesy of Lucette and Lee Runsdorf. Photograph, Schecter Lee.)

The designs for Berlin work were printed and colored on a kind of graph paper, termed in the nineteenth century quadrille or point paper, each square representing a square of the canvas. Easily transferred from paper to canvas—a woman worked by counting the squares of each color and making a stitch for each square—the designs made it possible to work a piece of needlework very easily. She no longer had to create her own design or work out a color scheme; both came ready-made on the printed and colored paper pattern. Because they were expensive—the patterns were colored by hand—many were used by more than one woman or resold to the shop, which would in turn resell them.

A huge variety of designs for Berlin work—14,000 of them were created between 1830 and 1840[9]—provided a diversity of subjects and patterns. For pictures, biblical scenes, engravings, and well-known paintings like Leonardo da Vinci's *Last Supper* were popular, as were pastoral and medieval scenes. In the latter half of the century, large, garishly colored flowers, especially overblown roses, and exotic birds were also favorites. Worked on a wide mesh canvas with large stitches—usually tent or cross—Berlin work was not nearly as fine or subtle as the embroidery of earlier centuries. In their color schemes, both printed patterns and wools were harsh and, even to contemporary eyes, often displeasing. Miss Lambert, instructing her readers on their choice of colors in embroidery, urged them to "carefully avoid harshness, yet, by contrast, give a proper spirit to the whole; and above all, avoid that gaudiness of colouring, and glaring want of taste, so generally exhibited in the coloured paper patterns or Berlin. . . ."[10]

But in spite of its strident colors and busy designs, Berlin work remained popular through most of the nineteenth century, worked not only on canvas but, beginning around 1820, on a kind of perforated cardboard, usually off-white.[11] Also called Bristol board, it was used instead of canvas for bookmarks, needlecases, and other small pieces, as well as for large frameable mottos such as "What Is Home Without Mother," designed to be hung on the wall.

Advice on how to work on perforated board was offered along with other instructions for embroidery:

> It [perforated card] is used for many ornamental articles, and is easy to work on, and when nicely done is nearly equal to fine canvas work. It is very nice for children to employ themselves on. Beautiful book-markers . . . needle-books, etc., can be made with it. Be careful in working that the needles are not too large, or the holes will be broken through. The small patterns must be worked in silk, the larger can be done in wool, or silk and wool.[12]

The introduction of Berlin-work patterns meant, for the most part, the end of needlework samplers. Samplers continued to be made, but by the 1830s Berlin wool had become the yarn most often used to work them. These late pieces look very different from those made earlier in the century. Berlin wool samplers were worked on fairly coarse canvas, and in general with only one or two different embroidery stitches. They tend either to have fewer design elements than the earlier ones—often large areas of the canvas are left unstitched—or to be very complicated in design and color.

Other types of samplers were also made during this period, including plain sewing samplers intended to teach a young girl basic techniques. Presumably, she would refer back to her sampler later on as young ladies of the seventeenth century did for their embroidery stitches. These oddly shaped samplers—usually with a white cotton background and colored thread that made the stitching visible—included examples of tacking, gathers, ruffles, gussets, buttonholes, waistbands, and pockets. In some cases, parts of the work were left unfinished to show how it was done.

In England, sewing samplers were made in book form as well, with each cloth page demonstrating one technique. A miniature sampler (3 to 6 inches) might be included in this small stitching notebook, which each girl made "along with a miniature skirt, apron, and knitted stockings."[13]

Berlin work, like many fads before it, died out as quickly as it was born, with women turning to other pursuits. Eventually, it was followed by what today is called simply needlepoint, done on pre-marked canvas, with the designs printed or painted in full color ready to be worked.

Both these examples of plain sewing techniques were accomplished by Mary J. Donovan in Somerville, New Jersey—the rectangular one (OPPOSITE) in 1895, and the other in 1897, by which time she had mastered ruffles, pleats, and buttonholes. LEFT, 18″ × 30″; OPPOSITE, 24″ × 8″. (Courtesy of Margie Dyer. Photograph, Schecter Lee.)

A most unusual subject for a reticule—the well-appointed table is even equipped with a globe. Made of very fine beads with leather straps to hold the drawstrings. Early 19th century. 7½″ × 5″. (Courtesy of Sylvia Pines.)

BEADWORK

By definition, beadwork is ornament—both a leisure-time activity and an object of elaborate decoration conferring status upon the maker and the wearer. While eighteenth-century beadwork in America was available to a privileged few, it reached its apogee during the nineteenth century, and was often combined with knitting and crochet. By 1808, a Philadelphia magazine pronounced: "No lady of fashion now appears in public without a riticule which contains her handkerchief, fan, card-money, and essence bottle."[14]

"Riticule," a deliberate misspelling of "reticule," referred to the popular drawstring bag carried by fashionable ladies throughout the nineteenth century. Known also as "indespensables," they were frequently satirized by men as examples of women's vanity. Beaded reticules enjoyed an enduring popularity, and continued to be used until World War I.

Four typical examples of the 1820s–40s style of bags of the fringed, drawstring variety. Height, 5″ to 9″. (Courtesy of the Litchfield Historical Society.)

This crocheted miser's purse with steel beading was made in the 1840s–50s. Its allover geometric patterns are typical of those found on many such purses. Length, 14". (Courtesy of the Brooklyn Museum.)

The miser's purse, also known as the long purse, ring purse, or stocking purse, came into fashion during the 1780s and was the first portable container designed to hold money for both men and women. (Before the eighteenth century, barter rather than currency had been the rule; few people carried cash.) Whether beaded, knitted, or crocheted, all miser's purses contained a slit in the middle (for the insertion of money) and two rings of steel, silver, or gold. The rings prevented the loss of coins and bills, as they kept them from passing into the middle section, which was often looped over a belt. The different sized and shaped ends made it easy to distinguish coins in the dark— "when it was necessary to pay a coin to a coachman, waiter, or some other tradesman, the correct coin could be withdrawn by feeling the end of the purse. The straight flat end with a fringe might contain the silver coins and the diamond, round, gathered, or tasseled end might contain the gold coins."[15]

A collection of 18th- and 19th-century beaded misers' purses from the Litchfield Historical Society. Length, 6″ to 12″.

Most miser's purses have geometric designs, but some were made with exquisite floral designs or rows of looped beads. *Godey's* and *Peterson's* regularly carried instructions and illustrations that clever (and patient) women could easily follow.

In attempting to make a beaded purse, a woman first had to select her beads, all of which were imported from Europe and were numbered according to size. She could choose from a wide range of beads, sold in bunches: transparent, opaque, iridescent, bugle, jet, gold, and cut steel. The smart needlewoman assembled beads of uniform size, ensuring a fine, even surface. Women usually consulted patterns, stringing row upon row of minute beads on silk or cotton thread. In 1904, Mary White recalled that "the needles were like slender wire. Indeed, my grandmother used broom-wire from a neighboring factory to knit her bags and purses with, for it was impossible to get needles that were fine enough."[16]

Many female academies included beadwork in their curricula; for instance, beaded bags were made at Miss Sarah Pierce's Academy in Litchfield, Connecticut, as early as the 1820s. Numerous bags survive with similar scenes and motifs, suggesting a common design source. By necessity, the practice of sharing assignments in class was widespread. While some women found designs in needlecraft books or magazines, others relied on handwritten instructions handed down by family and friends. Some of these patterns remained well-kept secrets, as this tale from nineteenth-century New England village life demonstrates:

In one New England town Matilda Emerson reigned a queen of bag makers; her patterns were beyond compare; one of a Dutch scene with a windmill was the envy of all who beheld it. She was a rival with Ann Green

A trio of American beaded bags. The two 19th-century florals are worked in delicate shades and complicated patterns. The reticule with a Grecian architectural scene is composed of fine beads and is in its original frame. c. 1900–20. Each bag approximately 10″ × 6″. (Courtesy of Evelyn Haertig. Photograph, Schecter Lee.)

for the affections of the minister, a solemn widower, whose sister kept house for him and his three motherless children. Matilda gave the parson's sister the written rules for a wonderful bead bag (the design having originated in Boston), a bag which displayed when finished a funereal willow tree and urn and grass-grown grave, in shaded grays and purple and white on a black ground; a properly solemn bag. But when the parson's sister assayed to knit this trapping of woe, it proved a sad jumble of unmeaning lines, for Ann Green had taken secretly the rules from the knitter's work box, and had changed the penciled rules in every line. When the hodgepodge appeared where the orderly symbols of gloom should have been seen, the sister believed that Matilda had purposely written them wrong in order to preserve her prestige as a bag knitter and she so prejudiced her brother that he coldly turned from Matilda and married, not Ann, but a widow from another town.[17]

Beaded bags depicting mourning scenes, Greco-Roman architecture, and floral-strewn landscapes closely followed prevailing fashions in art and costume. Some early nineteenth-century bags made of finely strung beads were enhanced by the proud beadmaker's name and date. While simple drawstring bags were completed at home, purses with complicated constructions were sent out to factories for finishing. Today beaded bags are regarded as elegant evening accessories, but originally they were carried by women whenever a purse was needed. Treasured for their beauty, they were kept in the family. In nineteenth-century New England, "All thrifty Wakefield women once carried beaded bags; bright woven things, come down as heirlooms."[18]

Beadwork and petit point tray decorated in the Kate Greenaway style: five little girls hang on to each other's skirts in a game of follow-the-leader. Except for the children's faces, executed in petit point, the tray is worked in beads. c. 1890. 20½″ × 9″. (Courtesy of the Margaret Woodbury Strong Museum.)

A rare pair of decorated Huron mittens. The delicate moosehair embroidery is worked on smoked buckskin— an art taught to the Hurons by the Ursuline nuns. c. 1800. Height, 12″. (Courtesy of William Channing. Photograph, Schecter Lee.)

Along with purses and bags, women spent hours working on beaded pictures—with varying degrees of success. Many designs came from the popular Berlin patterns of the day. In 1842, Miss Lambert in *The Hand-Book of Needlework* spoke of the necessity of obtaining the right color beads for shading faces and flowers.[19] Landscapes, sentimental scenes, and portraits of pets and people, often encased in ornate frames, decorated the parlors of Victorian homes.

Although Victorian beadwork was often characterized by flamboyant, oversize motifs, late eighteenth- and nineteenth-century work done by the Moravian Sisters in Pennsylvania displays a delicacy akin to moosehair embroidery. In Salem, beadwork was taught along with other needle arts to young girls in the early nineteenth century. One visitor to a boarding school in 1828 commented: "After an early dinner visited the Academy . . . we examined and admired the beautiful embroidery, beadwork, &c &c which was to be preserved and shown as specimens of taste and industry—with feelings (I doubt not) of pride by both parent and child."[20]

By mid-century Indian beadwork patterns began influencing beadwork designs in academies and the home, and their beauty was duly noted by the arbiters of fashion. As early as 1861 a widely read book on the subject noted that "The bead-work of the North American Indians is among the most beautiful. The Canadian Indian women sell large quantities to the visitors to the Falls of Niagra [sic], and a great deal of it finds its way to our large cities."[21]

The bold geometric patterns of the Plains found their way onto ladies' handbags, along with the floral motifs of the Great Lakes. By the turn of the century, beadwork fanciers readily admitted their debt to tribal decoration and enthusiasm for Indian handicrafts. However, even the novelty of Indian-derived designs could not prevent the gradual disappearance of beadwork in modern life. For a while the larger wooden beads sparked new interest; the magazine *Modern Priscilla* advised: "The large wood bead . . . is particularly adapted to the fruit designs. . . . The work is so very realistic that it cannot fail to be popular, and another thing in its favor is that the designs work up very rapidly."[22]

The cluttered Victorian look that inspired beaded candlesticks, vases, bell-pulls, and pole screens was declared passé, for as *House Beautiful* (1905) suggested, "The embroidered piano-cover is passing. Musicians prefer an instrument to be as bare as possible."[23] A woman might carry her grandmother's bag to the theater, but she no longer would tolerate a "beaded house."

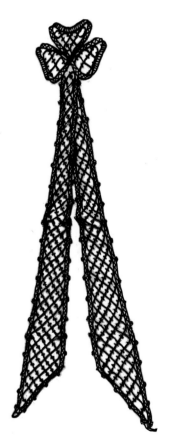

Jet sashes and collar ornaments could be bought at the notions counter, allowing the dressmaker to save time by cutting out and affixing these "ready-made" appliqués to cloaks, capes, and dresses. Note how the black jet beads were basted to cotton to protect them from breakage. Late 19th century. 38″ × 16″. (Courtesy of the Litchfield Historical Society.)

The round needlebook is an example of the type of perforated cardboard smalls that were very popular at the height of the Berlin work craze. Height, 3″. (Courtesy of Rosalind S. Miller. Photograph, Schecter Lee.)

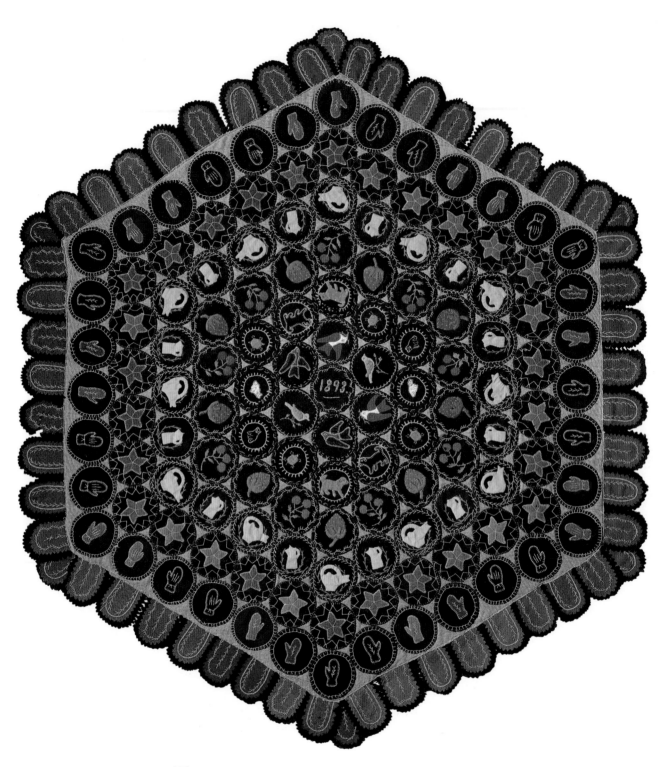

To make this table rug in 1893, the maker sewed circles of cloth
to the tan background, using the feather or buttonhole stitch, and
appliquéd motifs chosen from everyday life on each circle. Few
penny rugs are so profusely decorated. 42″ × 47″. (Courtesy of the
Shelburne Museum. Photograph, Ken Burris.)

NINE

RUGS

THE EARLIEST
FLOOR COVERINGS

R*ugs for the bed,* heavy carpet-like covers, were common in eighteenth-century colonial homes, but rugs for the floor were not. While today we take them for granted, floor rugs and carpets came relatively late into the Western world. Writing of seventeenth-century England, France, and Holland, Peter Thornton suggests their rarity even in Europe: "One gets the impression that carpets were commonly kept in storage and only brought out on important occasions or when the family was in residence."[1]

In addition to being used as bed coverings, rugs—at first imported from the East via England, and later made in England—covered the tops of tables and chests. Floor carpets were distinguished from those meant for tabletops, as eighteenth-century newspaper ads for floor coverings illustrate: ". . . printed carpets for tables . . . a quantity of stout carpeting both for floors and stairs, handsome oyl cloths for Tables" (*Boston Gazette,* 1760).[2]

What did cover the floors in many early homes was clean sand, sifted and swept each morning into graceful patterns—lines, circles, even herringbone designs. Merchants sold this sand, both for cleaning floors and to cover them, at competitive prices:

Scouring Sand for Floors . . . the Larger the Quantity the less The Price.

Sand for Floors and Scouring.[3]

Straw or rush matting and painted floorcloths made of heavy canvas were other alternatives in use by the middle of the eighteenth century. They continued to be used well into the nineteenth century, in a variety of patterns, mostly in imitation of other materials. The following designs were offered in an ad in *The Connecticut Courant* (a newspaper) in 1809: "Egyptian, Hieroglyphic, Rock, Bengal, Roman Pavement [presumably a grained marble design] and large Octogon patterns."[4] Floor cloths were sometimes spun, woven, and decorated at home, although they were made and sold in shops too. Samuel Perkins & Son of Boston offered "painted floor cloths or canvass carpets" for sale in 1816, by which date they were very popular:

> A large and elegant assortment of Painted Floor Cloths, without seams, some in imitation of the Brussels Carpeting, from $1.37½ to $2.25 per square yard, warranted to be of the best materials and well seasoned. These carpets possess a decided advantage over all others, as they are more durable, and in warm weather much more comfortable, easier Kept clean, and in hot climates, the only Kind that are not subject to injury from insects. . . ."[5]

Several types of carpets were imported from England in the eighteenth century, most commonly the Kidderminster, Scotch, or ingrains, (flat, woven and reversible), Brussels and Wilton (with a pile surface), and Oriental rugs, mostly from Turkey. None of these eighteenth-century rugs has survived, but contemporary inventories and advertisements are evidence that they were in use. Diaries and reminiscences of the period suggest, however, that floor carpets in the eighteenth century were very much a rarity, found only in the homes of the wealthy. A detailed inventory of 1773 for the house of Governor William Tryon in Fort George, New York, gives some idea of the number of rugs in use in the governor's mansion. Most of the rooms list a large Scotch or Wilton carpet, with his daughter's bedchamber containing "1 small Scotch carpet." "His Excellency's Dressing Room" has a Turkey carpet, and even the housekeeper's room boasts a rug, in her case, "1 Old Turkey Carpet."[6]

For the average person, rugs on the floor were such a rarity that many humorous stories survive about visitors who come into a house, see a carpet in the middle of the room, and proceed to walk around the edges rather than step on it. At first, carpets were placed in the center of the room and were not, like today's, wall-to-wall. The chairs and tables were placed around the perimeter, making the carpet an impressive centerpiece.

A Philadelphia lawyer, T. Matlack, recalled at age ninety-five the first carpet he had ever seen, in about 1750. A "Scotch carpet," it belonged to a Mrs. Shoemaker, a friend who had gotten it "as a rare present from England . . .[it] was deemed quite a novelty then."[7]

STRIPED WOOL AND RAG CARPETS

If store-bought carpets were beyond the reach of most Americans before the development of the domestic carpet industry in the 1830s and '40s, homemade rugs were not. It seems likely that the earliest type was the plain rag carpet, two of which, valued together at 8 shillings, were listed in 1777 in the Middleton, Massachusetts, inventory of Colonel Archelaus Fuller.[8] Such carpets were made of collections of rags cut into narrow lengths and sewn together in long strips that were then wound into balls before being loom-woven. Made of combinations of different types, weights, and colors of fabric, most rag rugs were woven in what was called a hit-and-miss design, although sometimes the rags were dyed first, either all in one color, or in several colors to form stripes. The most visually striking of the woven carpets are the brightly colored striped or checked type, for which the wool yarn—frequently homespun—was specially dyed, and the chosen colors arranged in rainbows of vibrant shades.

Made throughout the nineteenth century, rag rugs are a living folk craft today, still providing a way of recycling worn-out clothing and leftover fabric scraps.

In the Northeast, where homes were permanent dwellings, strips of rag carpet were sewn together to create wall-to-wall rugs. Single lengths were used in hallways and as stair-runners. As the nineteenth-century pioneers began moving westward, they took their rag carpets with them and found them to have many more uses than they had dreamed of. Emma Hill, who went to Kansas by prairie schooner in the 1870s, had a dirt floor and dirt roof in her first prairie home. But after spreading hay over the dirt, she laid down her rag carpet and "put the tool chest, the trunks, the goods box made into a cupboard and the beds all around the wall to hold down the carpet as there was nothing to tack it to. . . . So we were real cozy and comfortable."[9]

Cotton rag rugs or rag carpet runners were often used in halls or on stairs. They also were sewn together with other runners to form room-size carpets. Shenandoah Valley, Virginia. c. 1875. 144″ × 40″. (Courtesy of Stella Rubin. Photograph, Schecter Lee.)

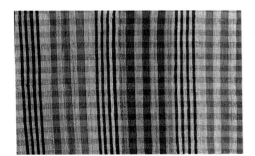
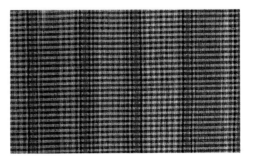

Iowa women hung rag carpets over their doorway openings to preserve warmth. In southern Indiana, they laid wall-to-wall rag carpet over heavy layers of straw in houses that were built up on stone pillars to keep out the bitter winter cold. In the spring, the carpet was taken up, the straw thrown out, and the floors left bare for summer.[10]

Preparing the rags was a time-consuming job, for which Utah women gathered together in "sewing bees":

> A group of friends would be invited to the home, and would be seated around a large basket of prepared rags (washed, and possibly dyed), where, for hours, they would sew and wind, while their tongues kept time to their flying needles. Luncheon would be served by the hostess, after which the sewing and visiting would continue until the original basket of soft fluffy rags had become one of hard balls ready to go to the weaver.[11]

HOOKED AND SEWN RUGS

An early 19th-century yarn-sewn and embroidered rug whose lush foliage and flowering garden, complete with birds, paint an idyllic picture. 42" × 24". (Courtesy of the Shelburne Museum. Photograph, Ken Burris.)

Judging from contemporary paintings and written sources, the woven carpets of striped wool or rags were stitched together to form large wall-to-wall rugs; but smaller area rugs were also coming into use, worked with a needle or hook rather than on the loom.

Where these smaller rugs were used has long been a mystery. Frequently referred to as table rugs, they probably were not actually used that way, as no evidence has so far turned up to support the idea. The earliest rugs, made in the first part of the nineteenth century, were some of the first floor—as opposed to bed—

rugs and are referred to in contemporary documents as hearth rugs: "The first reference to a floor rug quoted in the Oxford English Dictionary is dated 1810: 'a little rug for yr. hearthstone.' John Cogswell, a Boston cabinetmaker, had . . . '1 Hearth Rug' in a living room in 1818."[12] They were made especially to fit in front of the fireplace and protect the floor—or possibly an imported carpet—from stray sparks. Popular in exhibitions of ladies' handiwork at local agricultural fairs, these rugs were frequently praised by the judges for their beauty and economy. "At the Northampton [Mass.] Cattle Show in 1826, 'The hearth rugs were much admired for their beauty and appearance of durability.'"[13] Small rugs must, however, have been used in other areas as well—and quite early. The 1773 inventory of Governor Tryon's home, for example, lists "2 Side Bed Carpets" in one of the bedchambers.[14]

Area rugs were worked in an almost endless variety of needlework techniques, all in use earlier than the technique of hooking. Appliquéd or embroidered rugs, or rugs combining both kinds of needlework, are known to have been made very early. In Brimfield, Massachusetts, "The first carpets were introduced about 1802. They were made of square pieces of cloth sewed together, and ornamented with various patterns cut from differently colored cloth, and sewed on. . . ."[15]

The best known nineteenth-century embroidered carpet is the room-size (12 by 13½ feet) Caswell carpet made in Castleton, Vermont, by Zeruah Higley Guernsey Caswell between 1833 and 1835. Made entirely at home—she first grew and sheared her own sheep for the wool—the rug has seventy-six squares plus a removable hearth rug section, each embroidered in chain stitch with a different motif. Most of the colorful designs, all on a black ground, are of flowers or leaves, but the maker has also included shells, birds, butterflies, a young couple, and several squares with puppies or cats. Interestingly, the small animals perch on striped backgrounds, almost certainly meant to represent the popular striped rugs

A fine needlepoint rug, wool on linen, with a bamboo stitched border and a 2¾" wool fringe. Anna Baker of Bakersfield, Vermont, made this rug about 1810. 60" × 25". (Courtesy of the Shelburne Museum. Photograph, Ken Burris.)

Appliquéd pots of carnations and wildflowers decorate this woolen table cover, which is close to 6 feet long. New England. 1830–40. 30″ × 68″. (Collection of Grace and Elliott Snyder. Photograph courtesy of Thos. K. Woodard, American Antiques & Quilts.)

of the day and suggesting, as Homer Eaton Keyes believed, that those were the kind of rugs in Zeruah Caswell's own home. The embroidered blue tabby cat is said to have frightened the Guernseys' house cat once she had a good look at the rug: "The insulted pussy arched her back and spit spitefully at the worsted feline."[16]

Before the 1830s, no hooked rugs were made, although several other techniques are sometimes mistaken for hooking. A yarn-sewn piece, sewn with a needle and heavy wool yarn, may look like a hooked rug from the front, but a glance at the back, which shows only small yarn stitches with large spaces between them, quickly distinguishes it from a hooked rug. (Hooked rugs look almost exactly the same on both sides, as the hook leaves wide fabric loops on the back as well as the front, and the design is repeated there.)

Yarn-sewn rugs are sewn with the same technique as bed ruggs, a continuous running stitch. Much smaller and lighter, though, they are made on homespun linen foundations as opposed to the heavier, often wool, backings of bed ruggs, necessary for warmth. Other techniques, such as several types of shirring, are also used. Caterpillar or chenille shirring, bias, and pleated shirring are variations, all done with the fabric strips stitched down on the top of the rug to form the pile.

As with the yarn-sewn examples, the small stitches on the back are the clue to the technique used.

Best known of all the hand-worked rugs are the hooked variety. We have no firm evidence of when or where the first hooked rugs were made, although we do know that the technique developed during the 1840s in several places, notably the Maritime Provinces of Canada, French Quebec, New Hampshire, and along the Maine coast. Possibly the rugs evolved from the mats sailors made on their long sea voyages, at first using shipboard tools intended for making sturdy ropes.

Whatever its origins, hooked rugmaking reached its height in the 1850s when Asian jute used to manufacture inexpensive burlap, including burlap bags, was first imported into the United States. Burlap, with its wide, loose weave, made a perfect foundation for rug hooking, and burlap sacks, used for grain, were the perfect size for a rug when they were slit open and laid flat. Much better than the tightly woven linen or hemp used for yarn-sewn rugs, burlap made the actual job of hooking both easier and faster.[17]

Of all the types of stitchery, it was perhaps the hooked rug—not strictly a form of needlework since a hook is used—that gave women the most opportunity

Appliquéd table cover. This example of hearts and flowers made of wool, cotton, linen, and silk dates from the first quarter of the 19th century. 21″ × 28½″. (Collection of Grace and Elliott Snyder. Photograph courtesy of Thos. K. Woodard, American Antiques & Quilts.)

A shirred rug: the central urn with its profusion of flowers and fruits is a typical motif of the 1800–50 period. Shirring on linen, the technique used here, predated hooking. Made by Mrs. Stephenson of Edenton, Vermont, c. 1850. 30″ × 42″. (Courtesy of the Barbara Johnson Collection.)

The fisherman's knot and fish on this rug suggest the owner's occupation. The chimney smoke and hen add a touch of realism. 19th century. 41½″ × 28½″. (Courtesy of the Barbara Johnson Collection.)

The maker of this lively rug depicted the house and outbuildings of her farm, including the barnyard with its roosters. While the perspective of the scene is far from realistic, it is much more accurate than that on many homemade rugs. Berwick, Maine, dated 1886. 35″ × 50″. (Courtesy of Joy and Jack Piscopo.)

The pile on this floral basket hooked rug is of uniform height, making it atypical of its region, Waldoboro, Maine (known for hooked rugs with sculpted pile). The design is derivative of theorem paintings popular about 1810–40. Wool and cotton. c. 1860. 30″ × 42″. (Courtesy of Kelter-Malcé. Photograph, Schecter Lee.)

"Log Cabin—Straight Furrow" quilt designs were often adopted
by rug hookers, especially the varieties of Log Cabin. c. 1880.
49″ × 34″. (Courtesy of the Barbara Johnson Collection.)

A geometric hooked rug: abstract designs surrounded by multicolored stripes called "hit or miss" mark this as a 20th-century piece. Cotton and wool. 34″ × 50″. (Courtesy of the Barbara Johnson Collection.)

to create freely whatever struck their fancy. While quiltmaking allows for creativity in the choice of colors, fabrics, and pattern, the patchwork medium carries its own inherent restrictions, unlike the hooked rug, where almost anything is possible.

Some women chose geometric designs—blocks, clamshells, stripes in bold or muted colors; others found pleasure in a variety of floral designs, which they drew themselves, or had drawn by a more talented neighbor. Most ambitious were the rugmakers who chose to immortalize, in scenic rugs, their homes or farms or pets, creating colorful pictorial records of their lives.

Many women were perfectionists when it came to rugmaking, and insisted on getting their designs exactly right. The story is told of a Nova Scotia rugmaker who posed her cat on the burlap foundation of her rug and outlined him for her design. The cat, however, was not very cooperative: "He was lying on it [his tail], so it didn't show in the picture. But no cats grow without tails, so my old man held it out nice and straight, then I just stuck it on here."[18]

Hooked rugs were made in many shapes besides the predominant rectangular: squares, ovals, rounds, even hexagons and octagons were created. Especially popular were half circles for door mats, many of which carried messages of "Welcome" or "Call Again." One such is described in *New Chronicles of Rebecca*, published in 1907: "Rebecca could see the Cames' brown farmhouse from Mrs. Baxter's sitting-room window . . . inside the screen door of pink mosquito netting was a wonderful drawn-in [hooked] rug, shaped like a half pie, with 'Welcome' in saffron letters on a green ground."[19]

Room-size hooked rugs, much less common than the area ones, could take several years to make, but for those who could spare the time, they seemed well worth the effort. One nineteenth-century woman designed a floral pattern and then painted the design on the floor of an upstairs bedroom to make sure she liked it before using it in her rug.[20]

Making hooked rugs was already a popular activity by the 1860s, when the introduction of burlap pieces with pre-stenciled patterns made it possible for even greater numbers of women to take up the craft. One of the first people to mass-produce and sell pre-printed burlap rugs was Edward Sands Frost, a peddler from Biddeford, Maine, who decided he could draw rug patterns as well as his wife. Frost made stencils from scrap tin, stamped his patterns on burlap, and began selling them door-to-door. "The news of my invention of stamped rugs spread like magic . . . I at once became known as Frost, the rug man . . . I failed to find a man who dared to invest a dollar in them; in fact, people did not know what they were for, and I had to go from house to house . . . for I found the ladies knew what the patterns were for."[21] Before he sold his business in 1876, Frost had made 750 zinc stencils capable of printing 180 designs.

Of all the types of hand-worked rugs, braided ones are among the oldest, being found as early as the first quarter of the nineteenth century. Like rag rugs, braided ones used up whatever scraps and worn-out clothing were available, and were relatively easy to make. Three or more narrow strips, their edges carefully turned under, were braided and then stitched to or worked into another braid to form one long strip. The braid was then wound around itself to form a circle or oval or whatever shape the maker wanted. Some of the most interesting braided rugs are those of three, four, or more circles attached together, usually to form a large flower-like circle, although other shapes are sometimes found.

The second half of the nineteenth century gave rise to all sorts of area rugs, many of them pictured in *Godey's Lady's Book* or *Peterson's Magazine* with detailed instructions, down to the appropriate color choices. Penny or button rugs, made of three layered circles (the size of large, old-fashioned pennies), outlined with buttonhole stitches and secured to a plain foundation with a large cross-stitch, were much in vogue from the 1850s well into the twentieth century. They tended to be made in one of two color schemes—browns, tans, and earth tones, or black combined with the neon-like brights the Victorians loved. They were made in many shapes: rectangles, ovals, rounds, hexagons, and octagons. In the 1920s, when there was a surge of interest in American handicrafts, Ella Shannon Bowles described these rugs:

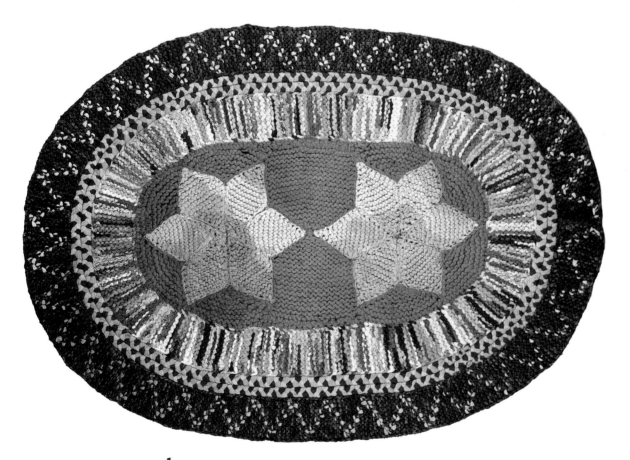

An early 20th-century Amish braided and knit rug from Lancaster County, Pennsylvania. The star motif and somber colors are hallmarks of Amish textiles. 29″ × 42″. (Courtesy of Kelter-Malcé. Photograph, Schecter Lee.)

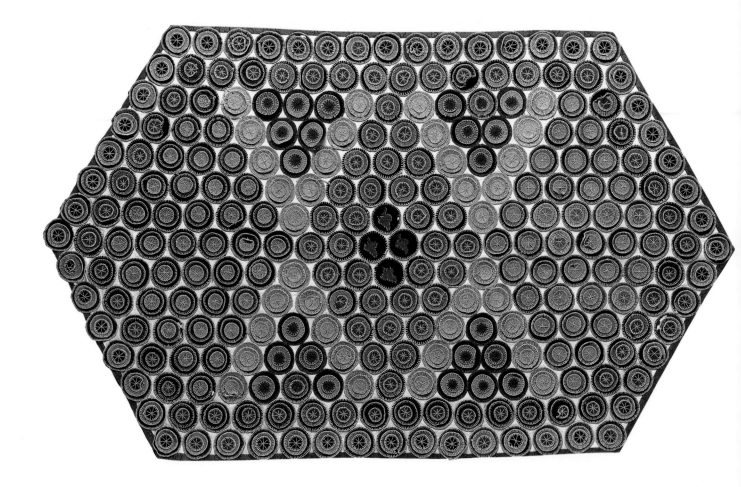

A woolen penny rug constructed of cloth "pennies" cut from men's suits and coarse blanketing. c. 1875–1900. 32″ × 53″. (Courtesy of Harold and Judith Weissman. Photograph, Schecter Lee.)

I feel certain that these were invented by some economical woman who wished to use up scraps of cloth too small for braiding and too heavy for drawing in [hooking]. My grandmother had two octagonal button rugs which ornamented the floor of the shuttered parlor. . . . Grandmother evidently had an eye for harmony; both of those rugs were carefully carried out in shades of brown, tan, and fawn.[22]

Crocheted and knitted rugs, or rugs combining both techniques, sometimes with embroidery, were also popular.

In 1854, *Godey's* gave instructions for using up small cloth scraps by knitting them into a rug:

Hearth-rugs are sometimes made by cutting cloth into strips ½ an inch wide and 2″ long, and knitting them together with string. This is done by inserting the piece of cloth exactly at the middle, in the loop of the knitting, and drawing it very tight; it is rather hard finger-work, and some make the rug by sewing the strips of cloth on to a piece of old carpet or any other strong material that may be at hand. This sort of rug will in winter form a very comfortable addition to a poor man's fireplace. Or the bits may be knitted into smaller pieces for door-mats.[23]

The hundreds of cloth pieces gave these rugs a shaggy surface, hence their name, shaggy or fluff mats.

Larger scraps could be used to make appliquéd crawling rugs for children. *Dainty Work for Pleasure and Profit*, published in 1893, explained how such a rug was to be put together. The foundation, it suggested, could be a piece of felt or flannel, or "an old dress skirt," with the appliqués of brightly colored scraps cut in the shape of toys, animals, and familiar playthings. "Picture books and cards" were possible sources for designs, to be "further embellished by adding a few embroidery stitches occasionally." Such rugs were the perfect thing for "little tots who can just crawl about, investigating everything on their hands and knees. They will spend any amount of time patiently trying to pick a small toy, drum or wheel-barrow off the rug—sometimes developing a little temper when they don't succeed."[24]

Like other nineteenth-century women, the Shaker sisters made and sold rugs of recycled materials. They made most of the popular types, but with some distinguishing characteristics that identify their rugs as Shaker. Their hooked rugs, for example, almost always have several rows of braiding bordering the central hooked section, and the backs may be finished with narrow Shaker-woven tape.

Another type, believed to be of Shaker origin, is the raveled knit rug, made by stitching down strips of partially unraveled knit material to a firm cloth foundation, usually mattress ticking. These striking rugs were made in stripes or geometric patterns in bright colors alternating with black, and seem unlikely pieces to have come from people who in their own dwellings were restricted in their use of color: "Carpets are admissable, but they ought to be used with discretion, and made plain. Mother Lucy says two colors are sufficient for one carpet. Make one strip of red and green, another of drab and gray, another of butternut and gray. The binding yarn may also be of two colours, and also the binding *if necessary*. . . ."[25] [italics ours]

Handmade rugs, mostly from cloth scraps, sometimes dyed and sometimes not, have been popular for the better part of two centuries, and continue to be so. The tradition of hooking, begun in the mid-nineteenth century, has had two revivals, in the 1920s and again with the Bicentennial. Rag carpets are still made on hand looms in western Maryland in the traditional ways, and some of the women who make them remember wall-to-wall striped rag carpeting in the homes of their childhood. As strongly as quilting, rugmaking continues today, with some women following regional traditions and others going to class to learn a skill their mothers had already lost.

Two Men in a Boat—an unusual Grenfell rug. It has been suggested that the rectangles represent the hunted whales or seals. The colors are typical of these Newfoundland rugs, but the abstract designs and double border are not. c. 1900–25. Grenfell Industries, Newfoundland, Labrador. 30″ × 25″. (Courtesy of the Barbara Johnson Collection.)

A family portrait! Rugs with similar verses and sentiments were popular in the 1920s and 1930s. 33″ × 50″. (Courtesy of the Barbara Johnson Collection.)

Both wool and cotton have been used as hooking material for this rug, dubbed "Trotting Pony," made about 1875. 29″ × 43″. (Courtesy of the Shelburne Museum. Photograph, Ken Burris.)

"Quilting Bee." Scenic rugs with people in them are among the rarest designs. This late 19th–early 20th century rug is especially interesting because the costumes are from an earlier period. Altogether a loving celebration of the home—complete with the inclusion of three rugs within the rug. 38″ × 17″. (Courtesy of the Barbara Johnson Collection.)

A miniature hooked rug. So small a rug was probably used as a table mat, or to cover a chest. The birds and tulips are a typical Pennsylvania German motif. Cotton-on-burlap foundation. Pennsylvania. c. 1875. 20″ × 10½″. (Courtesy of Jerry Grossman. Photograph, Schecter Lee.)

A panorama of the maker's favorite animals have been appliquéd onto this 19th century Pennsylvania rug. 30″ × 42″. (Courtesy of M. Finkel & Daughter.)

"The Cow Jumped Over the Moon": nursery rhymes were popular subjects for hooked rugs in the first half of the 20th century. 44″ × 30″. (Courtesy of Lloyd Williams.)

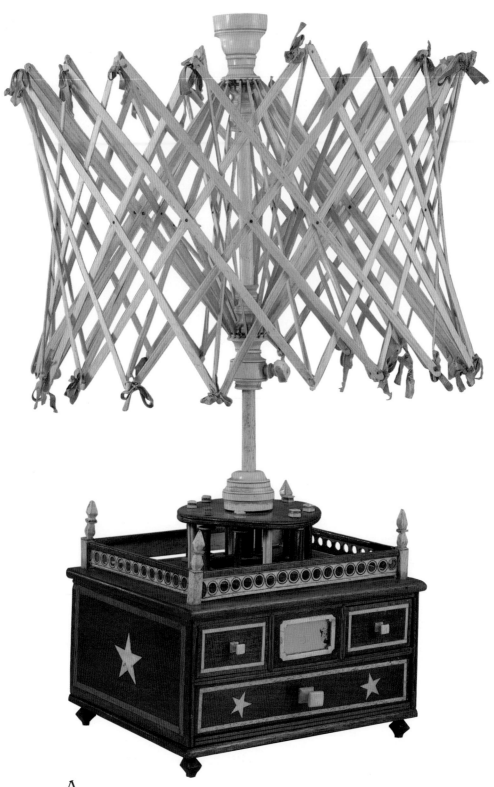

A whalebone and whale ivory swift mounted on an inlaid and mirrored sewing box. Swifts are used to rewind a skein of yarn onto a bobbin or in a ball. An umbrella swift, like this scrimshaw one, folds up when not in use and can be adjusted to hold any size skein. Scrimshaw swifts were usually made aboard whaling ships during long sea voyages. New England. 19th century. (Courtesy of Sotheby Parke Bernet.)

TEN

IMPLEMENTS OF LOVING LABOR: NEEDLEWORK TOOLS AND ACCESSORIES[1]

O*f all the* tools a needlewoman used, none was more essential or precious to her than her needle. So valuable was a needle throughout the medieval period that even a wealthy woman had only one; it was so necessary to daily life that the loss of it could turn an entire household upside down, as happens in the sixteenth-century English comedy *Gammer Gurton's Needle.*

"It is as scandalous for a woman not to know how to use her needle as for a man not to know how to use his sword," declared Lady Mary Wortley Montagu in eighteenth-century England, and few of her contemporaries would have challenged that view.

The use of the needle was taught to very little girls, as young as four or five, usually at a dame school, and was deemed a crucial part of their education. In 1935, one very old lady recalled how in her childhood all the little girls were required to carry their needle to and from school each day, and were punished if they forgot it. When one of her friends forgot hers, she managed to find a straight pin to "sew" with, "with which she had every appearance of sewing industriously," spending the hour looking for all the world as if she were doing her stitching. By luck, she was never found out.[2]

Many adult women found a comfort in hand stitching that nothing else could provide. Despite the invention in the mid-nineteenth century of the sewing machine, they still enjoyed sewing by hand. Writing in 1880, one woman described its virtues:

It [the needle] is more helpful . . . than the cigar, than the glass of sherry, or tumbler of beer. The plain seam is a sedative. . . . [Her] thoughts can go ambling off into fields of imagination as she sits over a bit of plain work! She can plan a charming romance or lay down the project of some helpful reform, as she draws her needle mechanically in and out of her seam.[3]

The art of making needles was a specialized, skilled craft. Even with the introduction of needlemaking machines in the second quarter of the nineteenth century, it remained a long, tedious process with much of the work done by hand. Miss Lambert, in her mid-nineteenth-century needlework handbook, described the process in some detail, so impressed was she that such a small object required so many steps in its manufacture:

Every sewing needle . . . passes through the hand of one hundred and twenty different operatives, before it is ready for sale. . . . The operation of piercing and trimming the eyes is performed by clever children with astonishing rapidity, who become so dexterous as *to pierce with a punch a human hair, and thread it with another* [her italics] for the amusement of visitors.[4]

As early as the eighteenth century, needles were manufactured in a large variety of types and sizes: sharps, the common sewing needle; long-eyed sharps, of which the Whitechapel variety, named for the area in London where the needle trade was centered, was preferred for embroidery; blunts, tapestry needles with an oval eye and blunt end; and betweens, shorter than sharps but not as short as blunts. In the tropics, where steel—the material of the majority of needles—might rust, needles were made of gold or silver.[5]

A needle of good quality made the stitching process smooth and pleasurable, while one of poor quality made it laborious. English needles were known to be superior, but women differed as to which company's product was best. Mrs. Pullan, in her manual of 1859, declared that she had "never been able . . . to use any manufacture but those of Messrs. Boulton & Sons, of Redditch, England."[6] Miss Lambert, in her book, explained how to judge quality:

It is easy to distinguish good English needles from spurious imitations; because the former have their axis coincident with their points, which is readily observed by turning them between the finger and thumb.

The truer the eye—whether diamond-shaped or round—the less it cuts the thread, and the easier it passes through the work.[7]

Even in temperate climates, needles were subject to rust if left out in the air. For that reason, and because they were so easily misplaced, small, airtight cases were a necessity. Containers for individual needles were made in two basic types, with the many differences in shape or material making for great variety. Long, thin cases were oval, round, or oblong and were made of silver, gold, leather, mother-of-pearl, beadwork, straw, wood, ivory, and bone. Needlecases were also made in

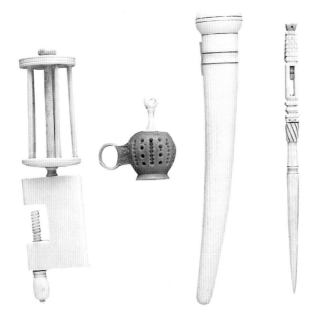

various shapes, including human figures, fish, and miniature umbrellas. These last frequently had a tiny Stanhope lens, named after its inventor, embedded in the handle, through which a photograph could be seen when the lens was held up close to the eye. Often sold as souvenirs, they had pictures of resorts, cities, and other well-known sights. From the 1860s until World War I, needlecases as well as tape measure holders, and other needlework tools came with these miniature viewers.[8]

Needlebooks were the other popular type of needle container. They resembled small books, with flannel leaves to protect the needles and keep them clean. Like the cases, they came in a variety of materials, their decoration elaborate or simple, in keeping with the period taste. Many were made at home, following the instructions that frequently appeared in nineteenth-century ladies' magazines, and they always included the inner flannel or felt leaves, often scalloped and outlined in buttonhole stitch, and a ribbon tie. Needlebooks, like cases, were treasured for their contents, but judging from a whimsical piece in *The Ladies' Repository* of 1872, "Reminiscences of an Old Needle Book," for themselves as well. In this memoir, the narrator, a Needle Book, discusses her happy life, and the great care her mistress has taken of her: "For many years I was favored with a place by her side or in her reticule wherever she went, whether for an afternoon visit or a month, and I never failed to attract attention and excite admiration. . . . My needles were always ready for every good work . . . and, too, many of my needles, like Dorcas, have gladdened the hearts of the poor."[9]

When mass-produced needles began appearing in paper packages, special cases in diverse shapes, including one that looked like a miniature lidded knife box, were introduced to hold the packets. These, too, were made of elegant materials, including ivory, silver, tortoise shell, and leather. One woman described a gift her mother received in 1809 as "the first of those little morocco [leather] cases full of needles she had ever seen, where the papers were all arranged in sizes, on a slope, which made it easy to select from them."[10]

As with her needles, all of a woman's needlework tools were of great value to her, and thus were kept in a special place, most often a workbox or fitted case, as beautifully made as she could afford. Workboxes came in various sizes, depending on how many pieces they were meant to hold. Most held needles, scissors, thimble, crochet and tambour handle and hooks, small cakes of beeswax to smooth thread, and an emery filled with sand for keeping needles clean and rust-free. More elaborate cases included tatting shuttles, silk winders of mother-of-pearl, ivory, or bone, a stiletto, a bodkin (the needle-like tool used for lacing ribbon or cord), and a powder pot or scent bottle. These last two were used to dry perspiration on the hands in order to keep one's needlework clean.

Smaller sewing cases of a shape and size to carry easily in the hand were often very elegant, and were sometimes referred to by the French name, *étui*. Sarah Pitt, of Williamsburg, Virginia, advertised such cases for sale in the 1760s: "Morocco etwees [*sic*] with instruments complete, plated or silver locks."[11]

These small, fitted cases, which were often imported from France or England, were made of inlaid wood, leather with or without silver mountings, or ivory, with

19th-Century flat sewing case and workbox. LEFT: Lined with purple silk in the lid and purple velvet to hold the sewing tools, this elegant case is probably French. Made of inlaid wood, it holds a silver needlecase, scissors, stiletto, thimble, and bodkin. c. 1800–50. 4¾″ × 2⅝″. RIGHT: A decorated steel box topped with a sewing bird is very unusual; sewing birds with clamps to attach them to a table or other work surface are more common. The inside of the lid contains a pincushion. Steel with silver and gilt decoration. c. 1850–1900. Height, 14½″. (Courtesy of Lillian and Jerry Grossman. Photograph, Schecter Lee.)

silk and velvet linings and silver or silver gilt tools. With the decline of fine needlework in the second half of the nineteenth century, cases appeared in shapes other than flat or oval, many of them less practical than the earlier ones had been, and intended more for display than use.

Aside from the needle, there was no more important tool, especially for plain sewing, than the ordinary straight or common pin. Pins, to which we pay little attention, were made by hand and highly valued in the seventeenth century, as a Salem, Massachusetts, inventory of 1684–85 shows. In the Corner Chamber was listed "1 Bedsted, 10 Shillings," while another entry for the same estate reads: "1 dozn. pins. 9 shillings. 1 dozn. ditto, 10 shillings," indicating that twelve pins, at least in this case, were worth as much as a bedstead.[12] Before the 1820s when an Englishman invented a machine for making pins in one piece, pins came in two

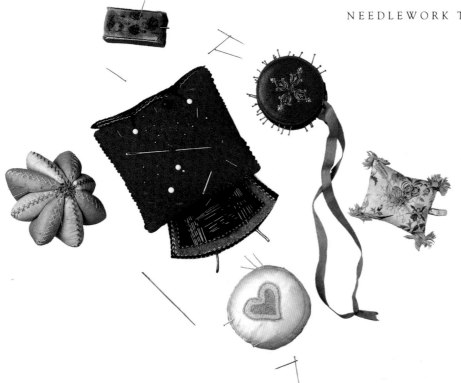

A group of late 18th- and 19th-century embroidered and decorated pincushions and needlecases were truly prized possessions. 2″ to 6″. (Courtesy of the Shelburne Museum. Photograph, Ken Burris.)

pieces, and the head had to be clamped onto the shaft. Until the 1830s, when the manufacture of one-piece pins was begun in Connecticut, most pins sold in America had been imported. The earliest ones were sold loose, and wrapped in paper, but by the 1740s, they were packed in boxes, and by the 1780s, on sheets of paper.

Pins came in a large variety of types and sizes, with names that have long gone out of the language: corkins, middlings, shorts, whites, lillikins, and the smallest size, called minikins or minifers. There were also special black pins for mourning costumes, and lace pins.[13]

Both adults' and infants' clothing was frequently fastened with straight pins, a practice that must have made many a baby unhappy. One mother at least, determined to keep her infant free from pin pricks, found a unique solution: "We were very eager to go [and see the woman's baby] and wanted to hold it and carry it around the room. She was willing but asked us if we had any pins on us anywhere. She said she had the nurse sew the baby's clothes on every morning so that if she cried she would know whether it was pains or pins."[14]

Small objects of great importance, pins seemed almost to have a kind of supernatural power. There were proverbs about them:

A group of early 20th-century needlework tools, including glass-headed pins. The two tape measures were advertising give-aways for garages. Height of pins and tape measures, 1″–2″; scissors 5″–8″ long. (Courtesy of Jean Hoffman–Jana Starr Antiques. Photograph, Schecter Lee.)

These tiny infant pincushions or pillows would have been given to new mothers. The leaf designs on the one at the right are three-dimensional, with some of the pins stuck deeper into the cushion than others to achieve this effect. 6″ × 8½″, 7″ sq., and 6½″ × 7½″. (Courtesy of Six-Sept Corporation. Photograph, Schecter Lee.)

If you see a pin, and let it lie,
You'll need a pin before you die.

and superstitions too: ". . . an elderly Scotch lady who even in these enlightened days always walks around back of any stray pin she may chance to spy upon the ground carefully avoiding stepping past its point, so as to avert the danger pointing her way."[15]

The problem of where to keep pins, which were always getting lost, was solved in a number of ways. In the fourteenth century, there were silver pincases called "epinguiers," in the sixteenth, pyn-pillows, and in the eighteenth, pin-poppets, little metal or wooden cases especially for pins.[16] Besides cases, boxes, and pinballs, there were pincushions in a multitude of shapes, sizes, and materials. Paper, fabric, canvaswork, knitting, embroidery—all were used to make pincushions; hearts, stars, balls, and square pillow shapes were among the most popular.

A special type of pincushion, much larger than the usual 2- or 3-inch size, is the layette pincushion, popular in the eighteenth and nineteenth centuries as a gift to new mothers. These cushions were stuck with pins arranged to form a design or verse, and as pins were so expensive, the great number that went into the arrangement was a welcome gift.

Baby pincushions typically bore both a design and a message, like this one described by Anna Winslow in her diary:

These metal sewing birds held a piece of cloth in their beaks, leaving the seamstress with both hands free, allowing her to hold the cloth taut with one hand and stitch with the other. They attached to the work table with a clamp and thumbscrew, both of which were often decorated in embossed designs. Steel, brass, and cast iron. 1850–60. Height, 4″–5″. (Courtesy of Lillian and Jerry Grossman. Photograph, Schecter Lee.)

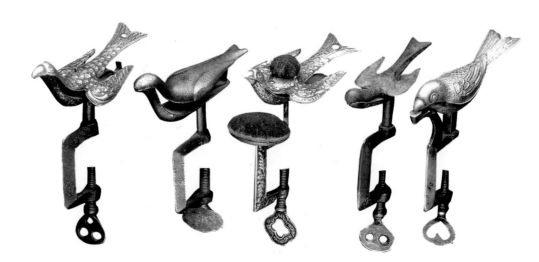

My aunt stuck a white sattan pincushin for Mrs. Waters. On one side, is a planthorn with flowers, on the reverse, just under the border are, on one side stuck these words, JOSIAH WATERS, then follows on the end, Decr 1771, and on the next side and end are the words, Welcome Little Stranger."[17]

"Welcome Little Stranger" was probably the most commonly used motto on such pillows, although several lines of verse and elaborate designs were also popular. *Godey's*, in 1860, offered directions for an "Infant's Pincushion" and suggested the following lines:

> May thy fragrance ever be
> Like the rosebud in the tree
> With a luster more sublime
> And thy every virtue shine[18]

Along with their pins, needles, sewing cases, and workboxes, women throughout history have treasured a variety of needlework tools. Many of those used in America were imported from France, England, or Germany, as some still are. Unless marked, or documented in some way, it is usually difficult even for experienced eyes to distinguish domestic from imported tools and cases. Whatever their origins, the tools women have used to do their needlework have remained almost as precious to them and frequently as fine as the work they have created.

With its cast-iron base and steel ribs, this swift is typical of the late 19th century. An angel above the elaborately decorated base balances the upper parts on its head. Height, 17″. (Courtesy of Lillian and Jerry Grossman. Photograph, Schecter Lee.)

The care lavished on these 18th-century knitted infant bonnets is extraordinary. Note the beaded flowers and leaves and the delicate lace edging around the two bonnets. 6½″ × 7″. (Courtesy of the Shelburne Museum. Photograph, Ken Burris.)

ELEVEN

KNITTING, CROCHET, AND LACE

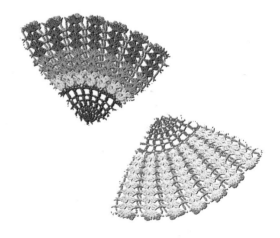

KNITTING

In *colonial America,* knitting was the fireside occupation of women and children. Since large families required an endless supply of stockings, caps, scarves, and mittens, knitted goods represented an important form of handiwork. Children were taught to "narrow" and "widen" by the age of six. Many boys were expected to knit stockings and suspenders as part of their round of daily chores, and girls were given "stints" to finish before they were allowed to play. For their first attempts girls often picked garters, those long narrow strips that wound around the legs to keep stockings in place, and had the advantage of being concealed, thus hiding inevitable mistakes. Girls took their knitting to school, gossiping with friends during recess over the clack of their needles. The pressure to finish work is often mentioned in pioneer diaries: "I had to knit my own stockings and the stockings for all the children younger than myself. Each day mother would give me a stint of thirty rounds and then I could play. Some days it would take me all day to knit, and on other days I would hurry and do it in a few hours. . . ."[1]

Knitted stockings were important enough to be included in eighteenth-century inventories. A Pennsylvania will included instructions for two sons to provide their mother with "a pair of woolen stockings and two pair of shoes yearly." Another Pennsylvania will stipulated "Yearly sheep shall be kept for her to make thereout for her necessary stockings."[2] Clearly, stockings were a measure of affluence, with most men owning two or three pairs, and the wealthy even more.

As early as the eighteenth century, some families produced enough knitted goods to barter or sell surplus items. Occasionally the men of the family would

Three pairs of children's knitted socks, found in New England, probably made in the third quarter of the 19th century. Height, 18″ to 20″. (Courtesy of Stella Rubin. Photograph, Schecter Lee.)

help with the "feetings" to earn a little tobacco money, and there were even a few like John Lougee, an emigrant from the isle of Jersey who established himself in Exeter, New Hampshire, as a knitter whose articles merited local acclaim.[3] Wealthy families might hire outside knitters to supplement their own output of linen and woolen stockings. An advertisement in the September 26, 1748, issue of *The New-York Gazette* reveals the importance of a local knitter and her wares:

> All sorts of Stockings new grafted and run at the Heels, and footed; also Gloves, mittens and Children's Stockings made out of stockings; Likewise plain work done by Elizabeth Boyd, at the Corner House opposite to Mr. Vallete's.

After stockings, mittens headed the list of items most desired by the Yankee peddlers, who took them in exchange for calicos, linens, and household goods. It is reported that as a young man, Benedict Arnold traveled along the Hudson River into Canada trading his father-in-law's knitted goods which had been made by farm women in Connecticut.[4]

While the invention of knitting machines in the early nineteenth century created large industries, it did not immediately affect home production. Until the 1880s, many factories still relied upon local women to finish the toes and heels of stockings by hand. Women in rural areas continued to acquire otherwise unobtainable goods by knitting them themselves. Moving west, they relieved the boredom and anxiety that accompanied the wagon trains by knitting, as the following encounter along the Oregon Trail reveals:

> She said she liked to sew and I said I'd rather crochet. She wished we could be together long enough so she could teach me to knit—I should be work-

ing on my man's winter socks right now; she was. Right then she took a half-knitted sock out of her apron pocket and, stopping only for a breath between needles, she worked as fast as she talked.[5]

In the West the accomplished knitter was as much in demand as the laundress and cook. At times knitters substituted buffalo wool for sheep wool, mixing it with raccoon fur to produce warm and serviceable stockings.[6]

Pioneer girls often made their pin money by knitting socks, which were very much in demand in mining and lumber camps. It took one pound of yarn to knit a pair of socks. When fingers flew, one pair could be made in a day. Often the heel and toe of the sock was knit double to give better wear. Socks were sold in dozen lots at fifty cents a pair. Ladies hose for special occasions, were made of finer yarn, often being knit to make a ribbed design, or with stripes running around the hose.[7]

Women in Shaker communities spent a major portion of their lives sewing and knitting clothing and accessories both for their own use and for sale to the outside world. Polly Ann Reed noted in her diary of 1872, "went to the shop and knit all day—finished off [my] sixth neckerchief."[8] The Shakers responded to the fashions of the times and kept careful records of popular items. In the 1850s, knitted stockings and needlebooks were among their most successful wares. In 1891, knitted silk and raccoon fur gloves were in such demand that one sister reportedly knitted forty-seven pairs in a year.[9] Using very thin needles, Shaker women knitted stockings as tubes with the feet done by hand and the heels reinforced by gussets. As with all Shaker products, the knitted stockings were famous for their quality.[10]

As the nineteenth century progressed, knitting became more of an art than a necessity. Periodicals and handbooks provided patterns and encouragement. The first pattern book was published in 1843 by J. S. Redfield in New York as part of a

Harrison Sanborn would have had little excuse for losing his mittens, as his name was worked into the cuffs. New England. c. 1840s. 10″ × 4½″. (Courtesy of Stella Rubin. Photograph, Schecter Lee.)

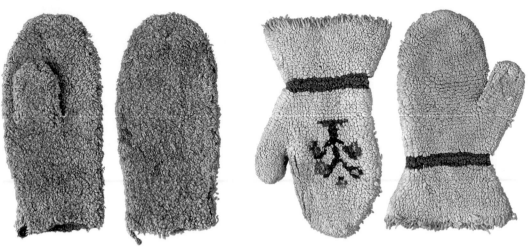

These handsome mittens were definitely in fashion for cold New England winters, and were worn by both men and women. Late 19th century. 12″ × 6″. (Courtesy of Sandra Vlodek. Photograph, Schecter Lee.)

series, titled "No. 4. Knitting, Netting, and Crochet," and was reviewed by the *Court Gazette:* "A more useful work can hardly be desired." In 1846 Sarah Hale, in a self-congratulatory editorial in *Godey's Lady's Book,* announced: "We are sure of the thanks of all ladies, young as well as old, for calling their attention to this useful and elegant branch of female art. No other periodical attends to these things."

While Sarah Hale exaggerated the claim of exclusivity (almost identical sets of instructions appeared in *Peterson's Magazine*), she certainly promoted knitting over the next twenty years by including patterns for infants' and children's clothing, accessories for the home, and fashionable articles for men and women. Even instructions for knitted flowers and fruit were featured in a series running from 1851 through 1853. Instructions for no fewer than six types of knitted shawls appeared in *The Ladies' Complete Guide to Needle-work and Embroidery* by Miss Lambert in 1859. *Godey's* also put its stamp of approval on the shawl, declaring in an editorial in May 1858, "Scarcely any article of apparel or decoration is so universally worn as the shawl." All sorts of knitted items for the home appeared in various periodicals, including knitted bedspreads and knitted edgings for table-

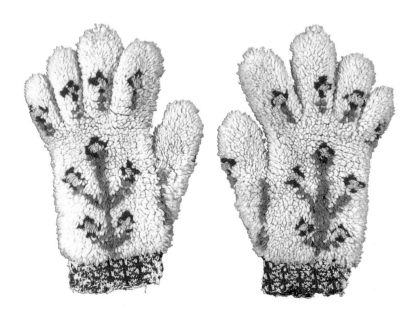

The knitter may have yearned for the warmer days of spring when she decorated these shag gloves with a profusion of flowers. New England. Late 19th century. 12″ × 6″. (Courtesy of Jeannine Dobbs. Photograph, Schecter Lee)

cloths and bed linens. Among the prettiest pillowcases were those whose knitted strips were set off by bands of colored cloth sewn beneath them. Women treasured the "work-pages" of the magazines, relying on them for gift ideas. In the 1870s in Utah, Clarissa Young Spencer recalled, "Our newest supplies in winter clothing were usually given us as Christmas gifts. Among them were pretty knitted gaiters and stockings, mittens and waistbands, also neck pieces and nubians [a fancy scarf that measured 3½ yards long by ½ yard wide]."[11]

The inclusion of knitted initials in scarves, mittens, and stockings not only followed the time-honored custom of marking textiles but also became a fashionable means of displaying the knitter's skill. Magazines such as *The Delineator* in

A group of 19th-century childrens' cotton and wool mittens, socks, and "wristers" that were truly "labors of love." (Courtesy of the Shelburne Museum. Photograph, Ken Burris.)

1894 published patterns of initials, spreading the series over a number of months. In New Hampshire one old-time knitter, Peggy Davis, was famous for being able to knit the letters of the alphabet into her mittens. A neighbor showed a pair of mittens that she had made for him to a gentleman who bet him that an old blind woman in another town could do the very same thing. After practicing in the dark for several nights, Peggy Davis presented her neighbor with a pair of perfect mittens in which she had arranged the letters of the alphabet to read:

> Money will make you many friends,
> But do not praise them high;
> For should misfortune make you poor,
> Such friends will pass you by.[12]

Mrs. Mary Jane Richer of Gaston, Vermont, knitted this lamb's
wool afghan in 1883. She included five panels of intricate cross-
stitch embroidery along with her initials and the date. 72″ × 69″
(Courtesy of the Shelburne Museum. Photograph, Ken Burris.)

Because of their added warmth and style, shag mittens were especially popular in New England. Ruth Henshaw noted in a diary entry in 1803 that she had made her father "a pair of shag mittens, that is a pair all over fringed, which is the new mode of knitting mittens."[13]

Home-knit stockings also followed the fashions of the times. During most of the nineteenth century, women favored black or white stockings or, less frequently, striped or blue-and-white twisted yarn combinations. Good black knee-length stockings held in place by elastic or knit garters edged in black lace were considered stylish. Mothers incorporated fancy stitches in the white cotton "Sunday best" stockings they made for their children, and knitted mittens with hooked-in patterns of colored yarns, checkerboard and herringbone designs. In some communities women spent many pleasurable hours together knitting stockings, a pastime that resembled the quilting bee. In the early nineteenth century in Narragansett, Rhode Island, "It was customary for the young ladies of the neighborhood to give social tea parties of an afternoon, at which we assembled at an early hour, dressed in our best, with our go-abroad knitting work, usually fine cotton, clocked hose. Some of these clocks comprised elaborate patterns."[14] The fascination for fancy "clocks" did not escape the notice of stocking manufacturers. In Annapolis, Maryland, a news item appeared in the August 30, 1764, edition of the *New-York Gazette:*

> There has lately been made and sold at Mr. Beall's Stocking Manufactory in this City, a large Quantity of Thread Stockings with this Device instead of the Clock, ➡ ➡ ➡

Wool afghan knitted during World War I and donated to the Red Cross at Debarkation Hospital #3 in New York City. Dated 1918. (Courtesy of Ken and Robin Pike.)

During the Civil War, Southern women resumed knitting as a means of providing needed clothes for their families. Since the blockade prevented them from even purchasing thread, they were forced to "manufacture" their own. In Alabama, resourceful homemakers outdid themselves in creating knitted garments that they decorated with crochet.

> After dark, when one could not see to sew, spin, or weave, was usually the time devoted to knitting and crocheting, which sometimes lasted until midnight. Capes, sacks, vandykes, gloves, socks and stockings, shawls, underclothes, and men's suspenders were knitted. The makers ornamented them in various ways, and the ornamentation served a useful purpose, as the [homemade] thread was usually coarse and uneven and the ornamentation concealed the irregularities that would have shown up in plain work.[15]

Women carried their knitting on social visits and it is reported that a trip home by a soldier on furlough or sick leave prompted a visit by every woman in the community. As they listened to news from the army, they would knit clothes for their "boys."[16] After the war, when supplies gradually became available, knitting once again became a pastime rather than a necessity.

Although knitting was not one of the major textile arts of the American Indians, some tribes wore knitted leggings and mittens. Among the Navajo, men knitted leggings out of blue, white, and black yarns, employing tight stitching to ensure long wear. They called a design knitted into the stockings "KHI ITOIN," or "the road that runs up the side of the leggings."[17] Before trading posts supplied steel knitting needles, the Navajo used highly polished wooden needles made from twigs. Among the Pueblo Indians, knitting was established in the seventeenth century, when the Spanish settlers introduced the craft. The Pueblo were required to supply the colonists with knitted stockings, which they continued to make well into the twentieth century.

CROCHET

Crochet was generally regarded as a decorative form of knitting, a European pastime that gained popularity in the mid-nineteenth century. One of the first American booklets featuring crochet patterns was published in 1845. The preface announced: "It is customary among the German ladies to have at hand some light piece of work, with which they can at any time be employed.—Our American ladies will doubtless find the custom worthy of imitation . . . and many new stitches are now offered to the ladies of America with which we flatter ourselves, they have never been acquainted."[18]

A book published in 1840, *My Crochet Sampler*, defined crochet as "a species of knitting originally practiced by the peasants in Scotland, with a shepherd's

A woman in Landis Valley, Pennsylvania, crocheted a table cover depicting these scenes of everyday life in the early 20th century. Note the Model-T type cars. 66″ × 70″. (Courtesy of Joy Piscopo.)

hook,—aided by taste and fashion, [that] has within the last seven years, obtained the preference over all other ornamental works of a similar nature."[19]

A great number of booklets containing patterns and instructions for knitting and crochet appeared in the Victorian era. A few manuals felt it fitting to offer guidance in correct behavior as well as crochet patterns. In 1887, *The Starlight Manual of Knitting and Crocheting* included a motto or admonition on each page, such as: "Don't say 'Somewheres,' 'Anywheres,' etc. for 'Somewhere,' 'anywhere,' etc., etc. Nothing is more vulgar."[20]

Many of the ladies' magazines devoted one or two pages each month to crochet. In addition to the more commonplace caps and jackets, designs for such esoteric articles as "Crochet Handle for Riding Whip" (*Godey's*, October 1865), "Crochet Jacket for a Greyhound" (*Godey's*, May 1873), and "Window-Blind Tassel in Crochet" (*Peterson's*, September 1860) reflected the growing demand for fancywork. Regional fads abounded: in the South around 1860, women delighted in making rattle necklaces for baby gifts out of tiny snuff boxes which they covered with multicolored crocheted yarn, and in New York crocheted purses made the front page of *Harper's Bazaar* in 1868 and 1870. Even on the frontier, where time for ornamental work was limited, "edgings were crocheted from spool thread for trimming underwear . . . and handkerchiefs. Wider crocheting was used for pillow cases, bottoms of skirts, and white aprons."[21]

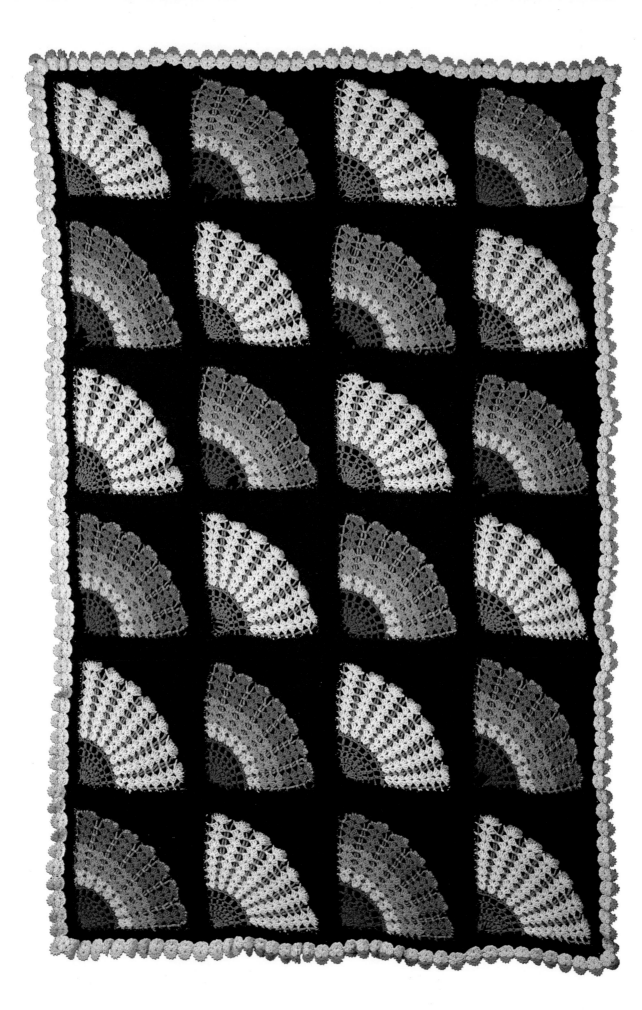

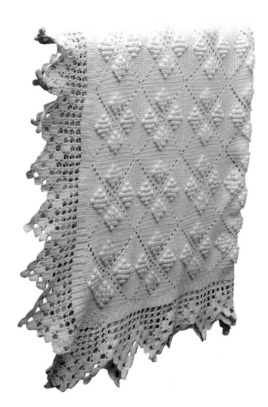

Two late 19th-century knitted and crocheted spreads hang from a hand-hewn drying rack. The Victorian vogue for elegant white bed coverings would have made these intricate counterpanes preferable to "old-fashioned" quilts and woven coverlets. Left, 82″ × 90″; right, 82″ sq. (Courtesy of Laura Fisher. Photograph, Schecter Lee.)

The passion for fancywork, while meeting with general approval, caused its detractors to comment in print about reported excesses. *The Household,* a newspaper published in Vermont and "dedicated to the interests of the American Housewife," editorialized in its May 1875 edition: "But when you find a housewife crocheting a tidy, sitting in the midst of dirt, with neglected children, pleading that she is so fond of fancy work, but she never did like housework, don't you ache to take her by the shoulders and shake some sense of responsibility as a wife and mother into her soul?"

LACE

The "sombre attire" of the Mayflower pilgrims did not have a lasting influence upon American costume. From Massachusetts to Virginia, the well-dressed colonist wore clothing adorned with lace and "passements" of gold and silver. Inventories and wills frequently mention the elaborate lace trimmings that graced neckcloths, caps, whisks, ruffs, gorgets, and handkerchiefs. How well a family fared was reflected in the amount of lace that decorated their clothing. In Virginia, gentlemen considered themselves undressed without gold lace ruffles, while in New Amsterdam, Dutch colonists spared little expense in acquiring lace trimmings. Among Philadelphians, "laced ruffles, descending over the hand, was a mark of indispensable gentility. They then wore short sleeves to their coats purposely to display their

OPPOSITE:
"Fans," an enduring design in quilts and fabrics from the Victorian era through the Art Deco movement, received an added impetus from the popularity of Oriental motifs. Here, a crocheted afghan in brilliant colors made about the turn of the century shows why this design attracted so much attention. 40″ × 61″. (Courtesy of Robert Gottlieb. Photograph, Schecter Lee.)

fine linen . . . and laced ruffles."[22] Women's aprons, dresses, handkerchiefs, and caps were either adorned by or made completely of lace.

Although an edict of the General Court of Massachusetts in 1634 banned the owning of lace, persons of wealth and position were allowed to indulge in "woolen, silk, and linen apparel" trimmed with "gold, silver, and thread lace." While most lace was imported, the wording of the edict of 1634 (lace is forbidden to be "*made*" as well as "owned" or "worn") implies that American lacemaking was well established in the seventeenth century.[23] It is interesting to note that censure for lace adornment lasted only as long as it took for the less exalted classes to be able to afford lace for themselves. Indeed, the eighteenth century is noted for the arrival of a number of skilled lacemakers in America, who advertised all kinds of lacework supplies and instruction.

In Pennsylvania, Reynier Jensen, a lace manufacturer and printer from the Netherlands, gave up lacemaking upon his arrival in 1697, but ran the colony's Quaker press. He is cited as having influenced generations of Pennsylvania design.[24] Almost a century later another lace manufacturer from the Netherlands arrived in New York, announcing in the *New-York Daily Advertiser* (Sept. 5, 1795): "David de la Pierre, Fringe and Lace Manufacturer, from Amsterdam has removed to No. 64 Stone Street where he continues to make all sorts of coach laces . . . and trimmings of all sorts."

An advertisement placed by Elizabeth Wilson in the *Pennsylvania Ledger and Weekly Adviser* (May 20, 1775) announced instruction in a wide variety of lacework techniques: "Dresden Work, Pointing, Bobbing and Netting Lace."

However, it was not New York or Pennsylvania but Ipswich, Massachusetts, a community largely composed of emigrants from the English Midlands with a heritage of lacemaking, that became the only meaningful center of American handmade lace. The women of Ipswich made a type of lace called bobbin lace. They

OPPOSITE:

A French woman, possibly a Creole, worked this exquisitely delicate Washington–Lafayette handkerchief to celebrate Lafayette's triumphal visit to America in 1824. 18 " sq. (Courtesy of the Litchfield Historical Society.)

Lace pillow and bobbins with black trimming lace. Miss Nina Hall Brisbane of Charleston, South Carolina, learned to make pillow bobbin lace from the nuns at St. Augustine's Convent there about 1870, when she was in her thirties. Note the perforated lace pattern on the roll of heavy paper— somewhat like today's construction paper. (Courtesy of the Litchfield Historical Society.)

held round pillows on their laps, stretching over them thin pieces of parchment in which the design had been pricked with pins. Thread attached to bobbins was then fastened to the pins in the design with the ensuing meshes forming the lace. By 1786, Ipswich workers were producing 42,000 yards of silk lace a year, using simple patterns suitable for trimmings.[25] From their efforts developed one of America's first cottage industries. Local annals report one "Aunt Mollie" Caldwell picking up lace once a week from Ipswich housewives, taking it to Boston by stagecoach, and bringing back in return such requested items as tea, coffee, sugar, and French calico.[26]

Because England did not allow the export of lacemaking machinery, disgruntled emigrants were forced to bring over machines clandestinely, in parts, hoping that they could reassemble them in America. Smugglers, risking fines and long prison terms, sometimes hid machinery in Yorkshire butter tubs.[27] The first factory opening (Medway, Massachusetts, 1818) was quickly followed by a second in Ipswich in 1824. The introduction of machine-made net signaled the end of bobbin lace in Ipswich, for women found it quicker and more pleasurable to "work" the net with darning and tambour stitches. This type of lace, known as Limerick lace, was made both in America and Ireland, attaining its peak of popularity from 1810 to 1840.[28] In New England, fashion dictated the wearing of "worked-lace veils" to church. Advertisements of the early nineteenth century mention a variety of lace and reveal its importance to women. In New York, the *Commercial Advertiser* ran a continuing notice through 1824:

> Lace Embroidered to any required pattern, White or Black Bobbinet, Patent Silk and Blond Veils, Dresses, Caps, Pelerines, Flounces, Edgings, Insertings, &c.
> Also—All kinds of LACE altered, joined, mended and dressed.
> Embroidery on Lace and Fine-Work taught by
>
> Misses Manly
> 45 Warren-Street

OPPOSITE, TOP:

Mary W. Peck wore this veil at her wedding in 1827, in Litchfield, Connecticut. She probably learned lacemaking at Miss Pierce's Academy, where she was listed as a student in 1811. The linen thread used to work the veil seems more like silk in texture than linen. 48″ × 38″. (Courtesy of the Litchfield Historical Society.)

Fashionable boarding schools included lacework in their curricula by the mid-eighteenth century. Unfortunately, few of the fragile cutwork samplers that were the test of a student's skill survived. Cutwork (sometimes called pointing) required the enclosing of an area of linen background material with a securing stitch. Then the enclosed area was cut out and filled in with various buttonhole stitches. These lacework inserts required infinite patience and dexterity, not to mention extraordinary eyesight.

In the South, where the appreciation of lace became a passion, many schools offered instruction in lacemaking. As early as 1777, an advertisement in the *South Carolina and American General Gazette* announced that "Clara Trotti . . . makes thread lace of all breadths, and to any pattern. She proposes opening a school for the instruction of young ladies in lacemaking, and will make it her study to give satisfaction and be thankful of all favours."

In 1738, Jane Voyer advertised in the Charleston *South Carolina Gazette* that she "undertakes the mending of laces." The following year she included a statement in her ad that "any young ladies that have a mind to learn embroidery, lacework . . . may be carefully taught after the best manner. . . ." The ardor for lacework continued throughout many Southern ladies' lives, their spare moments gently occupied in making lace according to the latest fashion. The early 1740s saw the birth of a vogue for lappets, which consisted of two lengths of shaped lace that hung down gracefully on either side of the head. It is reported that Eliza Lucas of indigo-production fame enjoyed making lappets in her leisure time. She spent

> the first hour after dinner . . . at music, the rest of the afternoon in Needle Work till candle light. . . . Tis the fashion here to carry our work abroad with. . . . You may form some judgement what time I can have to work on my lappets. I own I never go to them with a quite easy conscience as I know my father has an aversion to my employing my time in that poreing work, but they are begun and must be finished. . . .[29]

Throughout the South, Spanish lacework enjoyed an enduring popularity. Often made of embroidered netting, it was mainly fashioned for shawls and veils. Its fame spread through Mexico into New Orleans and eventually reached virtually every small town in the South. A Spanish heritage of scalloped edges, extensive foliage, and bouquets of flowers emanating from baskets or knots of ribbons inspired profusions of imaginative stitches—"The veils were yard squares of delicate white or black lace, heavily bordered and lightly spotted with flowers, while the shawls were sometimes nearly double that size, and of much heavier lace, as they had need to be, to carry the wealth of decorative darning lavished upon them."[30]

The demand for lace continued throughout the nineteenth century. In Louisville, Kentucky, J. Bacon & Sons (a prosperous wholesale house that had grown out of a peddler's pack) advertised all over the South that it carried "10,000 yards of cotton laces, 50,000 yards of fancy laces, 10,000 yards of Spanish laces, 25,000 yards of fancy laces in cream and white . . . etc." Women added lace trimmings and bindings on their dresses at every seam and around every pocket and collar.[31]

OPPOSITE, BOTTOM:

Elizabeth Hannah Canfield made this veil about 1830, possibly while she attended Miss Sarah Pierce's Academy in Litchfield, Connecticut. (Courtesy of the Litchfield Historical Society.)

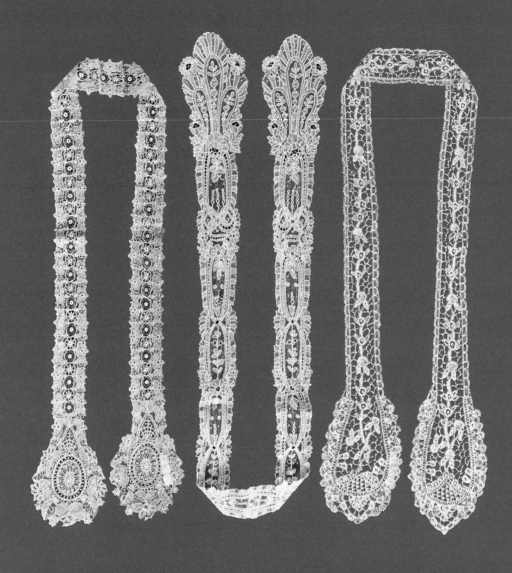

Most American lacemaking derived from European techniques, and women eagerly copied imported examples. The imitative lacework of Catherine Van Houten (1808–1874) in Paterson, New Jersey, is typical. Envying a lace cape in the Paris-bought trousseau of a friend, she reproduced it exactly in the six weeks before her own wedding.[32] In addition to tracing patterns from European laces, many women availed themselves of the instructions found in such popular periodicals as *Godey's* and *Harper's Bazaar*. At the turn of the century, needlework magazines were filled with European lace patterns.

During the same period, some American Indian women, guided by the Sibyl Carter Lace Association, were making an extensive variety of bobbin, needlepoint, and tape lace. Sibyl Carter was an Episcopalian missionary who, with the encouragement of Bishop Henry Whipple of Minnesota, began teaching lacemaking to Ojibwa women in 1890. By 1908, classes were being held for many tribes in the Midwest, New York, and the Far West.[33] Except for examples containing "Indian" designs, lacework made by these women appears identical to that made by many other groups. The somewhat primitive designs of tipis, mothers with papooses, hunters carrying bows and arrows, and men paddling canoes appear almost startling in conventional lacework. While Miss Carter and her teachers often chose popular patterns of the day, she noted that Indian lacemakers sometimes chose their own designs "from carpets, church windows, from leaves and flowers . . . and geometrical patterns from their beadwork."[34]

Although many Indians depended on lacework for much-needed income, most American women by the turn of the century regarded this craft as a diversion that was too time-consuming to learn. For those who wished to try their hand at modern point lace, tape lace, crocheted and knitted laces, drawn work, filet, and the many other types of lace, a host of patterns were available in popular publications such as *Needlecraft Magazine* and *Home Needlework Magazine*.

The shape of this lacework suggests it was used as a cap or an insertion in blouse or dress fronts. Such late 19th-century needle lace was partly based on the buttonhole stitch. 13″ × 10½″. (Courtesy of Rosalind S. Miller. Photograph, Schecter Lee.)

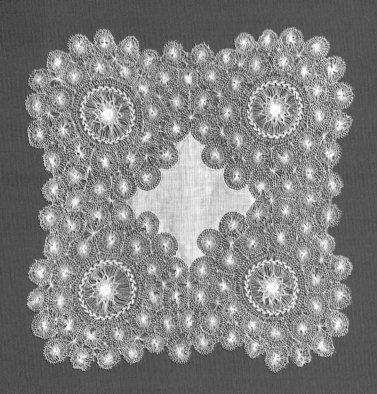

Lace doilies or coasters
characterized by a tenerife-
type embroidery with hem-
stitched, fringed edges.
c. 1880–90. Each 4″ to 5″ sq.
(Courtesy of Rosalind S. Miller.
Photograph, Schecter Lee.)

A late 19th-century
handkerchief made from single
disks composed of a tenerife-
type lacework, often seen in
ladies' magazines of the
period. 6″ sq. (Courtesy of
Rosalind S. Miller.
Photograph, Schecter Lee.)

This elaborately worked
collar of embroidered net with
buttonhole edging was
probably made in the late 19th
century. The flowers, which
can be described as re-
embroidered, have blossoms
whose definition is achieved
by needle and thread alone.
Height, 17½″. (Courtesy of
Rosalind S. Miller.
Photograph, Schecter Lee.)

Chippewa Indians making bobbin lace in Minnesota about 1900. (Courtesy of the Museum of the American Indian, Heye Foundation, New York City.)

A linen and lace mat, found in New York State, and probably made by an Oneida woman about the turn of the century. 6″ sq. (Courtesy of Lillian Grossman. Photograph, Schecter Lee.)

An unfinished lace collar worked on a pattern printed on a strip of pink cotton. Two kinds of factory-made lace are appliquéd over the pattern, providing an unusual "document" of how this type of work was done—requiring little skill and less labor than the earlier handmade lace. c. 1880–1900. 9″ × 16″. (Courtesy of the Litchfield Historical Society.)

Indian lacemakers, working in front of a "Churn Dash" quilt at the Redwood Mission, Morton, Minnesota, 1897. (Courtesy of the Minnesota Historical Society. Photograph, E. A. Bromley.)

Children's handkerchiefs from four different sets, skillfully arranged in colorful blocks, make up this unusual late 19th-century quilt. 90" × 92". (Courtesy of Laura Fisher. Photograph, Schecter Lee.)

TWELVE

PRINTED HANDKERCHIEFS, BANNERS, AND FLAGS

The depiction of events and famous people on such mundane textiles as ordinary handkerchiefs left a lively record of the nation's political, cultural, and social climate during the late eighteenth and nineteenth century. The earliest known American printed handkerchief not surprisingly pictures George Washington. Said to have been made by the famous Philadelphia printer, John Hewson, at the request of Mrs. Washington, the image was based on a 1775 print by C. Shepard, who in turn had copied a portrait of Washington by Alexander Campbell. As early as 1774, Hewson, noting the popular demand for printed handkerchiefs, had advertised in the *Pennsylvania Gazette* that he sold the necessary patterns. After Washington's death, memorial handkerchiefs resembling popular needlework pictures of the day chronicled sorrowful scenes of towering urns and monuments surrounded by mourning women and weeping willow trees.

European factories printed thousands of handkerchiefs commemorating events that appealed to the burgeoning American market. Migrating workers from these firms brought their printing techniques to America, sometimes directly copying the old designs. Since few early handkerchiefs bore factory marks, it is often difficult to determine the country of manufacture. Many English printing firms, perhaps taking heed of the success of commemorative export china, designed handkerchiefs depicting famous American heroes, battles, and holidays. Both American and European companies used designs from engravings and portraits. Broadsides, printed on silk or cotton, copied in their entirety famous documents such as the Declaration of Independence and the inaugural address of Thomas Jefferson. The many advertisements for printed handkerchiefs appearing in early newspapers attest to their popularity. A notice in the *Farmers Cabinet* (1823) announced a wide selection of designs: "John Moore has just received and now offering for sale a handsome assortment of printed handkerchiefs of the same patterns as those which were in such demand last year."

In 1915, Mrs. Eustace Bellecour of White Earth, Minnesota, wore a dress made out of an uncut roll of flag material. American Indians' fascination for the Stars and Stripes is documented by many old photographs showing shirts, leggings, and dresses made of flags and bunting, as well as a wealth of objects decorated with flag motifs. (Photograph courtesy of the Minnesota Historical Society.)

A printed silk broadside containing the full text of Washington's Farewell Address, produced by M. Fithian of Philadelphia in 1832. 18″ × 23″. (Courtesy of the New-York Historical Society.)

This printed pink-on-white cotton kerchief, attributed by some scholars to John Hewson of Philadelphia, is thought by others to have been manufactured in England or Holland. c. 1777. 33″ × 30″. (Courtesy of the New-York Historical Society.)

Pride in the new nation inspired handkerchiefs depicting the inauguration of George Washington, his death, maps and plans of the city of Washington, a visit to America by General Lafayette, and battles from the War of 1812. The scenes of naval and land battles, contrived to boost patriotic fervor, were manufactured almost immediately after the actual events took place.

Political and commemorative handkerchiefs reached a large audience; easily printed and distributed, they became an effective tool that remained in use into modern times. The first political handkerchief was introduced during Andrew Jackson's presidential campaign in 1832. By 1852, Nathaniel Hawthorne noted that Franklin Pierce's "portrait is everywhere in all the shop windows and in all sorts of styles, on wood, steel, and copper, on horseback, on foot, in uniform, in citizen's dress, in iron medallions, in little brass medals and on handkerchiefs."[1]

Bandannas (turkey red, tie-dyed cotton or silk handkerchiefs), ranging from 12 to 24 inches square, evolved into an important accessory to the political scene. Almost every man and boy carried a red bandanna in his coat pocket. Political conventions appeared to be a rolling sea of red cloth as people waved their handkerchiefs in support of their candidates. "In 1888 Grover Cleveland's running mate [Allen G. Thurman] was an old Democrat and he used none but bandanna handkerchiefs. As a mark of loyalty, millions of Democrats bought silk ones for their

The primitive appeal of this silk campaign bandanna glorifying General Harrison lies in the log cabin scene and in the border of hard cider barrels—both symbols of the 1840 campaign. 28″ × 24″. (Courtesy of the New-York Historical Society.)

girls and even flew red bandannas from the buggy whips of their favorite horse-drawn vehicle."[2]

Thurman, known as "The Knight of the Red Bandanna," inspired many songs concerning his affinity for these objects. He encouraged his supporters to wear their bandannas around their heads at the Chicago Convention. One advertisement of campaign handkerchiefs available in 1888 lists:

Thurman Bandannas

Harrison, "Red, White, and Blue" Bandannas

"Protection" Campaign Handkerchiefs [with the motto "Protection to Home Industries"]

"Free Trade" Bandanna Handkerchiefs [motto: Public Office a Public Trust]

"Voter's" Silk Bandanna in red or red, white and blue "appropriate for either Republican or Democrat."

Commemorative handkerchiefs celebrating anniversaries, fairs, and festivals were produced in great numbers. Most successful were the Centennial handkerchiefs of 1876—there were at least six cotton versions connected to this well-

A 19th-century kerchief depicts in pink on a white ground cotton the story of "The House That Jack Built." 13″ × 14½″. (Courtesy of the New-York Historical Society.)

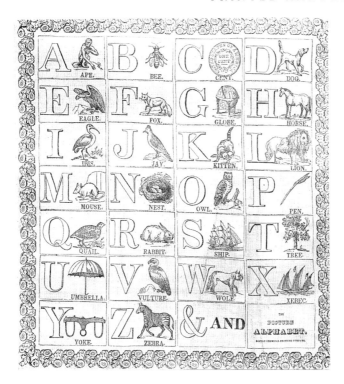

The Boston Chemical Printing Company manufactured this cotton "Picture Alphabet" about 1850–55 to instruct and delight young readers. 12″ × 10¾″. (Courtesy of the New-York Historical Society.)

"Uncle Tom's Cabin" contains no less than twenty-five scenes from Harriet Beecher Stowe's powerful novel. This children's educational kerchief was printed in brown ink on a white ground, c. 1870. 19½″ × 16½″. (Courtesy of the Cooper-Hewitt Museum, Smithsonian Institution.)

attended event. Many of these handkerchiefs were saved and re-used as center medallions in quilts or occasionally as backings for quilts.

Rarer are those handkerchiefs containing maps, charts, and pages from almanacs. As early as 1812, the *Philadelphia Mercantile Adviser* in its issue of December 30 listed "fancy map handkerchiefs." One early handkerchief, "Post Roads and Towns," depicted a table of towns from Maine to Georgia with the distances calculated between the various cities.

Among the most appealing handkerchiefs are those printed for children. They were designed to instruct and instill moral virtues as well as to entertain: good behavior, industry, temperance, and the perils of evil were thought to be appropriate subjects to be printed on these small cotton squares. Educational handkerchiefs include alphabets, numbers, Sunday School lessons, multiplication tables, and moral tales. Handkerchiefs of shadow pictures, soldiers, Mother Goose rhymes, and scenes of children and/or animals playing were increasingly manufactured as nineteenth-century attitudes toward children became more permissive.

The earliest American flags and banners evolved from the British and included both trade banners and flags identifying various American troops during the Revolution. The Sons of Liberty, a clandestine patriotic society, used a striped red and white flag to signify rebellion. The inclusion of stars might have derived from the strong Masonic influence on banners. The first American flags, unlike later printed versions, were unique creations—hand-spun, hand-dyed, and hand-sewn. Early flag makers followed the very general instructions of the Flag Resolution of 1774: " . . . 13 stripes alternate red and white . . . 13 stars white in a blue field. . . ." Even though red, white, and blue had been established as the official colors, a variety of colors were used. Flag makers also took liberties with the number of stripes and the placement of stars.

The Civil War inspired a rash of "flag bees," at which women worked on outsize flags. "On one large stars and stripes, the Newcomb Flag, four generations

Two early-20th-century children's handkerchiefs probably printed by the same firm. Each 12″ sq. (Courtesy of Wendy Lavitt. Photograph, Schecter Lee.)

of a family toiled—the great-grandmother recalling, while at work, her memories of childhood during the War of 1812."[3]

Even though President Lincoln disapproved, many northerners defaced the flag by cutting out stars representing the seceded states. In the South, a contest was held in 1861 to choose a design for the Confederate flag. The flag chosen derived from the Union flag; the copying was intentional, as southerners felt that they, too, owned the right to the American flag. In both the North and South, miniature flags were pressed into Bibles for safekeeping during the hostilities. These flags, originally intended for children, were known as "Bible flags." Ironically, the flags on the stage of the theater where Lincoln was shot received instant notoriety and were exhibited around the country. One Midwest newspaper, *The Home Fair Journal* (June 28, 1865), promised: "The Two Assassination Flags.— The flag that caught Booth's spur, and the one that Lincoln caught hold of, have arrived and will be on exhibition. . . ."

Until 1905, when Congress forbade the defacing of the flag, portraits and mottos superimposed upon American flags cast them into popular political campaign banners. Even those political banners not using actual flags were red, white, and blue, and contained design elements of the American flag. By associating presidential candidates with "Old Glory," strategists hoped to reap political success.

The assortment of parade flags, trade banners, and school banners is as varied as the organizations themselves. Silk, cotton, and linen banners were hand-painted or printed in many colors. Among the most beautiful trade banners are a group of seventeen silk ones painted in 1841 for a parade of the Portland, Maine, Charitable Mechanic Association. The painter of fifteen of the banners, William Capen, Jr., captured the interests of early nineteenth-century labor organizations while also revealing the contemporary taste in ornamental painting.[4] Many fine artists of the day painted banners and signs as a means of earning a living, creating decorative works of art out of utilitarian objects.

A silk banner of the 13th regiment, 7th Brigade, 3rd Division of the Newmarket Virginia Infantry, made in 1799. (Courtesy of the Museum of Early Southern Decorative Arts, Winston-Salem, N.C.)

A volunteer-militia knapsack from Massachusetts with design elements often found on banners and flags. "MM" probably stood for "Massachusetts Militia." Orange painted canvas with linen shoulder straps. c. 1815–25. Height, 15½"; length, 12¾". (Courtesy of the Guthman Collection.)

A painted-silk regimental flag belonging to the State Fencibles of Pennsylvania, who organized in 1813. This flag probably dates to that year. 32½" × 37½". (Courtesy of the Guthman Collection.)

A mid-19th-century silk banner extolling the Washington Light Infantry on one side and virtue and valor on the other ("Virescat") with a naturalistic rendition of a palm tree worked in silk and metallic threads. Note the tiny acorns of gold metallic thread with gold beaded caps. 43″ × 34″. (Courtesy of the Litchfield Historical Society.)

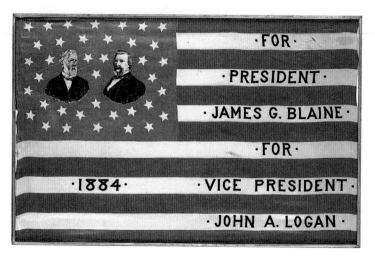

A silk flag banner for the Cleveland–Blaine campaign, distinguished by thirty-eight stars and the paired portraits of the candidates. The portrait of Blaine derived from an engraving printed in a newspaper, while that of Logan is from a photograph by C. M. Bell. 23″ × 15″. (Courtesy of Lillian and Jerry Grossman. Photograph, Schecter Lee.)

This full-length banner portrait of George Washington was printed in England, proof that foreign as well as American companies profited by the Centennial market. A young Washington, standing beneath the cracked Liberty Bell, holds the fateful message: "Washington/victory is ours/Paul Jones." 17½″ × 25″. Printed cotton, 1876. (Courtesy of the Cooper-Hewitt Museum, Smithsonian Institution.)

The focal point of this "Emancipation Day" celebration in Richmond, Virginia, is the banner of Abraham Lincoln surrounded by bunting and American flags waving in the breeze. (Courtesy of the Valentine Museum.)

This banner from Brockett Hollow School, in upstate New York, was originally used for school functions and later for reunions. Painted on cotton, c. 1880. 26″ × 34″. (Courtesy of J. S. Cocoman Antiques. Photograph, Schecter Lee.)

Oil-on-silk banner painted by William Capen, Jr., in 1841 for the Mechanic Association of Portsmouth, Maine. 33″ × 43″. (Courtesy of Richard Cheek.)

A blacksmith's banner, oil painted on silk by Joseph E. Hodgkins for the Portland, Maine, Charitable Mechanic Association parade in 1841. The reverse side features a well-muscled arm swinging a sledge, and another motto. 38″ × 35″. (Courtesy of Richard Cheek.)

A classic serape woven with natural yarns, indigo, and lac-dyed fibers, about 1855. The skillful execution of design and weave is typical of serapes of this period. 69″ × 53″. (Private collection.)

THIRTEEN

AMERICAN INDIAN
BLANKETS

NAVAJO BLANKETS

In *the Southwest,* the Spanish introduction of sheep raising to the Pueblo tribes during the early seventeenth century sparked the birth of Navajo weaving. Pueblo Indians captured in Navajo raids or conversely seeking refuge from the Spanish in Navajo lands taught their "adopted" tribe the techniques of weaving.

Destined to become world-famous for the arresting designs of their blankets, the Navajo originally wove simple, striped blankets that resembled those of the Pueblo. Unlike Pueblo men, Navajo males were not involved in weaving, but left the raising of sheep, the preparing of the wool, and the eventual weaving to the women of the tribe. By 1700, Navajo women not only supplied the needs of their own people but also wove for Spanish and intertribal trade. The dawn of an industry that would ultimately save the Navajo from economic and spiritual despair was duly noted by eighteenth-century Spanish travelers, who wrote home about the existence of Navajo blankets.

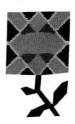

Throughout Navajo country various tribes considered textiles so important that weavings were used as currency and highly valued as gifts. As late as 1850, textiles compared favorably with human life, as attested by the sale of a captive slave, Rosalie Taveris, by the Apache and Comanche for "two striped blankets, ten yards of blue cotton drilling, ten yards of calico, as much cotton shirting, two handkerchiefs, four plugs of tobacco, a bag of corn, and a knife."[1]

Military men were among the first Americans to appreciate Navajo weaving. In 1847, J. T. Hughes recorded:

The chief presented Colonial Doniphan with several fine Navajo blankets. . . . Of these the colors are exceedingly brilliant, and the designs and figures in good taste. The fabric is not only so thick and compact as to turn rain, but to hold water as a vessel. They are used by the Navajos as a cloak in the day time, and converted into a pallet at night. Colonial Doniphan designs sending those which he brought home with him to the war department at Washington, as specimens of Navajo manufacture.[2]

The first sizable group of surviving blankets dates from what is known as the Classic Period (c. 1800–50). These blankets, designed to be worn around the shoulders, are largely composed of horizontal bands. Dramatic design elements in the form of rectangles and diamonds were sometimes woven into stripes of varying colors from natural and dyed wool.

The wool, originally from the Spanish Churro sheep, was fine and silky. Blankets of this period often contained yarn raveled from bayeta, the red English broadcloth imported by the Spanish. The Navajo's love of bayeta, a relatively expensive material, ensured its use by the finest weavers, who were inspired by it to create some of the most beautiful blankets of the nineteenth century.

After the tedious job of raveling the bolts of cloth (made available to the Navajo by trade), women wove the fibers into the wefts of their blankets. The rich yet soft shades of red derived from the natural dyes of lac and cochineal (dried, crushed bodies of insects mainly from the West Indies, Mexico, and the Orient). The Navajo of this period also used indigo for blue and, less frequently, homemade vegetal dyes. Shades of black, brown, gray, and white were achieved by carding undyed, natural yarns. When a weaver desired an intense black (not possible with natural wool), she used a black dye obtained from sumac, twigs, and leaves.

During the Classic Period, Navajo weavers supplemented bayeta with imported Saxony three-ply commercial yarns. The first commercial yarn available to the Navajo, Saxony was comparable in quality to bayeta. Since its coloring depended upon natural dyes and its texture remained soft, Saxony outranked later synthetic Germantown yarns (named after a manufacturing town in Pennsylvania). At the end of the Classic Period, American flannel, also known as "trader flannel," largely replaced bayeta; but its garish tints and tendency to mat made American flannel less attractive than the finer bayeta and Saxony-type yarns.

Among the most famous blankets of the Navajo were the "Chief Blankets." Approximately 70 inches wide by 50 inches long, these could actually be worn by any member of a tribe who could afford them, for the Navajo hierarchy did not include chiefs; however, their superior quality probably prevented all but the wealthiest of men from owning them. Several tribes, especially the Ute and the Sioux, vied for these prestigious blankets. At the end of the nineteenth century, trading posts received the highest prices for Chief Blankets. The Hubbell Trading Post reported fine quality Chief Blankets selling for the then substantial sums of $17.50 to $35.00 each.[3] Classic women's wearing blankets, distinguished from Chief Blankets by their smaller dimensions and narrower brown-and-gray background stripes (instead of brown and white stripes), were also highly valued.

Navajo weaver using the batten on an upright loom. Because the hogans in which they lived could not support a loom, the Navajo added side supports to a design adapted from the Pueblo. (Photograph, neg. no. 14473: P. E. Goddard. Courtesy Department Library Services, American Museum of Natural History, New York City.)

A Ute-collected First Phase Chief Blanket, woven from handspun, natural fibers and indigo-dyed yarns. Chief Blankets, although not actually worn only by chiefs, were so called because of their high value among many tribes. c. 1800–50. 68″ × 54″. (Private collection.)

A Second Phase Chief Blanket of lac-dyed bayeta, indigo-dyed yarns, and natural fibers. The plain stripes of the First Phase blanket now include horizontal bars within the stripes. c. 1860. 65″ × 50″. (Private collection.)

A Third Phase Chief Blanket, woven of indigo and cochineal-dyed yarns with natural fibers. Bold diamond-like designs have broken through the simple stripes of First and Second Phase Blankets. c. 1865–70. 63″ × 46″. (Private collection.)

    For means of identification, historians and collectors have divided the styles of Chief Blankets into three phases. Although a Chief Blanket was actually discovered in a Navajo grave about 1775, First Phase Blankets usually date from 1800–50.[4] These early blankets feature simple weft stripes of varying widths. The neighboring Ute particularly admired First Phase Blankets with bands of indigo. They collected so many pieces of this type that their blankets are now known as "Ute-style" First Phase Chief Blankets. Second Phase Chief Blankets (c. 1850–65) included rectangles as design elements. At first the small rectangles seemed almost lost within the stripes, but eventually they developed into larger motifs creating gridlike effects. In Third Phase Chief Blankets (c. 1865–80), rectangles evolved into diamonds, following a similar progression to the Second Phase rectangles. The early small diamonds gave way to explosive diamond shapes that dominated the visual field. Traders encouraged their finest weavers to copy the popular Third Phase Blankets, thus ensuring the longevity of their designs.

    While Chief Blankets reflected Pueblo origins, serapes hailed from a Spanish/ Mexican heritage. Although their evolution ran parallel to the development of the Chief Blankets, serapes incorporated more complex patterns based on zigzags, triangles, and diamonds. Design elements of the Mexican Saltillo Serape and the Spanish Rio Grande Serape influenced Navajo weavers, who adopted a simplified version of the Spanish/American aesthetic, often combining stripes and serape

Diamonds and zigzags are the main design components of this Saxony serape. c. 1850–65. 58″ × 81″. (Courtesy of the School of American Research, Santa Fe, N.M.)

Worn as a poncho, this finely woven blanket has a slit for the head and is composed of fibers dyed with lac, indigo, and (for the green) rabbitbrush. Its overall pattern is based on the concept of the interrupted stripe. c. 1845. 76″ × 50″. (Private collection.)

This blanket was probably made by a Navajo working for a Spanish family. It is of the type known today as a "Slave Blanket." Woven on Navajo looms, these reflected the Spanish aesthetics of the Mexican ruling class. This example is composed of a variety of yarns, including cochineal-dyed Saxony, natural fibers, and indigo-dyed and rabbitbrush-dyed yarns. c. 1854. 81″ × 56″. (Private collection.)

A handsome serape of the late Classic Period, making use of aniline-dyed yarns combined with traditional indigo-dyed yarns and natural fibers. c. 1870. 60″ × 84″. (Private collection.)

This Navajo "Eye-Dazzler" blanket is an interesting combination of
materials—white and brown undyed native handspun, indigo-dyed
native handspun, and red and orange native handspun dyed with
aniline. c. 1880s. (Courtesy of Tony Berlant.)

motifs in the same blanket. Unlike Chief Blankets, serapes are longer than they are wide.

The ponchos, considered among the rarer and more unusual of Navajo blankets, were of the finest weave and materials, and their elaborate patterns and skillful weaving ensured the highest prices—$50 to $100 by 1850.[5] By 1896 the following assessment stated:

> A balleta [bayeta] blanket . . . is worth $200 and not a dozen of them could be bought at any price today. It is seventy-three inches long by fifty-six inches wide and weighs six pounds. You can easily reckon that the thread in it cost something, at $6 a pound, and the weaving occupied a Navaho woman for many months. It is hardly thicker than an ordinary book cover, and is almost as firm. It is too thin and stiff to be an ideal bed-blanket, and it was never meant to be one. All blankets of that quality were made to be worn on the shoulders . . . and most of them were *ponchos*—that is, they had a small slit left in the center for the wearer to put his head through, so that the blanket would hang upon him like a cape. Thus it was combined overcoat, water-proof, and adornment.[6]

Early bayeta serapes (1830–50) were characterized by rows of horizontal bands usually containing terraced (stepped) zigzags from edge to edge. The corners of some serapes seem to have curving lines that have the appearance of stepped triangles. Many serapes retain the central diamond motif of Spanish/Mexican blankets. The 1860s witnessed the development of new patterns within the basic framework of serapes. These late serape styles seem to be more open in design and scale, utilizing "blocks instead of solid lines in terrace building."[7] New motifs—the cross, the "pine tree" diamond, a "T"-shaped element, and the block—were introduced along with synthetic dyes. The striking optical patterns of these late serapes forecast the Germantown Eye-Dazzlers of the coming decades.

Eye-Dazzlers (c. 1875–1900), so named for their exciting optical effects and bright colors, reflected the increasing availability of aniline dyes. The intense colors inspired "painted pictures with wool" that achieved spatial juxtapositions and three-dimensional illusions.[8] They also signified a change in the Navajo way of life, mirroring the turbulence of the internment at Bosque Redondo and its aftermath. Visually overwhelming weavings were grounded in rows of small details, most often diamonds. Outlining added to the drama of "radiating" diamonds with sawtooth edges. While some Eye-Dazzlers were made from heavier, hand-spun yarns, the best utilized Germantown yarn. Many traders and collectors dismissed the Eye-Dazzlers as too garish, feeling they were out of step with the then fashionable subtle hues of the Arts and Crafts movement. Other traders accepted the aesthetics of the Eye-Dazzlers while insisting upon blankets woven in the traditional way with Germantown yarns. Unfortunately, too many traders relegated these now valuable blankets into the same category as the "Pound Blankets," which were coarsely woven with poorly cleaned, low-grade yarns, and sold by weight.

The emergence of the Pound Blanket signaled a decline in quality weaving.

The era of the traders—the Transitional Period (c. 1890–1920)—was one of controversy. While many traders discouraged fine weaving by paying only by weight (inspiring Navajo weavers to pound sand and dirt into the ruglike blankets), others persuaded their best weavers to create new patterns with fine workmanship. The tastes of the traders were conditioned by Victorian sensibilities and encouraged weaving patterns derived from Frost hooked rugs, Turkish and Persian carpet designs and quilts. Indeed, by 1900 the wearing blanket had evolved into a rug for the floor, as traders found customers more apt to buy articles they could actually use in a den or gameroom. Many trading posts even featured "special order" weavings large enough for a porch or lodge.

The Navajo were no longer weaving blankets for themselves. It made economic sense for them to sell their valuable handwoven blankets to the traders and buy cheap, serviceable factory blankets for their own everyday use. As one old Tewa man remembered, "People wore new kind of clothes when the trains came."[9] The weaving of Pendleton blankets began when three brothers, Clarence, Roy, and Chauncey Bishop, took over their family's woolen mill in Pendleton, Oregon. They offered the Indians warm blankets made on a Jacquard loom in two styles:

A miniature Germantown "Eye-Dazzler" that was sold, half-finished on its loom, as a decorative wall hanging. While this example is tightly woven and well planned, quality varied widely on these small pieces. c. 1890. 22″ × 16″. (Courtesy of Wendy Lavitt. Photograph, Schecter Lee.)

Clah-Chese-Chili-Gi and his two wives, wearing Pendleton blankets, with a Teec Nos Pas style blanket in the background. Photographed by William Pennington about 1910. (Courtesy of Bob Kapoun Gallery.)

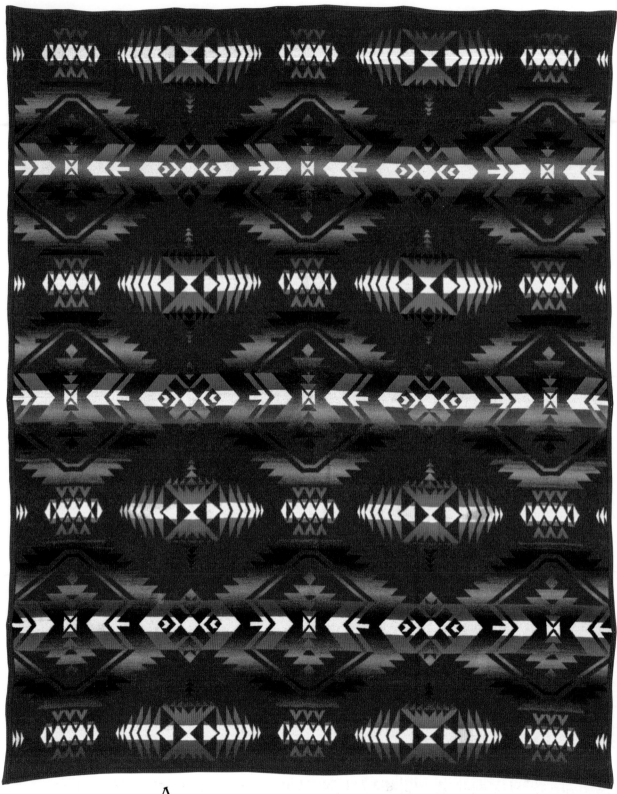

A typical Pendleton blanket whose "Indian" motifs and soft texture
found wide acceptance among Indians and Anglos. Early 20th century.
68″ × 72″. (Courtesy of Wendy Lavitt. Photograph, Schecter Lee.)

fringed, which were considered superior and worn as shawls, and unfringed, which were used as robes.[10]

Not surprisingly, the shifting fortunes of the Navajos affected their weaving. Even before the infamous scorched-earth policy of Kit Carson in 1863, the tribe had led a precarious existence. Their plundering had made them feared throughout the Southwest, but they still lived hand-to-mouth. As one soldier commented in 1852: "It seems anomalous that a nation living in such miserably constructed mud lodges should at the same time be making probably the best blankets in the world."[11]

Before the Navajo were rounded up and marched to Fort Sumner at Bosque Redondo, New Mexico, in 1864, they at least enjoyed a nomadic, free existence. During the Bosque Redondo years (1864–68) a once proud people came close to dying of starvation and despair. Repeated failures at raising crops or sheep forced them to rely on the government dole. Weaving all but ceased.

In 1868, after promising never to fight again, the Navajo were allowed to return home. The government gave them 30,000 sheep, hoping to spur the revival of weaving; however, the short, kinky, and greasy wool of the Rambouillet breed was unsuitable for spinning, and failed to stimulate a quick recovery. Moreover, the years at Bosque Redondo had brought the white man's ways and materials to the Navajo. Calico and velveteen dresses, machine-made blankets, aniline dyes, and the seemingly vast array of goods at the trading post all influenced the Navajo weaver:

An army officer wants "something fancy" and makes a sketch of his idea to guide the weaver. A trader's wife appears in a figured dress, or lays on her

Jicarilla Apache (Mrs. Reuben Springer and her daughter) wearing fringed Pendleton blankets, about the turn of the century. (Photograph, neg. no. 14308: P. E. Goddard. Courtesy Department of Library Services, American Museum of Natural History.)

living-room floor a rug fresh from an eastern factory. The trader exhorts his weavers to take heed of the new market, and displays catalogues of the latest linoleum patterns by way of inspiration. Soldiers in gaudy uniform and impressive regalia ride briskly about. Railroad trains come puffing and screaming down the slope of the continental divide. The whole world of the Navajo is born again. Can the people remain unchanged?[12]

During the reservation period, Navajo weavings began to appear with pictorial images illustrating the changes in daily life. Pictographs featuring livestock, trains, and houses competed in popularity with patriotic symbols of flags and eagles. However, pictographs were not woven in great numbers, for they did not meet the need for floor coverings and required considerable skill to execute.

Sand-painting rugs, as well as Yei and Yeibichai rugs, also featured pictorial images. These rugs—although based on Navajo ritual subject matter—were non-ceremonial, made solely for sale. The Yei figures in rugs sometimes represent supernatural beings found in sand paintings. They are usually depicted on a sand-colored or gray background and are surrounded by various symbols. Yeibichai rugs represent the line of Navajo dancers performing the Yeibichai dance from the Night Chant. At first many Navajo disapproved of using sacred symbols in weavings, even though the weavers always inserted "foreign" elements to secularize their work. One of the first Yei blankets to be exhibited by a trader caused the following reaction:

> Councils were held over the reservation to discuss the matter, and the trader was finally commanded to remove the blanket containing the offending emblems from the wall in his office. He refused, and for a time his life was deemed in jeopardy. But he was a fearless and obstinate man, and resisted all the pressure brought to bear upon him, though among themselves the Navajos still argued and discussed the sacrilege, and a shooting-scrape in which one man lost his life was the outcome.[13]

A decidedly Oriental influence and a dramatic border distinguish this finely woven Teec Nos Pas rug, made of handspun synthetic and natural colors. c. 1910. 83″ × 53″. (Private collection. Photograph, Christopher Selser.)

Juanita, a skillful Navajo weaver, shows her blankets to Governor W. F. M. Arny, in 1873. The American flag, a favorite motif in Indian art, obviously inspired the blanket in the center. More standard Navajo weavings are displayed in the background. (Photograph courtesy of the Museum of the American Indian, Heye Foundation.)

A photograph of one of the most famous Navajo weavers standing beside his masterpiece. This blanket, based on sacred sand painting, shattered Navajo tradition—decades passed before rugs derived from sand paintings were finally accepted. (Courtesy of Christopher Selser.)

The weaver of this pictorial rug was so captivated by an illustration in a 1921 issue of *The Delineator* that she created an approximation of the page in her weaving. Handspun synthetic dyes and natural handspun yarns. c. 1921. 93″ × 64″. (Private collection. Photograph, Christopher Selser.)

Gradually commercial success reduced the antagonism toward "ceremonial" weavings, and many are still being made today.

The legacy of the traders was the establishment of regional styles that in some areas still flourish. One of the earliest and most influential trading posts was started by Juan Lorenzo Hubbell in 1876 at Ganado. His efforts to standardize weaving led him to commission white artists to paint pictures of old Navajo blankets for his weavers to copy. He tried to improve the quality by limiting the weaver's palette to natural colors except for the intense crimson aniline dye that came to be known as "Ganado Red." A typical Ganado rug contained a central motif of one or more serrated diamonds, a variety of surrounding elements (crosses, zigzags, arrows, etc.), and black outlining. At one point Hubbell owned fourteen trading posts on the Navajo reservation and supplied rugs to the Fred Harvey chain of railroad

Dramatic designs worked in bright red (aniline-dyed) and natural yarns characterize Ganado rugs. The large symmetrical crosses contribute to the boldness of this example. c. 1900. 83" × 61". (Private collection. Photograph, Christopher Selser.)

Single-figure Yei rugs were popular from 1910 on. The feathers and arrows in the background were included to make the rug more "Indian." The Yei figure holds offerings to the Great Spirit. c. 1930. 3' × 5'. (Courtesy of William Channing. Photograph, Schecter Lee.)

Subtle tones and geometric symmetry are hallmarks of Two Gray Hills rugs, c. 1920s. (Courtesy of the School of American Research.)

hotels for use in their famous Indian rooms. When Hubbell in a reflective moment tried to explain the many hats a successful trader wore, he said: "Out here . . . the trader is everything from merchant to father confessor, justice of the peace, judge, jury, court of appeals, chief medicine man and *de facto* czar of the domain over which he presides."[14]

In 1897, J. B. Moore established the Crystal Trading Post, which became famous for its rugs resembling Oriental carpets. One of the first traders to sell by mail order, Moore claimed in his 1911 catalogue that his weavings "differ from all others in that we first buy the wool, select only the best and most suitable of it, ship it away, have it scoured and thoroughly cleaned, and shipped back. It is then spun into yarn and dyed in the yarn with a very superior and different dye too, than that used in the trade woven rugs . . . insuring even and absolute colors."[15]

Moore also featured rugs based on traditional designs, introducing dramatic borders containing such elements as the swastika, the cross, and a unique hook-shaped figure. The subdued color combinations and importance of symmetry in Crystal weavings probably influenced a neighboring trading post, Two Gray Hills.

Although the Two Gray Hills Trading Post opened in 1897, it wasn't until after 1912 that a distinctive regional style developed. Balanced geometric patterns in a monochromatic palette became its trademark. An emphasis upon precision workmanship eventually led to weavings so fine that they are considered tapestries.

During the past two hundred years the trail of Navajo weaving has led from finely woven shoulder wraps to rugs to tapestries destined for gallery walls. But throughout their history, the blankets have always been "expressions in art of the way The People [the Navajo] looked at the world."[16]

A classic 19th-century Chilkat blanket. The visual field is divided into a central section and two symmetrical adjoining panels. Every color change is outlined and bordered, adding to the stylized effect. 50″ × 65″. (Private collection. Courtesy of Eleanor Tulman Hancock. Photograph, Schecter Lee.)

THE CHILKAT BLANKETS

Among the Northwest Coast tribes, the Chilkat branch of the Tlingits were famous for their weaving. Spanish explorers in the 1770s noted the "woven scarf with fringe" that was highly prized by several native tribes. Chilkat blankets conferred status and wealth upon the owner much as a mink coat does to today's woman. Potlatches—great ceremonial occasions at which gifts were bestowed upon the guests and property destroyed by owners in ostentatious displays of wealth that the guests later tried to surpass—were resplendent with men wearing Chilkat robes. Although whole blankets were sometimes presented to the most honored guests, blankets were more often cut into strips and distributed—such pieces being valued far beyond their intrinsic worth.[17] To own a blanket "endowed a chief with great prestige; to give them away gave even greater glory, for only the wealthiest chiefs could afford to dispense with such valuable items. . . ."[18]

Chilkat blankets were considered so valuable that they often became a medium of exchange. Paul Kane, a Canadian traveler and painter, described one he was fortunate to obtain in the 1840s as "a blanket made from the wool of the mountain sheep. For one which I procured with great difficulty, I had to pay five pounds of tobacco, ten charges of ammunition, one blanket, one pound of beads, two check shirts, and one ounce of vermilion."[19]

By the last quarter of the nineteenth century the Chilkat blanket had been bartered, sold, or given as a gift among practically all the Northwest Coast tribes, and was known as a "dancing blanket" by the Tsimshian and a "fringe about the body" by the Haida and the Tlingit.[20]

These stylized, complicated blankets were created on a simple upright loom consisting of a horizontal bar attached to the tops of two poles. Unlike most tightly woven textiles, Chilkat blankets were woven from the top downwards, with a loose warp from which hung small bags containing the yarns. Women wove the twined blankets from a mixture of mountain goat wool, sinew, and shredded, softened bark, consulting patterns that were painted on boards by their menfolk. Unlike the Navajo who took pride in creating unique blankets within a traditional framework, Chilkat women never deviated from the pattern boards that were handed down through generations. A design comprised a single segment, later sewn together with other segments to form the blanket. Each blanket held ceremonial significance and echoed symbols seen on house fronts, totem poles, and storage boxes. Abstract animal symbols were systematically dissected into shapes that

From a postcard titled "Native Chiefs in Eastern Alaska," showing men in full regalia with Chilkat blankets draped over their shoulders. Early 20th century. (Courtesy of Wendy Lavitt.)

seem to present a visual CAT-scan of the figure. The blankets were usually symmetrical, one half being a copy of the pattern board, and the other half its mirror image. Both dyed and natural yarns were used, with soft hues of green, yellow, and aqua combined with black and white. The skilled weavers added the various colors from memory, as the pattern boards showed only the black part of the design. Other articles, including mats, shirts, dance aprons, and bags, were woven, but none achieved the eminence of the Chilkat blanket.

A Tlingit chief owned this button blanket with a killer whale design. Black wool, trimmed with red trade cloth. Found in Ketchikan, Alaska, and collected from Chief Kyan, its date of manufacture is unknown. 52″ × 68″. (Courtesy of the Museum of the American Indian, Heye Foundation.)

BUTTON BLANKETS

When fur-trading expeditions penetrated the Northwest Coast in the nineteenth century, the Indians coveted the shiny coins and brass buttons worn by military officers. They used them to decorate factory blankets from the Hudson's Bay Company, broadcloth, and flannel. The Northwest Coast tribes had long been accustomed to fastening bone amulets, puffin bills, dentalium, and abalone shells to garments as prized ornaments.[21] The introduction of iridescent pearl buttons by the traders inspired the development of a new form of ceremonial blanket that came to be known as the button blanket.

"I had some garments of blue cloth made with buttons sewed on in a curious manner which likewise fetched a good price," wrote Captain Joseph Ingraham in his 1790–92 journal describing his voyage to the Northwest Coast.[22] The date

established the practice of button decoration within the early days of trade. A drawing by an artist on a Russian expedition to Alaska and California about 1844 of a Tlingit funeral shows several button blankets—perhaps the earliest pictorial documentation of ceremonial blankets.[23]

Women appliquéd pieces of red flannel on blue or less frequently green broadcloth to represent symbolic clan figures. These forms were outlined by rows of buttons. While the basic design elements were simple, borders and additional motifs could involve thousands of buttons; making each blanket was a painstaking process. When commercial buttons were scarce, women fashioned makeshift buttons out of abalone shells.

Button blankets did not confer exalted status upon the wearer as did Chilkat blankets, yet they were nonetheless highly regarded and widely traded among Northwest Coast tribes. By the early twentieth century, button blankets were still being made, but their designs no longer held symbolic meaning.

An Indian brought this button blanket, along with some clothing he wanted to sell, to Vancouver in the 1880s. Red trade cloth appliqué decorated with trade buttons on a Hudson's Bay blanket. 55" × 44". (Courtesy of Arne Anton.)

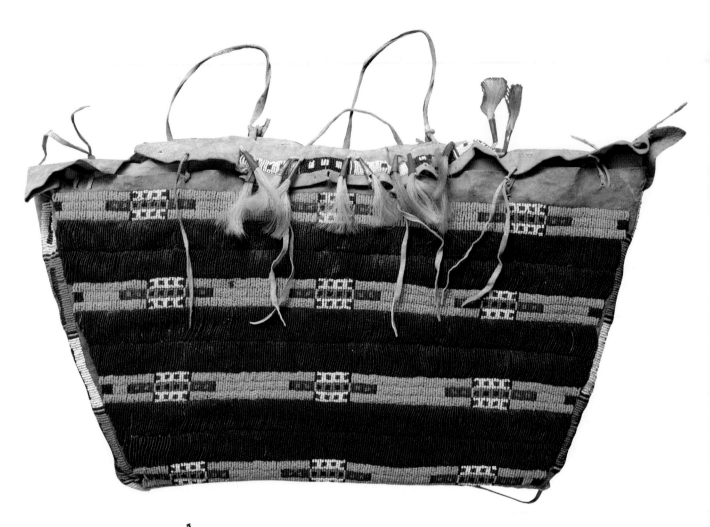

A Sioux beaded "possible bag," c. 1890. Possible bags were used to carry a variety of items: food, medicine and tools were common contents.

The detail (OPPOSITE) shows the difference between the spot, or appliqué, stitch (the multicolored band where each bead is sewn into the tanned rawhide) and the lazy stitch (the solid green area where several beads are strung onto a thread of sinew but not every bead is sewn down). 18″ × 13″. (Courtesy of Morningstar Gallery.)

FOURTEEN

AMERICAN INDIAN QUILLWORK AND BEADWORK

QUILLWORK

The women manifest much ingenuity and taste in the work which they
execute with porcupine quills. The colour of these quills is various, beautiful and durable, and the art of dying them [sic] is practised only by females.[1]

Early travelers noted that quillwork was an indigenous art of many
tribes, established long before the first explorers reached the New World. Using
an awl, or later a needle, women created intricate patterns with stitches resembling the backstitch, couched stitch, and chain stitch. Porcupine quills, sometimes
supplemented by bird quills, were used. For Plains tribes the bladders or intestines
of large animals served as pouches for storing the quills, which were carefully sorted
by size. Women decorated their pouches with quillwork and regarded them as
prized possessions, just as colonial needlewomen regarded their scrap bags. Besides
her pouch of quills a quillworker needed "a marker of bone, an awl, strands of
sinew, possibly a quill flattner [sic] usually made of bone or antler and an animal
skin dressed and ready to be decorated."[2]

Quillwork required patience and dexterity. Soaking quills in their mouths to
soften them sometimes made women ill.[3] For some Plains tribes, initiation into
honored quillwork societies (a tribal requisite for learning the craft) involved rules
that may have been based on health concerns. Among the Blackfeet,

it is said that quillworkers go blind if they ever throw a porcupine quill into
a fire, or if they do quillwork at night. It is also said that a quillworker will

prick her finger a lot with the quills if she sews any moccasins in her home. She is not supposed to eat certain food, such as porcupine meat, nor should she allow anyone to pass in front of her while she is quilling.[4]

Quilling societies ranked workers according to their skills and provided companionship akin to colonial spinning matches and pioneer quilting bees. Among the Cheyenne and Arapaho tribes, members of these societies were accorded a status equivalent to that of honored male warriors.[5]

Many designs derived from earlier woven quillwork, featuring geometric patterns. During the nineteenth century much curvilinear and some floral quillwork appeared in the Great Lakes and Woodlands areas. Although characterized by delicate, fine work, floral designs never were made in the same quantity as geometric ones. The Eastern and Great Lakes areas came to be known for a tremendous diversity of quillwork techniques. Although some women continued to use sinew, the introduction of the needle and thread caused the flowering of quill work art.

Iroquois child's moccasins, skillfully decorated with quillwork and beadwork. c. 1830. Height, 7″. (Courtesy of Gallery 10 of Arizona. Photograph, Schecter Lee.)

In the early days quills were either used in their natural state or colored with roots and vegetal dyes. In 1820, Daniel Harmon noted:

> To dye red or yellow, the Plains Indians make use of certain roots, and the moss which they find, on a species of the fir tree. These are put, together with the quills, into a vessel filled with water made acid by boiling

currants or gooseberries etc., in it. The vessel is then covered tight, and the liquid is made to simmer over the fire for three or four hours, after which the quills are taken out and dried and are fit for use . . . these colours never fade.[6]

Actually Harmon's observation of the amount of time required for dyeing was erroneous. Although dyes were boiled long enough to extract the color agents, quills could only be boiled a few minutes before dissolving.

The introduction of beads relegated quillwork to a secondary craft, eventually causing its demise as quillwork guilds gradually disappeared, or were in some cases replaced by beadwork guilds.

BEADWORK

"A good beader makes a good wife. I learned when I was ten. A girl who helped the grown-ups, who could tan and bead and quill well, was much honored. The men kept track of their brave deeds and us women used to keep a record of our kind of 'deeds.'"[7]

This recollection of Leading Cloud, a Sioux woman, expresses the importance, almost reverence, accorded to the art of beadwork by American Indian tribes. The

239

The dark green homespun strap of this Woodlands Indian powder horn is decorated with trade beads. Made in the late 18th century, it is a rare example of early beadwork. (Courtesy of the Guthman Collection.)

history of trade beads dates back to the days of Columbus. A long heritage of ornamentation led to an eager acceptance of beads offered by European expeditions in the seventeenth century. Fur traders introduced beads to the Eastern Woodlands Indians by 1675; moving westward, traders brought beads to the Plains Indians around 1800. These beads, each the size of a match head, were called pony beads. The appearance of smaller seed beads at different times in various areas inspired the beginning of an era of prolific, intricate beadwork.

Indian women easily adapted quillwork patterns, involving both outlining and covering large areas in beadwork. Instead of spending many hours dyeing porcupine quills, the women could simply select the colored beads they wanted from the trader's stock. Traders quickly learned which colors each tribe preferred and kept ample supplies that were sold by weight or by strings. As beads became more plentiful, prices dropped. A six-foot strand of small blue beads commanded one beaver skin in the Great Lakes area in 1760, but by 1807 two pounds of beads could be had for one skin.[8] Women used sinew for thread and worked upon buckskin and other hides. Even when cloth and cotton thread replaced earlier materials, Indian women cut the cloth according to their own designs and decorated them with the same motifs found on their hides.[9]

The prodigious amount of beadwork created by Indian women was accomplished with few exceptions by using only two stitches: the overlay stitch (also known as the spot, or appliqué, stitch) and the lazy stitch. Some tribes favored one stitch, others used both. The overlay stitch produced a smooth surface and worked well for delicate outlining and background coverage. A thread was strung with a few beads and laid upon the cloth or hide. A separate sewing thread fastened the bead thread to the material at regular intervals. This "overlaying" of the first thread by the second is similar to a couching stitch in traditional European embroidery. When working on tanned hide, careful beaders took pride in not carrying the stitch through to the underside, thereby assuring a clean backing. On the decorated side, beads were arranged tightly to conceal the threadwork. Members of the Woodlands, Plains, and Great Lakes tribes used this appliqué stitch for floral patterns.

The lazy stitch produced a distinctive ridged surface. In a series of parallel rows, each line, usually of six to twelve beads, was sewn down only at the ends of the row. As in the overlay on hide, stitch perforations were just below the surface, thereby obscuring any evidence of sewing. The lazy stitch was so well suited for covering large areas that many Plains tribes used it for blanketing all sorts of objects and clothing with beadwork.

The beads themselves were made of nearly indestructible glass in Venetian factories, sold to European exporters, and distributed by traders in exchange for furs and other goods. On the Plains, the earlier pony beads (1800–40) were usually available only in white, black, blue, or red; due to their rarity, they were used sparingly, often as an added trimming to quillwork. On the Plains beadwork, patterns initially resembled geometric quillwork. In the mid-nineteenth century the traders introduced seed beads to the Plains tribes in a dazzling array of colors.

A beaded strip centered on Northern Plains buffalo hide showing Crow or Nez Percé influence. These tribes often chose similar colors and employed the design element of the hourglass in their work. c. 1880s. Hide, 60″ × 36″; beaded strip, 52″ × 3″. (Courtesy of Morningstar Gallery.)

Although these varied somewhat in size, they were always considerably smaller than the pony beads. The stage was set for a period of innovation involving both materials (such as metallic, faceted beads) and designs. At times beads were used and re-used on newer objects, rendering it difficult for us to date an object solely by the beads themselves. However, it is possible to distinguish antique beadwork from modern examples. Beverly Hungry Wolf, a Blackfoot Indian, explains:

> The old-time seeds were made in Italy, and are known as "Italian beads" to merchants. They are of good glass, and the colors are very soft and subtle. They are of uneven shapes which gives the finished beadwork a special texture. Most modern beads are sold as "Czechoslovakian beads," since that is where they are made. They have pretty, even shapes and very bright colors, and can easily be told from the old style of beading.[10]

Many an Indian girl spent her first year in a cradle decorated by beads and beaded amulets. As a child she played with dolls whose beaded clothing mirrored adult costume. Often she began instruction in sewing and beadwork by making and decorating her doll's clothing. The easiest patterns were "straight lines, either continuous or interrupted . . . from which she progressed to diagonal patterns and the familiar 'otter-tail' pattern."[11] As she grew proficient, she graduated to her own simple garments and moccasins. A Fox Indian remembers:

> . . . when I was twelve years old, I was told, "Come, try to make these." [They were] my own moccasins. "You may start to make them for yourself after you know how to make them. For you already know how to make them for your dolls. That is the way you are to make them," I was told. She only cut them out for me. "This is the way you are to make it," I was told. Finally I really knew how to make them.[12]

A Sioux child's beaded cap, collected in South Dakota before 1915. The sprigged floral calico bonnet with typical Sioux geometric beadwork shows a true blending of cultures. Note how the styling of the hat with its ruffled edges resembles the pioneer poke bonnet. 7″ × 11″. (Courtesy of the Museum of the American Indian, Heye Foundation.)

The "octopus" bag, so called because of its shape, is a unique form found only among North American Indians. The Tlingit pouch, late 19th-century, was worn with a shoulder strap for both ceremonial occasions and everyday use. Height, 17″. (Courtesy of J. C. Antiques.)

Indian girls industriously applied themselves to the mastery of sewn and woven beadwork. Their eagerness reflected tribal customs, as their marriageability and standing in the community were enhanced by their needlework skills. The patterns they chose depended on tribal tradition and were usually geometric or floral in design. Among the Chippewa, "Every woman who did beadwork had patterns cut from stiff birch bark which she laid on the material to be decorated. . . . Patterns were pricked with a stiff fishbone around the outline and then cut with scissors."[13]

The use of floral patterns spread rapidly from the Eastern Woodlands through the Plains. Although floral realism reflected European influences, it also mirrored the Indian's perception of his or her environment. One early collector of beadwork in the 1880s reported that she "sat on a river bank and watched a Cree woman using only the natural juices from plants for ink and a stick for a brush, draw a flower from life, which she then used as the basis for a beaded design."[14]

Geometric beadwork of the Plains groups relied upon established designs, symbolic colors, and in some instances the desire to tell a story or express a thought. Designs with fixed meanings enabled a viewer to "read" the beaded article and understand the owner's life and deeds. The symbolic meanings of colors and geometric elements varied from tribe to tribe, although there is some overlap.

Reservation beadwork developed unique characteristics of its own, including pictorial depictions of flags, houses, men, and animals. Ironically, these non-traditional motifs were perceived by the burgeoning tourist market as typically "Indian." Soldiers and traders often commissioned their own designs and unusual items such as beaded medical bags, pocketbooks, and saddles. Ladies' magazines and store catalogues containing sewing patterns were eagerly seized upon by Indian

women, who adapted the patterns for their own use. Beaded sets of vests and trousers for boys, size 4–14, appearing in the 1897 Sears, Roebuck catalogue, and similar sets in issues of *Godey's Lady's Book* in the 1870s and 1880s, resemble Indian-made vests and pants of the period.[15]

Nowhere was the appeal to Victorian sensibilities more pronounced than in the "new" beadwork of the Iroquois, known as "embossed beading." Characterized by a dense application of beads resulting in a bas-relief effect, embossed designs tended to cover most of the background with florid motifs in rich but dark Victorian hues. Heavy beaded fringes and the use of translucent and metallic beads added to the feeling of ornamental excess. The purity and clean lines of old-time beadwork had been replaced by fussy accumulations of beads destined for the "what-not" shelf in the Victorian home.

Creek or Seminole bandolier bag sash with elaborate beadwork. The "bandolier" or shoulder bag might have derived from the decorated dearskin pouches worn by the Algonquin tribes before European exploration. Another theory suggests the bandolier bag copied the ditty bags used by British and French soldiers. c. 1840. (Courtesy of William Channing. Photograph, Schecter Lee.)

A strip of deerskin decorated with the geometric beadwork favored by the Sioux. Found in South Dakota, late 19th or early 20th century. 25″ × 33″. (Courtesy of the Museum of the American Indian, Heye Foundation.)

While the people of the Tlingit tribe are better known for outstanding blankets, their beadwork is also spectacular, as shown in this chest ornament or bib representing the killer whale. Worked on trade cloth, it was made between 1890 and 1910 in Alaska. (Courtesy of the Museum of the American Indian, Heye Foundation.)

The border design of this late 19th-century Hopi manta exemplifies
the use of negative space—the background equivalent to the
foreground in design importance—reminiscent of ancient Anasazi
textiles. Mantas were usually worn as wrap-around dresses or shawls.
57″ × 48″. (Courtesy of the School of American Research.)

FIFTEEN

OTHER AMERICAN INDIAN TEXTILES

PUEBLO INDIAN EMBROIDERY

The existence of Pueblo Indian embroidery dates from prehistoric times, making its unique form of decoration a truly indigenous art. Fourteenth-century murals found in Hopi country depict figures wearing kilts with border designs that appear to be embroidered ceremonial garments. During the three centuries of Spanish rule (1540–1846), embroidery flourished. The colonists introduced metal needles and actively encouraged decorative needlework for altar cloths and vestments.[1]

The majority of surviving embroidered garments date from the mid-nineteenth century. Although the weaving of mantas (cloaks or wrap-around dresses), blankets, kilts, belts, and sashes fell to Pueblo men, embroidering (except in Hopi villages) emerged as a female art. Many of the Pueblo made distinctive ceremonial shawls with embroidered geometric designs along the top and bottom edges. These designs included both secular and religious motifs deriving from textiles of the prehistoric era.

In the fifteenth century the Pueblo invented a unique backstitch that paralleled the warp rather than the weft and proved useful for quickly filling in large areas. To a lesser extent the herringbone, outline, and satin stitch were used as adjuncts to the Pueblo backstitch.

While neighboring tribes bartered goods and horses for the prized Pueblo textiles, the white man knew little about them. Unlike the Navajo, who often wore machine-made blankets, saving his own valuable weavings for the trader, the Pueblo Indian kept his most elaborately decorated clothing for himself. In 1879 an anthropologist noted that

247

the manufacture of cotton embroidered ceremonial blankets, dance kilts and sashes . . . white cotton blankets with red and blue borders . . . women's black diagonal cloth dresses . . . and wraps . . . and women's belts was a great industry among the Hopi Indians. The trading of these articles to all the Pueblo tribes from Taos to Isleta dates so far back that there is no knowledge handed down of the time when the Hopi goods were first introduced among the other Pueblos. The Zuni, too . . . carried the women's dresses, wraps and belts to Taos and the other villages.[2]

Both woolen and cotton clothing were embroidered, with early woolen mantas containing the same high quality yarns found in Navajo classic blankets. At Acoma, dark woolen mantas were embroidered with bayeta and indigo-dyed yarns in borders of contrasting colors that enlivened these otherwise somber garments. Spanish-influenced floral motifs are sometimes seen next to prehistoric designs of terraced triangles. Cotton textiles show greater variety in decoration and colors.

After 1880, Hopi dance sashes featured an embroidery known as Hopi brocade, whose technique originated in prehistoric times.[3] Like many Pennsylvania show towels, Hopi sashes were embroidered and fringed at both ends. Colored wefts floating over groups of warps produced an effect resembling traditional brocade. Embroiderers followed prescribed designs, except for a narrow band of brocade separating the decorated area from the plain background. This band became the embroiderer's "signature," bearing a design of his choice.

Twentieth-century Pueblo Indians incorporated Anglo forms of clothing into their lives, but they never abandoned the traditional, pre-Spanish embroidered garments. Although different from the older clothing, in that they are now made of synthetic materials, these garments still retain their distinctive embroidery.

A Navajo manta, c. 1860, that shows a Pan American design influence. The most striking feature of this shawl, which is made of lac-dyed bayeta, three-ply green Saxony, and indigo-dyed fibers, is its pink center formed by recarding and respinning bayeta with white fibers. The diamond-twilled dark blue borders resemble Hopi and Zuñi weaving. 54″ × 38″. (Courtesy of Morningstar Gallery.)

A Hopi man proudly displays two intricately embroidered white cotton mantas. c. 1900. (Courtesy of the Natural History Museum of Los Angeles County. Photograph, A. C. Vroman.)

P art of a Pueblo cotton breech cloth, heavily embroidered with colored yarns. The geometric designs bespeak their prehistoric Anasazi heritage. 20½″ × 16½″. (Courtesy of the School of American Research.)

The Oklahoma Osage were renowned for their skill in sewing "high-fashion" garments. This woolen shawl decorated with silk ribbon appliqués was made in the early 20th century. (Courtesy of the Denver Art Museum. Photograph, Otto Nelson.)

Dolls from the Osage tribe, wearing costumes decorated by typical Osage ribbonwork. Early 20th century. 15″ h. (Courtesy of the Denver Art Museum.)

RIBBON APPLIQUÉ

In 1762, a missionary's account of a Delaware woman's burial included a description of "her leggins lined with ribbons."[4] This cryptic notation is the earliest written reference to one of the most beautiful Indian crafts, known as ribbon appliqué. Eighteenth-century trade lists often include various cloths and woolens, but silk ribbons appear less frequently. In the nineteenth century, ribbons were routinely traded, and certain Woodlands, Plains, and Great Lakes tribes incorporated "European" appliqué techniques into their own designs with the coveted silk ribbons. The fancy for beads, ribbons, and other adornments reflected an appreciation of beauty and fashion by Indians of high rank. In 1850, an Indian chief at Fort Union offered his "good will" for a number of "status symbols": "Let me feel something soft over my shoulders. Bestow some glittering mark on my back, cover my bare head and let something gay appear there, that my young men may know that I am respected at the fort."[5]

Ribbon borders decorated a variety of garments, including blankets, shawls, leggings, moccasins, dance costumes, breech clouts, and shirts. While some ribbons were appliquéd in stripes or simple crisscrosses, other ribbonwork derived from geometric and floral designs found in beadwork and moosehair embroidery. Techniques drew upon traditions found in quillwork and beadwork, employing both curvilinear styles and rectilinear appliqué. It was not uncommon for a 12-inch border to consist of as many as twelve ribbons, each cut, sewn, and appliquéd so as to form overlapping patterns. In geometric ribbonwork the rows of triangles and diamonds somewhat resemble Seminole patchwork.

The elongated diamonds on these Osage breech cloth and leggings
are probably the result of Crow influence. c. 1870. Leggings, 35″ × 9″;
breech cloth, 40″ × 12″. (Courtesy of Morningstar Gallery.)

FIBER BAGS OF THE GREAT LAKES INDIANS

A rich heritage of twined-fiber weaving preceded the colorful woven bags made from wool introduced by the traders in the nineteenth century. For the fabrication of their bags the Great Lakes tribes gathered both vegetal and animal fibers, employing a variety of finger-weaving techniques. By the middle of the eighteenth century cotton twine appeared, supplementing native vegetal yarns. While rougher openwork bags were used for cleaning corn, softer, closely twined bags (usually decorated) were reserved for storing food. Typically, stylized animals and geometric forms competed for attention on opposite panels of the bags.

During the nineteenth century bags of raveled and respun wool yarn gradually replaced those made of hemp and nettle. The choice of wool paralleled the history of Navajo blankets, with native dyes and Saxony yarns giving way to aniline-dyed yarns.[6] It was not unusual to find both natural fibers and commercial yarns in a single bag. A new type of decoration evolved: bright horizontal bands containing geometric elements.

A wider range of color combinations and designs distinguishes late 19th-century Great Lakes utility bags from the earlier natural fiber bags. 15″ × 20″. (Courtesy of William Channing. Photograph, Schecter Lee.)

A woven bag from Oklahoma, made by members of the Sac and Fox tribes. This one represents the mythological Thunder Bird, who ruled the skies and brought storms and great war victories. Twined decorative bags of this type were usually made of nettles, buffalo hair, or various plant stalks. 15½″ × 20″. (Courtesy of the Museum of the American Indian, Heye Foundation.)

An early 19th-century woven bag with panther figures, made by the Menominee tribe in Wisconsin. Most bags of this type have a central decorated panel flanked by vertical bands. 22″ × 15″. (Courtesy of the Museum of the American Indian, Heye Foundation.)

A Seminole woman, resplendent in traditional costume, sewing in Everglades, Florida. This photograph was taken during the 1930s by Deaconess H. M. Bedell, a patron and promoter of Seminole arts. (Courtesy of the Museum of the American Indian, Heye Foundation.)

SEMINOLE PATCHWORK

During the eighteenth and nineteenth centuries the Seminole Indians residing in what is now Florida gave up their buckskin clothing in favor of cooler cottons. They were influenced by the colorful, practical garments of the Scottish Highlanders, who settled in the area as traders, soldiers, and homesteaders. The ruffles and flourishes of English military uniforms also appealed to Seminole sensibilities, inspiring the Indians to adopt an unusual blend of English and Scottish garb. From the Highlanders, Seminole men chose their long trade shirts worn without trousers. The skirtlike kilts of the Highlanders provided freedom of movement and were more suitable than trousers in the swamps.[7] By the middle of the nineteenth century Seminole women began to incorporate ruffles and bands of appliqué on tunics and dresses. When the anthropologist Clay MacCauley visited the Seminoles in 1880, he found the people wearing clothing made of "calico, cotton, ginghams, and sometimes flannels" ornamented by braids and stripes.[8]

The distinctive patchwork patterns that we know today evolved after the introduction of the hand-cranked sewing machine at the turn of the century. Seminole women crowded the trading posts to marvel at the invention that heralded a revolution in tribal clothing. Gratifying their love of ornament, they created a form of patchwork that depended upon the sewing machine. The large bands decorated by appliqué were replaced by strips of geometric designs that resembled patchwork. At first, wide bands of patchwork predominated, but by the 1920s the bands grew smaller and were composed of increasingly complicated patterns. A thriving tourist trade developed; it still exists today. Women sewed alone and in groups for this market, frequently naming their patterns for natural elements such as lightning, rain, trees, and animals.

Seminole patchwork has often been compared with traditional patchwork. Unlike pieced work, Seminole patchwork has always been made from single strips of hand-torn cloth instead of individual pieces of fabric. While a postage stamp quilt might contain three thousand individual 1-inch pieces, a single Seminole skirt can easily contain over four thousand 1-inch pieces.

Seminole designs derive from many sources. Undoubtedly contact with American settlers and runaway slaves (who found a safe haven among the sympathetic Indians) expanded the knowledge of quilting techniques and sewing skills. The bright colors and bold juxtapositions of African origin can be seen in Seminole garments. "Strip quilts," composed of rectangular scraps of fabric pieced together in colorful strips, were made by Southern slaves whose African heritage influenced their choice of color and design. This rich visual tradition is reflected in Seminole patchwork. In spite of these influences many historians feel this work is an indigenous art, the product of the Seminole eye, unlike any other decorative art in America.

A postcard from the 1930s or 1940s showing a Seminole woman at her hand-cranked sewing machine. (Courtesy of Wendy Lavitt.)

SEMINOLE INDIANS AT C
(HOUBL

In this postcard a young Seminole woman displays her handicraft. (Courtesy of Wendy Lavitt.)

An early postcard: a group of women, children, and one man, dressed in their colorful costumes. (Courtesy of Wendy Lavitt.)

NOTES

BIBLIOGRAPHY

INDEX

NOTES

CHAPTER ONE

1 W. R. Cochrane, *History of the Town of Antrim, New Hampshire, From Its Earliest Settlement to June 27, 1877 . . .* (Manchester, N.H., 1880), p. 275.

2 Catherine Fennelly, *Textiles in New England, 1790–1840* (Meriden, Conn.: Meriden Gravure Co., 1961), pp. 14–15.

3 Frances Little, *Early American Textiles* (New York: The Century Co., 1931), p. 78.

4 Quoted in ibid., p. 70.

5 James Birkit, *Some Cursory Remarks Made . . . in His Voyage to North America, 1750–51,* Yale Historical Manuscripts (New Haven, 1916), p. 11. Quoted in *Linen-Making in New England, 1640–1860* (North Andover, Mass.: Merrimack Valley Textile Museum, 1980), p. 15.

6 Bertha S. Dodge, *Tales of Vermont, Ways and People* (Harrisburg, Pa.: Stackpole Books, 1977), p. 50.

7 Kitturah Penton Belknap, quoted in Cathy Luchetti, and Carol Olwell, comps., *Women of the West* (St. George, Utah: Antelope Island Press, 1982), p. 136.

8 Ibid., pp. 141–42.

9 Marguerite Porter Davison, *Pennsylvania German Home Weaving,* Vol. 4 (Plymouth Meeting, Pa.: Mrs. C. Naaman Keyser, 1947), p. 7.

10 Richardson Wright, *Hawkers and Walkers in Early America* (Philadelphia: J. B. Lippincott, 1927), p. 105.

11 Alice Morse Earle, *Home Life in Colonial Days* (New York: The Macmillan Company, 1898), pp. 188–89.

12 Ibid., p. 192.

13 George Flower, *The Western Shepard* (New Harmony, Ind., 1841), pp. 17–18.

14 Luchetti and Olwell, comps., *Women of the West,* p. 138.

15 George J. Cummings, "A Leaf from the Life of a Farmer's Boy Ninety Years Ago," in *Old-Time New England,* January 1929, p. 100.

16 Ellen C. (Hobbs) Rollins, "The Country Store," in *Old-Time New England,* January 1930, p. 124.

17 Almon C. Varney, *Our Homes and Their Adornments* (Detroit: J. C. Chilton, 1882), p. 260.

18 Earle, *Home Life in Colonial Days,* p. 207.

19 Little, *Early American Textiles,* p. 70.

20 Quoted in Florence H. Pettit, *America's Indigo Blues* (New York: Hastings House, 1974), p. 98, and George Francis Dow, *The Arts and Crafts in New England: 1704–1755* (Topsfield, Mass.: The Wayside Press, 1927), p. 161.

21 Aaron Tufts, quoted in *All Sorts of Good Sufficient Cloth: Linen-Making in New England, 1640–1860* (North Andover, Mass.: Merrimack Valley Textile Museum, 1980), p. 24.

22 Quoted in Howard M. Chapin, "Calico Printing Blocks," *The American Collector,* Vol. 4, September 1927, p. 213.

23 Private manuscript by Anthony Arnold, quoted by D. Graeme Keith, "Cotton Printing," in Helen Comstock, ed., *The Concise Encyclopedia of American Antiques* (New York: Hawthorn Books, 1958), p. 299.

24 Ibid., p. 299.

25 *Pennsylvania Gazette*, July 9, 1788, quoted in the *Pennsylvania Museum Bulletin*, 26 (January 1931), p. 27.

26 See Florence H. Pettit, *America's Indigo Blues*, for a detailed account.

27 Florence H. Pettit, "The Printed Textiles of Eighteenth-Century America" (Glenbrook, Conn.: Irene Emery Roundtable on Museum Textiles, 1975 Proceedings, 1976), pp. 45–46.

28 Thomas Cooper, *A Practical Treatise of Dyeing and Callicoe Printing* (Philadelphia: Bobson, 1815), p. 327, quoted in Florence M. Montgomery, *Printed Textiles* (New York: Viking Press, 1970), p. 290.

29 James B. Finley, "Life in the Backwoods," *The Annals of America*, Vol. 8, 1850–57 (New York: Encyclopaedia Britannica, Inc.), p. 295.

30 Genevieve W. West in Kate B. Carter, comp., *Heart Throbs of the West*, Vol. 8 (Salt Lake City: Daughters of Utah Pioneers, 1947), p. 29.

31 Cited by Joanna L. Stratton, *Pioneer Women: Voices from the Kansas Frontier* (New York: Simon & Schuster, 1981), p. 68.

32 Vaughn L. Glasgow, "Textiles of the Louisiana Acadians," *Antiques*, August 1981, p. 339.

33 Ibid., p. 344.

34 Beverly Gordon, *Shaker Textile Arts* (London and Hanover, N.H.: University Press of New England, 1980), p. 41.

35 Prudence Morrell, "Account of a Journey to the West in the Year 1847," edited by Theodore E. Johnson, *Shaker Quarterly*, Summer–Fall 1968, p. 55.

36 J. S. Buckingham, *The Slave States of America*, Vol. 1 (1842), pp. 163–64.

37 *Hands That Built New Hampshire: Spinning and Weaving in New Hampshire*, WPA Writers Program (Brattleboro, Vt.: Stephen Daye Press, 1940), p. 157.

38 *Catalogue of Early American Handicraft*, Brooklyn Museum Press, February 1924 (unpaged).

39 Annie Clark Tanner, *A Mormon Mother* (Salt Lake City, Utah: Tanner Trust Fund, University of Utah Library, 1976), pp. 44–45.

40 St. John Crèvecoeur, *Sketches of Eighteenth Century America*, edited by Henri L. Bourdin, Ralph H. Gabriel, and Stanley T. Williams (New Haven: Yale University Press, 1925), pp. 122–23.

41 Georgiana Brown Harbeson, *American Needlework* (New York: Bonanza Books, 1938), p. 30.

42 Carter, comp., *Heart Throbs of the West*, Vol. 8, p. 23.

43 Pettit, *America's Indigo Blues*, p. 210.

44 Dena S. Katzenberg, *Blue Traditions* (Baltimore: The Baltimore Museum of Art, 1973), p. 12.

45 "About Spinning Wheels," *Harpers' Bazaar*, July 1, 1876, p. 427.

46 Carter, comp., *Heart Throbs of the West*, Vol. 1, p. 297.

47 Ibid., Vol. 9, p. 399.

48 Abbott Lowell Cummings, "Connecticut Homespun," *Antiques*, September 1954, p. 207.

49 Allen H. Eaton, *Handicrafts of the Southern Highlands* (New York: Dover Publications, 1973), p. 142.

CHAPTER TWO

1 Alice Morse Earle, *Customs and Fashions in Old New England* (Rutland, Vt.: Chas. E. Tuttle Co., 1973), p. 118 (reprint of 1893 Scribner's ed.).

2 Sally Garoutte, "Early Colonial Quilts in a Bedding Context," *Uncoverings 1980*, p. 19.

3 Earle, *Customs*, p. 115.

4 Florence Montgomery, *Textiles in America*, p. 336.

5 Peter Thornton, *17th Century Interior Decoration in England, France and Holland* (New Haven, Conn., and London: Yale University Press, 1978), p. 179.

6 Florence Peto, *American Quilts and Coverlets* (New York: Chanticleer Press, 1949), p. 11.

7 Thornton, p. 113.

8 Marion Day Iverson, "The Bed Rug in Colonial America," *Antiques*, Vol. 85, January 1964, p. 107. Linda R. Baumgarten, "The Textile Trade in Boston, 1650–1700," *Arts of the Anglo-American Community in the 17th Century*, pp. 228, 238.

9 *The Workwoman's Guide*, England, 1838, p. 200. Joan Evans has been researching rose blankets, and brought this to our attention.

10 Thornton, p. 113.

11 Montgomery, *Textiles in America*, p. 170, and Marion Day Iverson, "The Bed Rug in Colonial America," *Antiques*, Vol. 85, January 1964, p. 107.

12 Montgomery, p. 18.

13 Susan Burrows Swan, in *American Needlework*, p. 72, says a full set had 6 side curtains, but Florence M. Montgomery, in *Textiles in America, 1650–1870*, p. 18, says there were "4 curtains made wide enough to

enclose the bed and long enough to reach nearly to the floor."

14 H. B. Stowe, quoted in *Textiles in New England, 1790–1840* (Sturbridge, Mass.: Old Sturbridge Village, 1961), pp. 31–32.

15 Helen Maggs Fede, *Washington Furniture at Mt. Vernon* (Virginia: Mt. Vernon Ladies' Association of the Union, 1966), p. 18. Cited in Montgomery, *Textiles in America*, p. 205.

16 Swan, p. 88.

17 Florence Peto, *American Quilts and Coverlets* (New York: Chanticleer Press, 1949), p. 13.

18 Wadsworth Atheneum, *Bed Ruggs/1722–1833* (Hartford, Conn.: Wadsworth Atheneum, 1972), p. 16, and Earle, *Customs*, p. 114.

19 Wadsworth Atheneum, p. 17.

CHAPTER THREE

1 George Francis Dow, *Every Day Life in the Massachusetts Bay Colony* (Boston: SPNEA, 1935), p. 54. Sally Garoutte, in "Early Quilts in a Bedding Context," *Uncoverings, 1980*, records what she found in surveying seventeenth- and early eighteenth-century records of Plymouth, Providence, Hartford, and New Hampshire: of a total of 858 bedding items listed, only ten were quilts. Laurel Horton, in "19th Century Middle Class Quilts in Macon County, N.C.," *Uncoverings, 1983*, p. 93, notes that "in Macon County, as elsewhere during the early 19th century, blankets were cheap and available and quilts were special creations. A woman planning to spend the time and effort to make a quilt was likely also to have gone to the expense to purchase fabric especially for that quilt."

2 Garoutte, pp. 23–24.

3 George F. Dow, *The Arts and Crafts in New England, 1704–1775*, p. 170.

4 Florence M. Montgomery, *Textiles in America, 1650–1870* (New York: W. W. Norton, 1984), p. 279.

5 Mrs. Hersh points out the similarity to floor designs and gives a thorough analysis of the quilt's materials, design, and construction in "Some Aspects of an 1809 Quilt," *Uncoverings, 1982*, pp. 3–12.

6 Sarah Anna Emery, *Reminiscences of a Nonagenarian* (Newburyport, Mass., 1879), p. 32.

7 Patsy and Myron Orlofsky, *Quilts in America* (New York: McGraw-Hill, 1974), p. 208; Montgomery, *Textiles in America*, p. 314.

8 Caroline Howard King, *When I Lived in Salem, 1822–1866* (Brattleboro, Vt., 1937), p. 187.

9 *The Dictionary of Needlework*, 1882 edition, quoted in Orlofsky and Orlofsky, p. 79.

10 Both letters are quoted in Ellen F. Eanes, "Nine Related Quilts of Mecklenburg County, N.C., 1800–1840," *Uncoverings, 1982*, pp. 38 and 40.

11 Johanna Bergen, Kings County, L.I., June 11, 1826, quoted in Florence Peto, *Historic Quilts* (New York: The American Historical Co., 1939), p. 63.

12 Both of these customs are recounted in Peto, *Historic Quilts*, p. 146.

13 Mary E. Wilkins Freeman, in *The People of Our Neighborhood* (Philadelphia: Curtis Publishing Co., 1895), p. 121.

14 Sally Garoutte, in her article on "Early Quilts in a Bedding Context," p. 25, makes the point that the "need" was probably neither economic nor practical, based on her research in colonial wills and inventories.

15 Florence Peto, *American Quilts and Coverlets* (New York: Chanticleer Press, 1949), p. 19.

16 See Averil Colby, *Patchwork* (Newton Centre, Mass.: Charles T. Branford, 1958), pp. 96 and 101.

17 Alice Morse Earle, ed., *Diary of Anna Green Winslow: A Boston Schoolgirl of 1771* (Boston: Houghton Mifflin, 1894), p. 62.

18 Mary E. Wilkins Freeman, "Ann Lizy's Patchwork," in *Young Lucretia and Other Stories* (New York and London: Harper and Bros., 1889), p. 69.

19 Ruth McKendry, *Traditional Quilts and Bedcoverings* (New York: Van Nostrand Reinhold, 1979), p. 88.

20 Quoted in Susan Roach, "The Kinship Quilt," in Rosan A. Jordan and Susan J. Kalcik, eds., *Women's Folklore, Women's Culture* (Philadelphia: University of Pennsylvania Press, 1985), p. 59.

21 Kate B. Carter, comp., *Heart Throbs of the West*, Vol. 9, p. 398.

22 Quoted in C. Kurt Dewhurst, Betty MacDowell, and Marsha MacDowell, *Artists in Aprons* (New York: E. P. Dutton, 1979), p. 100.

23 Peto, *Historic Quilts*, p. xvii.

24 Emery, *Reminiscences of a Nonagenarian*, p. 28.

25 Glenda Riley, *Frontierswomen, The Iowa Experience* (Ames, Iowa: Iowa State University Press, 1981), p. 48.

26 McKendry, *Traditional Quilts and Bedcoverings*, p. 102.

27 Mrs. Matilda Pullan, *The Lady's Manual of Fancy Work* (New York: Dick & Fitzgerald, 1859), p. 95.

28 Miss Florence Hartley, *The Ladies' Hand Book of Fancy and Ornamental Work* (Philadelphia: J. W. Bradley, 1859), quoted in Virginia Gunn, "Victorian

Silk Template Patchwork," *Uncoverings*, *1983*, p. 17.

29 Mary E. Gostelow, ed., *The Complete Guide to Needlework Techniques and Materials* (London: Quill Publishing Co., 1982), p. 72.

30 Dr. William Rush Dunton, Jr., *Old Quilts* (Catonsville, Md.: privately published, 1947), p. 77.

31 *Godey's*, April 1864, p. 396.

32 Dena S. Katzenberg, *The Baltimore Album Quilt* (Baltimore: Baltimore Museum of Art, 1980), p. 64.

33 Ibid., p. 62.

34 Gunn, "Victorian Silk Template Patchwork," *Uncoverings*, *1983*, p. 9.

35 *Godey's*, January 1835, p. 40.

36 Quoted in Gunn, p. 21.

37 Quoted in Penny McMorris, *Crazy Quilts* (New York: E. P. Dutton, 1984), p. 12. This version of the story was told in the British magazine *The Queen* in the 1880s.

38 *Godey's*, May 1883, p. 462.

CHAPTER FOUR

1 Mary E. Gostelow, ed., *The Complete Guide to Needlework Techniques and Materials*, p. 172.

2 Marie Sophie von la Roche, from *Sophie in London*, *1786*, p. 76, quoted in Averil Colby, *Quilting* (New York: Charles Scribner's Sons, 1971), p. 127.

3 Caroline Howard King, *When I Lived in Salem*, *1822–66*, p. 192, quoted in Elisabeth Donaghy Garrett, "The American Home. Pt. III: The Bedchamber," *Antiques*, March 1983, p. 615.

4 Marie D. Webster, *Quilts: Their Story and How to Make Them* (Garden City, N.Y.: Doubleday, Page & Co., 1915), pp. 87–88.

5 Colby, *Quilting*, p. 148.

6 Susan Burrows Swan, *A Winterthur Guide to American Needlework* (New York: Crown, A Winterthur Book, 1976), p. 129.

7 Orlofsky and Orlofsky, *Quilts in America*, p. 184.

8 Sally Garoutte, "Marseilles Quilts and Their Woven Offspring," *Uncoverings*, *1982*, p. 117.

9 Quoted in ibid., pp. 118, 132.

10 Advertisement in *The Commercial Advertiser*, July 3, 1850.

11 Florence Peto, *American Quilts and Coverlets*, p. 23.

12 Jean Taylor Federico, "White Work Classification System," *Uncoverings*, *1980*, p. 69. She notes that "of the dozen embroidered [white work] bedspreads which have family histories in the DAR collection, they are predominantly from Virginia, South Carolina, and Kentucky. None of them is from the North, nor is any of metropolitan origin."

13 Laurel Horton, "Quiltmaking. Traditions in South Carolina," in *Social Fabric: South Carolina's Traditional Quilts* (Columbia, S.C.: University of South Carolina, McKissick Museum, n.d.), p. 160.

CHAPTER FIVE

1 Kate Milner Rabb, *Indiana Coverlets and Coverlet Weavers*, Indiana Historical Publications, Vol. 8, No. 8 (Indianapolis: Indiana Historical Society, 1928), p. 418.

2 Ibid., p. 413.

3 Nancy Dick Bogdonoff, *Handwoven Textiles of Early New England* (Harrisburg, Pa.: Stackpole Books, 1975), p. 53.

4 John W. Heisey, Gail C. Andrews, and Donald R. Walters, *A Checklist of American Coverlet Weavers* (Williamsburg, Va.: Colonial Williamsburg Foundation, 1978), p. 89.

5 Sandra Rambo Walker, *Country Cloth to Coverlets: Textile Traditions in 19th Century Rural Pennsylvania* (University Park, Pa.: Keystone Books, 1981), p. 8.

6 Alexander Hamilton, M.D., *A Gentleman's Progress: Itinerarium of Dr. Alexander Harrison, 1744* (Chapel Hill, N.C.: University of North Carolina Press, 1948), p. 93.

7 Heisey, Andrews, and Walters, p. 78.

8 Eliza Calvert Hall, *A Book of Handwoven Coverlets* (Boston: Little, Brown, 1912), pp. 206–7.

9 Sadye Tune Wilson and Doris Finch Kennedy, *Of Coverlets: The Legacies, The Weavers* (Nashville, Tenn.: Tunstede, 1983), p. 47.

10 Dorothy Sterling, ed., *We Are Your Sisters: Black Women in the Nineteenth Century* (New York: W. W. Norton, 1984), pp. 89–90.

11 Bogdonoff, p. 97.

12 Dorothy K. Burnham, *The Comfortable Arts: Traditional Spinning and Weaving in Canada* (Ottawa, Ontario: National Gallery of Canada, 1981), p. 92.

13 Earl F. Robacker, *Arts of the Pennsylvania Dutch* (New York: A. S. Barnes & Co., 1965), p. 75.

14 See pages 125–29 of *A Checklist of American Coverlet Weavers* for pictorial depictions of trademarks.

15 Patricia T. Herr, "Jacquard Coverlets," *Early American Life*, October 1982, p. 68.

16 Ibid.

17 Gloria Seaman Allen, "Jacquard Coverlets in the Daughters of the American Revolution Museum, Part I: New York Coverlets," *Antiques*, January 1985, p. 294.

18 Mabel Tuke Priestman, *Art and Economy in Home Decoration* (New York: John Lane Company, 1908), p. 122.

CHAPTER SIX

1 B. D. Bargar, ed., "Governor Tryon's House in Fort George," *New York History*, 1954, pp. 301–2.

2 *Treasures of Independence: Independence National Historical Park and Its Collections*, ed. John C. Milley (New York, 1980), quoted by Elisabeth Donaghy Garrett, "The American Home: Part IV: The Dining Room," *Antiques*, October 1984, p. 918.

3 Quoted in Marion Day Iverson, "Table Linen in Colonial America," *Antiques*, November 1959, p. 427.

4 Owned in 1641 by Mrs. Jose Glover of Cambridge, Mass. Ibid., p. 426.

5 Advertisement in *The Connecticut Gazette and the Commercial Intelligencer* (April 11, 1804), p. 2.

6 Quoted in Garrett, p. 917.

7 Elizabeth Warren Curtis, "The Colorful Victorian Tablecloth," *American Collector*, April 1940, p. 11.

8 April 1882, p. 233.

9 Alan G. Keyser, "Beds, Bedding, Bedsteads and Sleep," *The Rainbow (Der Reggeboge)*, Quarterly of the Pennsylvania German Society, October 1978, p. 12.

10 Catharine E. Beecher and Harriet Beecher Stowe, *The American Woman's Home* (New York: J. B. Ford & Company, 1869), p. 359.

11 Florence Hartley, *The Ladies' Hand Book of Fancy and Ornamental Work* (Philadelphia: J. W. Bradley, 1861), pp. 168–69.

12 Beverly Gordon, *Shaker Textile Arts* (Hanover, N.H.: University Press of New England, 1980), p. 93.

13 Jack T. Ericson, "American Pillowcases," *The Clarion*, Winter 1979, p. 36.

14 Keyser, p. 16.

15 Lilian Baker Carlisle, "Pennsylvania German Pillowcases," *Antiques*, April 1969, p. 556.

16 *Decorative Needlework of the Pennsylvania Germans* (catalogue), Hershey Museum of American Life, February 1979, p. 4.

17 Ellen J. Gehret, "O Noble Heart . . .", *The Rainbow (Der Reggeboge)*, July 1980, p. 1.

18 Ellen J. Gehret, *This Is the Way I Pass My Time* (Birdsboro, Penn.: The Pennsylvania German Society, 1985), p. 5.

19 Ibid., p. 11.

20 *Godey's*, February 1871, p. 183.

21 *Peterson's Magazine*, July 1883, p. 82.

22 Beecher and Stowe, p. 309.

23 *The Delineator*, April 1883, p. 244.

CHAPTER SEVEN

1 Caroline Howard King, *When I Lived in Salem, 1822–1866*, p. 155.

2 "Letter from a Brother to a Sister at a Boarding School," *Ladies Magazine*, November 1792, p. 260, quoted in Susan Burrows Swan, *Plain and Fancy* (New York: Holt, Rinehart and Winston, 1977), p. 40.

3 A Lady [Eliza Ware Rotch Farrar], *The Young Lady's Friend* (Boston: American Stationers' Co.; John B. Russell, 1837), p. 122, quoted in Swan, p. 40.

4 *American Samplers* (Boston: Society of the Colonial Dames of America, 1921), p. 105.

5 Emery, *Reminiscences of a Nonagenarian*, p. 21.

6 Susan Burrows Swan, *American Needlework*, p. 64.

7 Advertisement in *The Connecticut Journal*, April 18, 1793, quoted in Glee Krueger, *New England Samplers to 1840* (Sturbridge, Mass.: Old Sturbridge Village, 1978), p. 10.

8 Florence H. Pettit, *America's Printed and Painted Fabrics*, p. 148.

9 Laurel Thatcher Ulrich, *Good Wives. Image and Reality in the Lives of Women in Northern New England, 1650–1750* (New York: Alfred A. Knopf, 1982), p. 34.

10 Mary Gay Humphreys, *Catherine Schuyler* (New York: Charles Scribner's Sons, 1897), p. 73.

11 Quoted in Susan B. Swan, "Worked Pocketbooks," *Antiques*, February 1975, p. 298.

12 Ibid.

13 *The Boston Evening Post*, March 1742, quoted in Nancy Graves Cabot, "Engravings and Embroideries. The Sources of Some Designs in the Fishing Lady Pictures," *Antiques*, December 1941, p. 368. For a detailed discussion of the works in this group, see N. G. Cabot, "The Fishing Lady and Boston Common," *Antiques*, July 1941, pp. 28–31.

14 Ibid., p. 367.

15 *Pennsylvania Gazette*, Dec. 29, 1768, quoted in Swan, *Plain and Fancy*, pp. 233–34.

16 *Columbian Centinel* and the Boston *Independent Chronicle*, March 1803, quoted in Betty Ring, "Mrs. Saunders and Miss Beach's Academy," *Antiques*, August 1976, p. 305.

17 Swan, *Plain and Fancy*, p. 136.

18 Miss Lambert, *The Hand-Book of Needlework* (New York: Wiley & Putnam, 1847), p. 134.

19 Susan Burrows Swan, "Appreciating American Samplers, Part II," *Early American Life*, April 1984, p. 44.

20 Elisabeth Donaghy Garrett, *The Arts of Independence* (Washington, D.C.: The National Society, Daughters of the American Revolution, 1985), p. 78.

21 Betty Ring, *Let Virtue Be a Guide to Thee. Needlework in the Education of Rhode Island Women, 1730–1830* (Providence, R.I.: Rhode Island Historical Society, 1983), p. 37.

22 Swan, "Appreciating American Samplers, Part I," *Early American Life*, February 1984, p. 44.

23 Quoted in Hope Hanley, *Needlepoint in America* (New York: Charles Scribner's Sons, 1969), p. 50.

24 *Nancy Shippen: Her Journal Book*, ed. Ethel Armes (Philadelphia and London: J. B. Lippincott, 1935), pp. 40–41.

25 Quoted in Jane C. Giffen, "Susanna Rowson and Her Academy," *Antiques*, September 1970, p. 439.

26 Ring, *Let Virtue Be a Guide to Thee*, p. 97.

27 Krueger, *New England Samplers*, p. 24.

28 Swan, "Appreciating American Samplers, Part I," p. 45.

29 Krueger, *New England Samplers*, p. 5.

30 Quoted in Garrett, *Arts of Independence*, p. 87. Betty Ring, in "Mrs. Saunders and Miss Beach's Academy," *Antiques*, August 1976, p. 312, notes that students there also made embroidered silk globes, although she knows of no surviving examples made in New England.

31 *South Carolina Gazette* (Charleston), Aug. 1–8, 1754, quoted in Swan, *American Needlework*, p. 89.

32 The *American & Commercial Daily Advertiser* (Baltimore), March 29, 1814, quoted in Davida Tenenbaum Deutsch, "Samuel Folwell of Philadelphia: An Artist for the Needleworker," *Antiques*, February 1981, p. 420.

33 Jane C. Nylander, "Some Print Sources of New England Schoolgirl Art," *Antiques*, August 1976, p. 292.

34 Quoted in ibid., p. 293.

35 *The Young Lady's Book*, (Boston: A. Bowen, and Carter & Hendee), 1830, p. 300.

36 Sylvia Groves, *The History of Needlework Tools and Accessories* (London: Country Life, 1966), p. 25.

37 Betty Ring, *Let Virtue Be a Guide to Thee*, p. 158.

38 "Engravings in Silk: Printwork Embroideries of the Upper Hudson Valley," Exhibition catalogue, Rensselaer County Historical Society, Troy, N.Y., February 1984, n.p.

39 Eliza Southgate Bowne, *A Girl's Life Eighty Years Ago* (New York: Charles Scribner's Sons, 1887), p. 25.

40 Betty Ring, "Mrs. Saunders and Miss Beach's Academy," pp. 305–6.

41 Matthew D. Finn, *Theoremetical System of Painting, or Modern Plan, Fully Explained, in Six Lessons* (New York: James Ryan, 1830), pp. 10–11.

CHAPTER EIGHT

1 Quoted in Virginia Gunn, "Victorian Silk Template Patchwork in American Periodicals, 1850–75," *Uncoverings*, 1983, p. 21.

2 *Godey's*, February 1864, p. 198.

3 *Needle and Brush: Useful and Decorative* (New York: Butterick Publishing Co., 1889), p. 302.

4 Janet Ruutz-Rees, *Home Decoration* (New York: D. Appleton and Co, 1881), p. 87, quoted in Harvey Green, *The Light of the Home* (New York: Pantheon Books, 1983), p. 99.

5 Mrs. Matilda Pullan, *The Lady's Manual of Fancy Work*, pp. 198–200.

6 *Needle and Brush*, p. 34.

7 Mrs. C. S. Jones, quoted in Fred and Mary Fried, *America's Forgotten Folk Arts* (New York: Pantheon Books, 1978), pp. 154–55.

8 Fried and Fried, p. 155.

9 Susan Burrows Swan, *Plain and Fancy*, p. 206.

10 Miss Lambert, *The Hand-Book of Needlework*, p. 38.

11 Hope Hanley, *Needlepoint in America*, p. 81.

12 Florence Hartley, *The Ladies' Hand Book of Fancy and Ornamental Work*, p. 100.

13 Susan Burrows Swan, "Appreciating American Samplers, Part II," *Early American Life*, April 1984, p. 43.

14 Quoted in Evelyn Haertig, *Antique Combs and Purses* (Carmel, Calif.: Gallery Graphics Press, 1983), p. 175.

15 Ibid., p. 185.

16 Mrs. Mary Talbot White, *How to Do Beadwork* (New York: Doubleday, Page & Co., 1904), p. 104.

17 Alice Morse Earle, *Two Centuries of Costume in*

America, 1620–1820 (2 vols., New York, 1903; reprinted, 2 vols., New York: Arno Press, 1968), pp. 593–94.

18 Ellen C. (Hobbs) Rollins, "The Country Store," *Old-Time New England*, January 1930, p. 125.

19 Miss Lambert, *The Hand-Book of Needlework*, p. 248.

20 Diary of Juliana Margret Connor, 1827, Southern Historical Collection, the University of North Carolina Library, Chapel Hill, N.C. Cited by John Bivins, Jr., and Paula Welshimer, *Moravian Decorative Arts in North Carolina* (Winston-Salem, N.C.: Old Salem, Inc., 1981), p. 59.

21 Florence Hartley, *The Ladies' Hand Book of Fancy and Ornamental Work*, p. 25.

22 *Modern Priscilla*, October 1911, p. 47.

23 *House Beautiful*, November 1905, p. 30.

CHAPTER NINE

1 Peter Thornton, *17th Century Interior Decoration in England, France and Holland* (New Haven and London: Yale University Press, 1978), p. 146.

2 George Francis Dow, *The Arts and Crafts in New England, 1704–1775. Gleanings from Boston Newspapers* (Topsfield, Mass.: The Wayside Press, 1927), p. 170.

3 Advertisements in *The Boston News-letter*, 1746 and 1747, quoted in ibid., p. 213.

4 Dec. 13, 1809, quoted in Nina Fletcher Little, *Floor Coverings in New England Before 1850*, p. 22.

5 *Boston Daily Advertiser*, 1816, quoted in Dorothy Swan Malley, "Notes on Floorcloths in New England," *Antiques*, July 1968.

6 B. D. Bargar, ed., "Governor Tryon's House in Fort George," *New York History*, 1954, pp. 301–2.

7 *Annals of Philadelphia and Pennsylvania*, Vol. 1 (New York: Baker & Crane, 1844), p. 205.

8 Little, *Floor Coverings*, p. 29.

9 Joanna L. Stratton, *Pioneer Women: Voices from the Kansas Frontier*, pp. 55–56.

10 The facts about southern Indiana are from an unpublished lecture given by Professor Warren Roberts of the Folklore Institute at Indiana University in Bloomington.

11 Kate B. Carter, comp., *Heart Throbs of the West*, Vol. 2, p. 478.

12 Marion Day Iverson, "The Bed Rug in Colonial America," *Antiques*, January 1964, p. 108.

13 Jane C. Nylander, "The Hearth Rug," *Early American Life*, December 1983, pp. 50–51.

14 Bargar, p. 301.

15 The Rev. Charles M. Hyde, quoted in Little, p. 32.

16 Ella Shannon Bowles, *Handmade Rugs* (Garden City, N.Y.: Garden City Publishing Co., 1937), p. 182. She also quotes Keyes's view of the striped carpet.

17 Joel and Kate Kopp, *American Hooked and Sewn Rugs* (New York: E. P. Dutton, 1975), p. 37.

18 Ibid., p. 90.

19 Quoted in Bowles, p. 17.

20 Helene von Rosenstiel, *American Rugs and Carpets* (New York: William Morrow, 1978), p. 42.

21 *Descriptive Catalogue of E. S. Frost and Co.'s Hooked Rug Patterns* (Dearborn, Mich.: Greenfield Village and Henry Ford Museum, 1970), pp. 4–5.

22 Bowles, pp. 137–38.

23 *Godey's*, May 1854, p. 423.

24 No author or publisher, p. 215.

25 Edward D. and Faith Andrews, *Shaker Furniture: The Craftsmanship of an American Communal Sect* (New Haven: Yale University Press, Dover Publications, 1937), p. 54, quoted in Von Rosenstiel, *American Rugs and Carpets*.

CHAPTER TEN

1 The first phrase is from a poem by Patience Worth. Quoted in Gertrude Whiting, *Tools and Toys of Stitchery* (New York: Columbia University Press, 1928; Dover reprint, 1971, as *Old-Time Tools and Toys of Needlework*), p. 4.

2 "The Dame School," *Old Time New England*, January 1935, p. 104.

3 Quoted in Ella Shannon Bowles, *Homespun Handicrafts* p. 113.

4 Miss Lambert, *The Hand-Book of Needlework*, pp. 89–90.

5 Gay Ann Rogers, *An Illustrated History of Needlework Tools* (London: John Murray, 1983), p. 59.

6 Mrs. Pullan, *The Lady's Manual of Fancywork*, p. 181.

7 Miss Lambert, pp. 90–91.

8 Rogers, pp. 72–73.

9 Barbara Andrews, "Needle Cases," *The Antique Trader Annual of Articles*, Vol. 8, p. 389.

10 Sylvia Groves, *The History of Needlework Tools and Accessories*, p. 26.

11 *Virginia Gazette*, October 27, 1768, quoted in Hope Hanley, *Needlepoint in America*, pp. 42–43.

12 George F. Dow, *Every Day Life in the Massachusetts Bay Colony*, p. 278.

13 Richardson Wright, *Hawkers and Walkers in Early America* (Philadelphia: J. B. Lippincott, 1927), pp. 45–46.

14 Caroline Cowles Richards, *Village Life in America, 1852–1872: As Told in the Diary of a School-Girl*, 1913, reprinted, Williamstown, Mass., 1972. Quoted in Elisabeth Donaghy Garrett, *The Arts of Independence*, pp. 72–73.

15 Whiting, p. 141.

16 Ibid., pp. 150–53. See also Rogers, p. 141.

17 Alice Morse Earle, ed., *Diary of Anna Green Winslow*, p. 12.

18 *Godey's*, January 1860, p. 11.

CHAPTER ELEVEN

1 Hannah Dalton in Kate B. Carter, comp., *Heart Throbs of the West*, Vol. 9, p. 399.

2 Quoted by Ellen J. Gehret, *Rural Pennsylvania Clothing* (York, Pa.: G. Shumway, 1976), p. 225.

3 *Hands That Built New Hampshire: Spinning and Weaving in New Hampshire*, WPA Writers Program, p. 173.

4 Richardson Wright, *Hawkers and Walkers in Early America*, p. 23.

5 Hilda Faunce, *Desert Wife* (Lincoln, Nebr.: University of Nebraska Press, 1928), p. 14.

6 James B. Finley, "Life in the Backwoods," *The Annals of America*, Vol. 8, 1850–57 (New York: Encyclopaedia Britannica, Inc.), p. 296.

7 Robee Beutler Coleman in Carter, comp., *Heart Throbs of the West*, Vol. 2, p. 486.

8 Beverly Gordon, *Shaker Textile Arts* (Hanover, N.H.: University Press of New England, 1980), p. 27.

9 Ibid., p. 43.

10 Ibid., pp. 81–82.

11 Clarissa Young Spencer in Carter, comp., *Heart Throbs of the West*, Vol. 9, p. 331.

12 *Hands That Built New Hampshire*, pp. 172–73.

13 Cited by Catherine Fennelly, *Textiles in New England 1790–1840*, p. 12.

14 Emery, *Reminiscences of a Nonagenarian*, p. 77.

15 Walter L. Fleming, "Home Life in Alabama During the Civil War," *Southern History Association*, March 1904, p. 91.

16 Ibid., p. 97.

17 Charles Avery Amsden, *Navaho Weaving: Its Technic and Its History*, p. 108.

18 *A Winter Gift for Ladies* (G. B. Zieber & Co., 1845), p. 2.

19 Miss A. Lambert, *My Crochet Sampler* (New York: Lowitz, Becker & Cludius, 1849), p. 2.

20 *The Starlight Manual of Knitting and Crocheting* (Boston: Nonantum Worsted Co., 1887), p. 7.

21 Carter, comp., *Heart Throbs of the West*, Vol. 8, p. 21.

22 John Watson, *Annals of Philadelphia and Pennsylvania*, Vol. 1 (New York: Baker & Crane, 1844), p. 186.

23 Francis Morris, "Laces of the American Colonists in the Seventeenth Century," *Needle and Bobbin Club*, 1926, reprinted in *Lace Magazine of the World*, Supplemental Pages, no. 1, January 1981, p. 2.

24 Virginia Churchill Bath, *Needlework in America* (London: Mills & Boon, 1979), p. 16.

25 Zelma Bendure and Gladys Pfeiffer, *America's Fabrics* (New York: The Macmillan Company, 1946), p. 391.

26 Emily Noyes Vanderpoel, *American Lace and Lace-Makers* (New Haven: Yale University Press, 1924), p. 9.

27 Bath, *Needlework in America*, p. 306.

28 Ibid., p. 5.

29 Elise Pinckney, ed., *The Letterbook of Eliza Lucas Pinckney, 1739–1762* (Chapel Hill, N.C.: University of North Carolina Press, 1972), pp. 34–35.

30 Candace Wheeler, *The Development of Embroidery in America* (New York: Harper and Bros., 1921), p. 92.

31 Thomas D. Clark, *Pills, Petticoats and Plows* (Indianapolis and New York: The Bobbs-Merrill Co., 1944), p. 200.

32 Vanderpoel, *American Lace and Lace-Makers*, Plate 70.

33 Kate C. Duncan, "American Indian Lace Making," *American Indian Art Magazine*, Summer 1980, p. 29.

34 Ibid., p. 32.

CHAPTER TWELVE

1 Roy Franklin Nichols, *Franklin Pierce: Young Hickory of the Granite Hills* (Philadelphia: University of Pennsylvania Press, 1958), p. 209.

2 H. J. Blanton, *When I Was a Boy*, quoted by Herbert Ridgeway Collins, *Threads of History* (Washing-

ton, D.C.: Smithsonian Institution Press, 1979), p. 4.

3   Boleslaw and Marie-Louise Mastai, *The Stars and the Stripes* (New York: Alfred A. Knopf, 1973), p. 133.

4   William David Barry and Earle G. Shettleworth, Jr., "Portland, Maine, Trade Banners of 1841," *Antiques*, September 1984, p. 577.

CHAPTER THIRTEEN

1   Frank McNitt, *The Indian Traders* (Norman, Okla.: University of Oklahoma Press, 1962), p. 19.

2   J. T. Hughes, "Doniphan's Expedition," quoted by George Wharton James, *Indian Blankets and Their Makers* (New York: Dover Publications, 1974), p. 21.

3   McNitt, p. 210.

4   Joe Ben Wheat, "The Navajo Chief Blanket," *American Indian Art Magazine*, Summer 1976, p. 46.

5   Charles Avery Amsden, *Navaho Weaving: Its Technic and Its History*, p. 147.

6   Charles F. Lummis, *Some Strange Corners of Our Country*, quoted in James, p. 25.

7   Amsden, *Navaho Weaving*, Plate 99.

8   J. J. Brody, *Between Traditions* (Iowa City: Stamats Publishing Co. for the University of Iowa Museum of Art, 1976), unpaged catalogue.

9   Frederick H. Douglas, *Unpublished Field Notes, 1935–38*, quoted by Kate Peck Kent, *Pueblo Indian Textiles: A Living Tradition* (Santa Fe, N.M.: School of American Research Press, 1983), p. 15.

10   McNitt, p. 222.

11   Lieutenant J. H. Simpson, "Report on the Navaho Country," quoted by James, pp. 21–22.

12   Amsden, p. 213.

13   James, pp. 139–40.

14   Juan Lorenzo Hubbell, "Fifty Years an Indian Trader," *Touring Topics* (December 1939), quoted in Anthony Berlant and Mary Hunt Kahlenberg, *Walk in Beauty* (New York Graphic Society, 1977), p. 114.

15   McNitt, p. 254.

16   Berlant and Kahlenberg, p. 19.

17   G. T. Emmons, "The Chilkat Blanket," *Memoir of the American Museum of Natural History*, Vol. 3, part 4, 1907, p. 346.

18   Cheryl Samuel, *The Chilkat Dancing Blanket* (Seattle, Wash.: Pacific Search Press, 1982), p. 35.

19   J. Russell Harper, *Paul Kane's Frontier* (Austin, Tex.: University of Texas Press, 1971), p. 107.

20   Erna Gunther, *Art in the Life of the Northwest Coast Indian* (Portland, Ore.: Portland Art Museum, 1966), p. 77.

21   Ibid., p. 83.

22   Suzanne Yabsley, "Appliqué Button Blankets in Northwest Coast Indian Culture," *Uncoverings*, 1983, p. 44.

23   E. E. Blomkvist, Basil Dmytryshyn, and E. A. P. Crownhart-Vaughn, "A Russian Scientific Expedition to California and Alaska, 1839–1849," *Oregon Historical Quarterly*, No. 36, 1972, p. 150.

CHAPTER FOURTEEN

1   Daniel W. Harmon, *Sixteen Years in the Indian Country* (Toronto: Macmillan, 1957), p. 236.

2   Julia M. Bebbington, *Quillwork of the Plains* (Calgary, Alberta: Glenbow Museum, 1982), p. 14.

3   Beverly Hungry Wolf, *The Ways of My Grandmothers* (New York: William Morrow, 1980), p. 241.

4   Ibid., p. 243.

5   Bebbington, p. 16.

6   Daniel W. Harmon, *A Journal of Voyages and Travels in the Interior of North America*, edited by D. Haskel, Flagg, and Gould (Andover, Mass., 1820), pp. 377–78.

7   James A. Maxwell, ed., *America's Fascinating Indian Heritage* (Pleasantville, N.Y.: The Reader's Digest Association, 1978), p. 173.

8   Richard E. Flanders, "Beads in the Upper Great Lakes: A Study in Acculturation," *Beads: Their Use by Upper Great Lakes Indians* (Grand Rapids, Mich.: Grand Rapids Public Museum, 1981), p. 11.

9   Ibid., p. 11.

10   Beverly Hungry Wolf, *The Ways of My Grandmothers*, pp. 244–45.

11   Frances Densmore, "Chippewa Customs," *Bureau of American Ethnology Bulletin 86* (Washington, D.C.: Smithsonian Institution Press, 1929), p. 62.

12   Truman Michaelson, "The Autobiography of a Fox Woman," *U.S. Bureau of Ethnology 40* (Washington, D.C.: Government Printing Office, 1925), p. 303.

13   Frances Densmore, "Uses of Plants by the Chippewa Indians," *U.S. Bureau of Ethnology Annual Report 44* (Washington, D.C.: Government Printing Office, 1928), p. 390.

14   Emma Shaw Colcleugh quoted by Barbara A. Hail, *Hau, Kola!* (Bristol, R.I.: Eastern Press, 1980), p. 222.

15   Hail, *Hau, Kola!*, p. 84.

CHAPTER FIFTEEN

1 Kate P. Kent, "Pueblo Weaving," *American Indian Art Magazine,* Winter 1981, p. 35.

2 Matilda Coxe Stevenson, "Dress and Adornment of the Pueblo Indians," Bureau of American Ethnology manuscript (Washington, D.C.: Smithsonian Institution Press, n.d.), p. 118.

3 Richard Conn, *Native American Art in the Denver Art Museum* (Seattle, Wash.: University of Washington Press, 1979), p. 186.

4 Alice Marriot, "Ribbon Appliqué Work of North American Indians, Part I," *Bulletin of the Oklahoma Anthropological Society,* Vol. 6, March 1958, p. 58.

5 Mary Jane Schneider, "Plains Indian Clothing: Stylistic Persistence and Change," *Bulletin of the Oklahoma Anthropological Society,* Vol. 17, November 1968, p. 23.

6 Andrew Hunter Whiteford, "Fiber Bags of the Great Lakes Indians, Part II," *American Indian Art Magazine,* Winter 1977, p. 40.

7 Dorothy Downs, "British Influences on Creek and Seminole Clothing, 1733–1858," *Florida Anthropologist Society,* Vol. 33, 1980, p. 53.

8 Hilda J. Davis, "The History of Seminole Clothing and Its Multi-Colored Designs," *American Anthropologist,* Vol. 57, 1955, p. 974.

BIBLIOGRAPHY

Amsden, Charles Avery. *Navaho Weaving, Its Technic and Its History.* Glorieta, N.M.: The Rio Grande Press, 1934.

Andrews, Barbara. "Needle Cases." *Antique Trader Annual of Articles,* Vol. 8.

Andrews, Charles M. *Colonial Folkways: A Chronicle of American Life in the Reign of the Georges.* New Haven, Conn.: Yale University Press, 1919.

Annals of Philadelphia and Pennsylvania. Vol. I, New York: Baker & Crane, 1844.

Arthur, T. S. "The Quilting Party." *Godey's,* September 1849.

The Arts of Independence. Washington, D.C.: The National Society, Daughters of the American Revolution, 1985.

Atwater, Mary Meigs. *The Shuttlecraft Book of American Handweaving.* New York: The Macmillan Company, 1935.

Barbeau, Marius. "From Gold Threads to Porcupine Quills." *Antiques,* January 1944.

Bargar, B. D., ed. "Governor Tryon's House in Fort George." *New York History,* 1954.

Bath, Virginia Churchill. *Needlework in America.* London: Mills & Boon, Ltd., 1979.

Baumgarten, Linda R. "The Textile Trade in Boston, 1650–1700," in Quimby, Ian M. G., ed., *Arts of the Anglo-American Community in the 17th Century.* Charlottesville, Va.: University Press of Virginia, 1975.

——. *Beads: Their Use by Upper Great Lakes Indians.* Grand Rapids, Mich.: Grand Rapids Public Museum, 1981.

Bebbington, Julia M. *Quillwork of the Plains.* Calgary, Alberta: Glenbow Museum, 1982.

Beecher, Catharine E., and Stowe, Harriet Beecher. *The American Woman's Home.* New York: J. B. Ford & Company, 1869.

Bendure, Zelma, and Pfeiffer, Gladys. *America's Fabrics.* New York: The Macmillan Company, 1946.

Berlant, Anthony, and Kahlenberg, Mary Hunt. *Walk in Beauty: The Navajo and Their Blankets.* Boston: New York Graphic Society, 1977.

Birrell, Verla. *The Textile Arts.* New York: Harper & Row, 1959.

Bogdonoff, Nancy Dick. *Handwoven Textiles of Early New England.* Harrisburg, Pa.: Stackpole Books, 1975.

Bolton, Ethel Stanwood, and Coe, Eva Johnston. *American Samplers.* Boston: Massachusetts Society of the Colonial Dames of America, 1921.

Bonfield, Lynn A. "The Production of Cloth, Clothing and Quilts in 19th Century New England Homes." *Uncoverings,* 1981. Mill Valley, Calif.: American Quilt Study Group, 1982.

Bowles, Ella Shannon. *Handmade Rugs.* Garden City, N.Y.: Garden City Publishing Co., 1937 (first published 1927).

——. *Homespun Handicrafts.* Philadelphia and London: J. B. Lippincott, 1931.

Bowne, Eliza Southgate. *A Girl's Life Eighty Years Ago: Selections from the Letters of Eliza Southgate Bowne.* New York: Charles Scribner's Sons, 1887.

Brett, K. B. "Bouquets and Flower Arrangements in Textiles." *Antiques,* April 1955.

Brightman, Anna. "Woolen Window Curtains." *Antiques*. December 1964.

Brody, J. J. *Between Traditions: Navajo Weaving Toward the End of the Nineteenth Century*. Iowa City: Stamats Publishing Company, 1976.

Brooklyn Institute of Arts and Sciences. Catalogue of Early American Handicraft comprising costumes, quilts, coverlets, samplers, laces, embroideries, and other related objects; opening February 4, 1924. Brooklyn, N.Y.: Brooklyn Museum Press, 1924.

Bullard, Lacy Folmar, and Shiell, Betty Jo. *Chintz Quilts: Unfading Glory*. Tallahassee, Fla.: Serendipity Publishers, 1983.

Burnham, Harold B., and Burnham, Dorothy K. *Keep Me Warm One Night*. Toronto: University of Toronto Press, 1972.

Cabot, Nancy Graves. "The Fishing Lady and Boston Common." *Antiques*, July 1941.

Campbell, Juliet H. L. "What Becomes of the Pins," *Godey's*, October 1849.

Carlisle, Lilian Baker. "Pennsylvania German Pillowcases." *Antiques*, April 1969.

Carter, Kate B., comp. *Heart Throbs of the West*. 12 vols. Salt Lake City, Utah: Daughters of Utah Pioneers, 1940–51.

———. *Treasures of Pioneer History*. 6 vols. Salt Lake City, Utah: Daughters of Utah Pioneers, 1952–62.

Cerney, Charlene. "Navajo Pictorial Weaving." *American Indian Art* magazine, Winter 1976.

Chapin, Howard. "Calico Printing Blocks." *The American Collector*, September 1927.

Clark, Raymond B., Jr. "Historical Handkerchiefs." *New York History*, April 1955.

Clark, Thomas D. *Pills, Petticoats and Plows*. Indianapolis and New York: The Bobbs-Merrill Co., 1944.

Colby, Averil. *Patchwork*. Newton Centre, Mass.: Charles T. Branford, 1958.

Collins, Herbert Ridgeway. *Threads of History*. Washington, D.C.: Smithsonian Institution Press, 1979.

Conn, Richard. *Native American Art in the Denver Art Museum*. Seattle, Wash.: University of Washington Press, 1979.

Cooper, Grace Rogers. *The Copp Family Textiles*. Washington, D.C.: Smithsonian Institution Press, 1971.

Cummings, Abbott Lowell. "Connecticut Homespun." *Antiques*, September 1954.

Curtis, Elizabeth Warren. "The Colorful Victorian Tablecloth." *American Collector*, April 1940.

Davis, Hilda. "The History of Seminole Clothing and Its Multi-Colored Designs." *American Anthropologist*, Vol. 57, 1955.

Davis, Mildred J. *Early American Embroidery Designs*. New York: Crown, 1969.

———. *The Art of Crewel Embroidery*. New York: Crown, 1962.

Davison, Marguerite Porter. *Pennsylvania German Home Weaving*. Vol. 4. Plymouth Meeting, Pa.: Mrs. C. Naaman Keyser, 1947.

Davison, Mildred. "Hand-woven Coverlets in the Art Institute of Chicago." *Antiques*, May 1970.

———, and Mayer-Thurman, Christa C. *Coverlets*. Chicago: Art Institute of Chicago, 1973.

Dedera, Don. *Navajo Rugs*. Flagstaff, Ariz.: Northland Press, 1975.

Densmore, Frances. "Chippewa Customs." *Bureau of American Ethnology Bulletin 86*, Washington, D.C.: Smithsonian Institution Press, 1929.

Deutsch, Davida Tenenbaum. "Samuel Folwell of Philadelphia: An Artist for the Needleworker." *Antiques*, February 1981.

Dewhurst, C. Kurt, MacDowell, Betty, and MacDowell, Marsha. *Artists in Aprons*. New York: E. P. Dutton, 1979.

Dillmont, Thérèse de. *Encyclopedia of Needlework*. Mulhouse, France, n.d.

Dow, George Francis. *The Arts and Crafts in New England: 1704–1775*. Topsfield, Mass.: The Wayside Press, 1927.

———. *Every Day Life in the Massachusetts Bay Colony*. Boston: SPNEA, 1935.

Downs, Dorothy. "The Art of the Florida Indians." Exhibition Catalogue from the Lowe Art Museum, 1976.

———. "British Influences on Creek and Seminole Men's Clothing." *Florida Anthropologist Society*, 1980.

———. "Patchwork Clothing of the Florida Indians." *American Indian Art Magazine*, Summer 1979.

Duncan, Kate C. "American Indian Lace Making." *American Indian Art Magazine*, Summer 1980.

Dunton, William Rush, Jr. *Old Quilts*. Catonsville, Md., 1947 (published by the author).

Eanes, Ellen F. "Nine Related Quilts of Mecklenburg County, N.C." *Uncoverings*, 1982. Mill Valley, Calif.: American Quilt Study Group, 1983.

Earle, Alice Morse. *Costume of Colonial Times*. New York: Charles Scribner's Sons, 1894.

———. *Customs and Fashions in Old New England.*

Rutland, Vt.: Charles E. Tuttle, 1973 (reprint of 1893 Scribner's edition).

——. *Diary of Anna Green Winslow: A Boston School Girl of 1771.* Boston: Houghton Mifflin, 1894. Reprinted Williamstown, Mass.: Corner House Publishers, 1974.

——. *Two Centuries of Costume in America, 1620–1820.* 2 vols. New York: The Macmillan Company, 1903. Reprinted, 2 vols., New York: Arno Press, 1968.

Eaton, Allen H. *Handicrafts of the Southern Highlands.* New York: Dover Publications, 1973.

Emery, Sarah Anna. *Reminiscences of a Nonagenarian.* Newburyport, Mass.: William H. Huse & Co., Printers, 1879.

Ericson, Jack T. "American Pillowcases." *The Clarion,* Winter 1979.

Ewers, John C. *Blackfeet Crafts.* Vol. 9. Washington, D.C.: U.S. Office of Indian Affairs, 1945.

Federico, Jean Taylor. "White Work Classification System." *Uncoverings, 1980.* Mill Valley, Calif.: American Quilt Study Group, 1981.

Fennelly, Catherine. *Textiles in New England, 1790–1840.* Meriden, Conn.: Meriden Gravure Co., 1961.

——. *The Garb of Country New Englanders, 1790–1840.* Meriden, Conn.: Meriden Gravure Co., 1966.

Field, June. *Collecting Georgian and Victorian Crafts.* New York: Charles Scribner's Sons, 1973.

Finley, Ruth E. *Old Patchwork Quilts and the Women Who Made Them.* Newton Centre, Mass.: Charles T. Branford, 1957 (reprint of 1929 edition).

Finn, Matthew D. *Theoremetical System of Painting, or Modern Plan, Fully Explained, in Six Lessons.* New York: James Ryan, 1830.

Fiske, Patricia L., ed. *Imported and Domestic Textiles in Eighteenth Century America.* Proceedings of the 1975 Irene Emery Roundtable on Museum Textiles. Washington, D.C.: Textile Museum, 1975.

Fitzrandolph, Mavis. *Traditional Quilting: Its Story and Its Practice.* London: B. T. Batsford, 1954.

Freeman, Mary E. Wilkins. "A Quilting Bee in Our Village." *The People of Our Neighborhood.* Philadelphia: Curtis Publishing Co., 1895.

Fried, Fred and Mary. *America's Forgotten Folk Arts.* New York: Pantheon Books, 1978.

Frost, S. Annie. *The Ladies Guide to Needlework and Embroidery.* New York: Henry T. Williams, 1877.

Gallagher, Constance Dann. *Linen Heirlooms.* Newton Centre, Mass.: Charles T. Branford, 1968.

Gallagher, Dorothy. *Hannah's Daughters: Six Generations of an American Family, 1876–1976.* New York: Thomas Y. Crowell, 1975.

Garoutte, Sally. "Early Quilts in a Bedding Context." *Uncoverings, 1980.* Mill Valley, Calif.: American Quilt Study Group, 1981.

——. "Marseilles Quilts and Their Woven Offspring." *Uncoverings, 1982.* Mill Valley, Calif.: American Quilt Study Group, 1983.

Garrett, Elisabeth Donaghy. "The American Home, Part III: The Bedchamber." *Antiques,* March 1983.

Gehret, Ellen J. "O Noble Heart . . . An examination of a motif of design from Pennsylvania German embroidered hand towels." *Der Reggeboge (The Rainbow),* July 1980.

——. *Rural Pennsylvania Clothing.* York, Pa.: G. Shumway, 1976.

——, and Keyser, Alan G. *The Homespun Textile Tradition of the Pennsylvania Germans.* Harrisburg, Pa.: Historical and Museum Commission, 1976.

——. *This Is the Way I Pass My Time.* Birdsboro, Pa.: The Pennsylvania German Society, 1985.

Giffen, Jane. "Susanna Rowson and Her Academy." *Antiques,* September 1970.

Glasgow, Vaughn L. "Textiles of the Louisiana Acadians." *Antiques,* August 1981.

Godey's Lady's Book. Philadelphia: Louis A. Godey, 1830–98.

Gordon, Beverly. *Shaker Textile Arts.* London and Hanover, N.H.: University Press of New England, 1980.

Gostelow, Mary, ed. *Complete Guide to Needlework.* London: Quill Publishing Co., 1982.

Green, Harvey. *The Light of the Home.* New York: Pantheon Books, 1983.

Groves, Sylvia. *The History of Needlework Tools and Accessories.* London: Country Life, 1966.

Gunn, Virginia. "Victorian Silk Template Patchwork in American Periodicals, 1850–1875." *Uncoverings, 1983.* Mill Valley, Calif.: American Quilt Study Group, 1984.

Gunther, Erna. *Art in the Life of the Northwest Coast Indian.* Portland, Ore.: Portland Art Museum, 1966.

Haertig, Evelyn. *Antique Combs and Purses.* Carmel, Calif.: Gallery Graphics Press, 1983.

Hail, Barbara A. *Hau, Kóla!* Bristol, R.I.: Eastern Press, 1980.

Hall, Carrie A., and Kretsinger, Rose G. *The Romance of the Patchwork Quilt in America.* Caldwell,

Idaho: The Caxton Printers, Ltd., 1935. (Reprinted by Bonanza Books.)

Hall, Eliza Calvert. *A Book of Hand-Woven Coverlets*. Rutland, Vt.: Charles E. Tuttle, 1966 (reprint of 1912 edition).

Hands That Built New Hampshire: Spinning and Weaving in New Hampshire. WPA Writers Program. Brattleboro, Vt.: Stephen Daye Press, 1940.

Hanley, Hope. *Needlepoint in America*. New York: Charles Scribner's Sons, 1969.

Harbeson, Georgiana Brown. *American Needlework*. New York: Bonanza Books, 1938.

Hartley, Florence. *The Ladies' Hand Book of Fancy and Ornamental Work*. Philadelphia: J. W. Bradley, 1861.

Heisey, John W., Andrews, Gail C., and Walters, Donald R. *Checklist of American Coverlet Weavers*. Williamsburg, Va.: Colonial Williamsburg Foundation, 1978.

Herr, Patricia T. "Jacquard Coverlets." *Early American Life*. October 1982.

Hersh, Tandy. "Some Aspects of an 1809 Quilt." *Uncoverings, 1982*. Mill Valley, Calif.: American Quilt Study Group, 1983.

Holm, Bill. *Crooked Beak of Heaven*. Seattle, Wash.: University of Washington Press, 1972.

———. "A Working Mantle Neatly Wrought: The Early Historic Record of Northwest Coast Pattern-Twined Textiles—1774–1850." *American Indian Art Magazine*, Winter 1982.

Holmes, Margaret. "American Weavers: Their Problems and Their Growth." *DAR Magazine*, December 1979.

Homespun to Factory-Made: Woolen Textiles in America, 1776–1876. North Andover, Mass.: Merrimack Valley Textile Museum, 1977.

Horton, Laurel. "Quiltmaking Traditions in South Carolina." *Social Fabric: South Carolina's Traditional Quilts*. Columbia, S.C.: University of South Carolina, McKissick Museum, n.d.

Houck, Shirley. *The Delhi Jacquard Coverlets*. Walton, N.Y.: The Reporter Company, 1982.

Humphreys, Mary Gay. *Catherine Schuyler*. New York: Charles Scribner's Sons, 1897.

Hungry Wolf, Beverly. *The Ways of My Grandmothers*. New York: William Morrow, 1980.

Irwin, John. "Origins of 'Oriental' Chintz Design." *Antiques*, January 1959.

Iverson, Marion Day. "Table Linen in Colonial America." *Antiques*, November 1959.

———. "The Bed Rug in Colonial America." *Antiques*, January 1964.

James, George Wharton. *Indian Blankets and Their Makers*. New York: Dover Publications, 1974.

Katzenberg, Dena S. *And Eagles Sweep Across the Sky*. Baltimore: The Baltimore Museum of Art, 1977.

———. *The Baltimore Album Quilt*. Baltimore: The Baltimore Museum of Art, 1980.

Kent, Kate Peck. *Pueblo Indian Textiles: A Living Tradition*. Santa Fe, N.M.: School of American Research Press, 1983.

———. *The Story of Navajo Weaving*. Phoenix, Ariz.: McGrew Printing and Lithographing Co., 1961.

King, Caroline Howard. *When I Lived in Salem, 1822–1866*. Brattleboro, Vt., 1937.

Kolodny, Annette. *The Land Before Her*. Chapel Hill, N.C.: The University of North Carolina Press, 1984.

Kopp, Joel and Kate. *American Hooked and Sewn Rugs*. New York: E. P. Dutton, 1975.

Krueger, Glee. *New England Samplers to 1840*. Sturbridge, Mass.: Old Sturbridge Village, 1978.

———. *A Gallery of New England Samplers*. New York: E. P. Dutton, 1978.

Lambert, Miss A. *My Crochet Sampler*. New York: Lowitz, Becker & Cludius, 1849.

———. *The Hand-Book of Needlework*. New York: Wiley & Putnam, 1847.

———. *The Ladies' Complete Guide to Needle-work and Embroidery*. Philadelphia: T. B. Peterson & Bros., 1859.

Lefevre, Edwin. "American Exposition Handkerchiefs." *American Collector*, October 1938.

———. "Washington Historical Kerchiefs." *Antiques*, July 1939.

Lewittes, Esther. "A Mexican 18th Century Wool Rug." *Antiques*, April 1955.

Little, Frances. *Early American Textiles*. New York and London: The Century Co., 1931.

Little, Nina Fletcher. *Floor Coverings in New England Before 1850*. Sturbridge, Mass.: Old Sturbridge Village.

Luchetti, Cathy, and Olwell, Carol, comps. *Women of the West*. St. George, Utah: Antelope Island Press, 1982.

Lyford, Carrie A. *Iroquois Crafts*. Vol. 6. Washington, D.C.: U.S. Office of Indian Affairs, 1945.

———. *Quill and Beadwork of the Western Sioux*. Vol. 1. Washington, D.C.: U.S. Office of Indian Affairs, 1940.

Lyman, Lila Parrish. "Knitting: a Little-Known Field for Collectors." *Antiques*, April 1942.

Macswiggan, Amelia. "Bead Embroidery." *The Antiques Journal*, July 1971.

Malley, Dorothy Swan. "Notes on Floor Cloths in New England." *Antiques*, July 1968.

Marein, Shirley. *Flowers in Design.* New York: Viking Press Studio Book, 1977.

Markoe, William. *The Historical Development of the American Flag.* Washington, D.C.: Public Affairs Press, 1952.

Maxwell, Gilbert. *Navajo Rugs.* Palm Desert, Calif.: Desert-Southeast, Inc., 1963.

McKendry, Ruth. *Traditional Quilts and Bedcoverings.* New York: Van Nostrand Reinhold, 1979.

McMorris, Penny. *Crazy Quilts.* New York: E. P. Dutton, 1984.

McNitt, Frank. *The Indian Traders.* Norman, Okla.: University of Oklahoma Press, 1962.

Michie, Audrey. "Charleston Textile Imports, 1738–1742." *Journal of Early Southern Decorative Arts*, May 1981.

Montgomery, Florence M. *Printed Textiles—English and American Cottons and Linens—1700–1850.* New York: Viking Press, 1970.

——. *Textiles in America, 1650–1870.* New York: W. W. Norton, 1984.

Montgomery, Pauline. *Indiana Coverlet Weavers and Their Coverlets.* Indianapolis: Hoosier Heritage Press, 1974.

Morris, Francis. "Laces of the American Colonists in the Seventeenth Century." *Needle and Bobbin Club*, 1926, reprinted in *Lace Magazine of the World*, Supplemental Pages, no. 1, January 1981.

Murray, Anne Wood. "The Elegant Handkerchiefs." *Antiques*, June 1965.

Needle & Brush: Useful and Decorative. Metropolitan Art Series. New York: Butterick Publishing Co., 1889.

Nylander, Jane C. "The Hearth Rug." *Early American Life*, December 1983.

——. "Some Print Sources of New England Schoolgirl Art." *Antiques*, August 1976.

Orchard, William C. *Beads and Beadwork of the American Indians.* New York: Museum of the American Indian, Heye Foundation, 1975.

Orlofsky, Patsy and Myron. *Quilts in America.* New York: McGraw-Hill, 1974.

Parker, Rozsika, and Pollock, Griselda. *Old Mistresses: Women, Art & Ideology.* London: Routledge & Kegan Paul, 1981, and New York: Pantheon Books, 1981.

Parslow, Virginia. "James Alexander, Weaver." *Antiques*, April 1956.

"The Patchwork School," in *The Pot of Gold and Other Stories.* Boston: D. Lothrop, 1892.

Peto, Florence. *Historic Quilts.* New York: The American Historical Co., 1939.

——. *American Quilts and Coverlets.* New York: Chanticleer Press, 1949.

Pettit, Florence H. *America's Indigo Blues.* New York: Hastings House, 1974.

——. *America's Printed and Painted Fabrics.* New York: Hastings House, 1970.

Pohrt, Richard. "The Indian and the American Flag." *American Indian Art* magazine, Spring 1976.

Pullan, Mrs. Matilda. *The Ladies Keepsake, or Treasures of the Needle.* London: Darton & Co., 1851.

——. *The Lady's Manual of Fancy Work.* New York: Dick & Fitzgerald, 1859.

Riley, Glenda. *Frontierswomen. The Iowa Experience.* Ames, Iowa: Iowa State University Press, 1981.

Ring, Betty. *Let Virtue Be a Guide to Thee.* Providence, R.I.: Rhode Island Historical Society, 1983.

——. "Mrs. Saunders and Miss Beach's Academy." *Antiques*, August 1976.

——. "Needlework Pictures at Bassett Hall." *Antiques*, February 1982.

Roach, Susan. "The Kinship Quilt." *Women's Folklore, Women's Culture.* Philadelphia: University of Pennsylvania Press, 1985.

Rodee, Marian E. "Multiple Pattern Germantown Rugs." *Indian Art Magazine*, Summer 1978.

Rogers, Gay Ann. *An Illustrated History of Needlework Tools.* London: John Murray, 1983.

Rogers, Madeline. "Jacquard Coverlets: Where Genealogy and Textiles Meet." *American Art and Antiques*, January–February, 1979.

Rush, Beverly, with Whitman, Lassie. *The Complete Book of Seminole Patchwork.* Seattle, Wash.: Madrona Publishers, 1982.

Safford, Carleton L., and Bishop, Robert. *American Quilts and Coverlets.* New York: Weathervane Books, 1974.

Samuel, Cheryl. *The Chilkat Dancing Blanket.* Seattle, Wash.: Pacific Search Press, 1982.

Schneider, Mary Jane. "Plains Indian Clothing: Stylistic Persistence and Change." *Oklahoma Anthropological Society*, November 1968.

Schoelwer, Susan Prendergast. "Form, Function and

Meaning in the Use of Fabric Furnishings: A Philadelphia Case Study, 1700–1775." *Winterthur Portfolio,* Spring 1979.

Schorsch, Anita, ed. *Art of the Weaver.* New York: Universe Books, 1976.

Scoon, Carol. "A Fine Collection of Historical Textiles." *American Collector.* September 1947.

Nancy Shippen. Her Journal Book. Ed. Ethel Armes. Philadelphia and London: J. B. Lippincott, 1935.

Sickels, Elizabeth Galbraith. "Thimblemakers in America." *Antiques,* September 1967.

Standard, Mary Newton. *Colonial Virginia: Its People and Customs.* Philadelphia: J. B. Lippincott, 1917.

Stearns, Bertha M. "Early New England Magazines for Ladies." *New England Quarterly,* July 1929.

Sterling, Dorothy, ed. *We Are Your Sisters: Black Women in the Nineteenth Century.* New York: W. W. Norton, 1984.

Straight Tongue: Minnesota-Indian Art from the Bishop Whipple Collections. Exhibition Catalogue of the Science Museum of Minnesota. St. Paul, 1981.

Stratton, Joanna L. *Pioneer Women: Voices from the Kansas Frontier.* New York: Simon & Schuster, 1981.

Stribling, Mary Low. *Crafts from North American Indian Arts.* New York: Crown, 1975.

Swan, Susan Burrows. *A Winterthur Guide to American Needlework.* New York: Crown, a Winterthur Book, 1976.

———. *Plain and Fancy. American Women and Their Needlework, 1700–1850.* New York: Holt, Rinehart and Winston, 1977.

———. "Worked Pocketbooks." *Antiques,* February 1975.

———. "Appreciating American Samplers—Parts I and II." *Early American Life,* February and April 1984.

Textiles in New England, 1790–1840. Sturbridge, Mass.: Old Sturbridge Village, 1961.

Thornton, Peter. *17th Century Interior Decoration in England, France and Holland.* New Haven and London: Yale University Press, 1978.

Tillotson, Harry Stanton. *The Exquisite Exile, The Life and Fortunes of Mrs. Benedict Arnold.* New York: Lothrop, Lee & Shepard Co., 1932.

Ulruch, Laurel Thatcher. *Good Wives. Image and Reality in the Lives of Women in Northern New England, 1650–1750.* New York: Alfred A. Knopf, 1982.

Vanderpoel, Emily Noyes. *American Lace and Lace-Makers.* New Haven: Yale University Press, 1924.

Varney, Almon C. *Our Homes and Their Adornments.* Detroit: J. C. Chilton, 1882.

Vollmer, John E., Keall, E. J., and Nagai-Berthrong, E. *Silk Roads. China Ships.* Toronto: Royal Ontario Museum, 1983.

Von Rosenstiel, Helene. *American Rugs and Carpets.* New York: William Morrow, 1978.

Wadsworth Atheneum. *Bed Ruggs/1722–1833.* Introduction and Essay by William L. Warren. Hartford, Conn.: Wadsworth Atheneum, 1972.

Walker, Sandra Rambo. *Country Cloth to Coverlets.* University Park, Pa.: Pennsylvania State University Press, 1981.

Wardle, Patricia. *Guide to English Embroidery.* London: Her Majesty's Stationery Office, 1970.

Watson, John. *Annals of Philadelphia and Pennsylvania.* Vol. 1. New York: Baker & Crane, 1844.

Webster, Marie D. *Quilts: Their Story and How to Make Them.* Garden City, N.Y.: Doubleday, Page & Co., 1915.

Wheat, Joe Ben. "The Navajo Chief Blanket." *American Indian Art Magazine,* Summer 1976.

Wheeler, Candace. *The Development of Embroidery in America.* New York: Harper and Bros., 1921.

Whiting, Gertrude. *Tools and Toys of Stitchery.* New York: Columbia University Press, 1928. Reprinted Dover Publications, 1971, as *Old-Time Tools and Toys of Needlework.*

Whiteford, Andrew Hunter. "Fiber Bags of the Great Lakes Indians, Part II." *American Indian Art Magazine,* Winter 1977.

———. "Tapestry-Twined Bags, Osage Bags and Others." *American Indian Art,* Spring 1978.

Wildscut, William, and Ewers, John C. *Crow Indian Beadwork.* New York: Museum of the American Indian, Heye Foundation, 1959.

The Workwoman's Guide. 2nd edition, London: Simpkin, Marshall; Birmingham: Thos. Evans, 1840. Reprinted, Ouston Ferry, Doncaster, S. Yorks. Bloomfield Books and Publications, 1975.

Wright, Richardson. *Hawkers and Walkers in Early America.* Philadelphia: J. B. Lippincott, 1927.

Yabsley, Suzanne. "Appliqué Button Blankets in Northwest Coast Indian Culture." *Uncoverings, 1983.* Mill Valley, Calif.: American Quilt Study Group, 1984.

The Young Lady's Book: A Manual of Elegant Recreations, Exercises and Pursuits. Boston: A. Bowen, and Carter & Hendee. Philadelphia: Carry & Lea, 1830.

The Young Lady's Friend (by a Lady). Boston: American Stationers' Co., John B. Russell, 1837.

INDEX

M

N

O

R

S